Applications in Human Resource Management

Cases, Exercises, & Skill Builders

Applications in Human Resource Management

Cases, Exercises, & Skill Builders

STELLA M. NKOMO
University of North Carolina–Charlotte

MYRON D. FOTTLER
University of Alabama at Birmingham

R. BRUCE MCAFEE
Old Dominion University

Fourth Edition

South-Western College Publishing
an International Thomson Publishing company I(T)P®

Cincinnati · Albany · Boston · Detroit · Johannesburg · London · Madrid · Melbourne · Mexico City
New York · Pacific Grove · San Francisco · Scottsdale · Singapore · Tokyo · Toronto

Team Leader: Dave Shaut
Executive Editor: John Szilagyi
Developmental Editor: Ohlinger Publishing Services
Marketing Manager: Joe Sabatino
Production Editor: Kelly Keeler
Manufacturing Coordinator: Dana Schwartz
Internal Design: Jennifer Marsh-Lambert
Production House: DPS Associates, Inc.
Printer: WebCom Limited

Printed in Canada
3 4 5 6 7 8 9 10

International Thomsom Publishing Europe
Berkshire House
168–173 High Holborn
London, WC1V7AA, United Kingdom

International Thomson Editores
Seneca, 53
Colonia Polanco
11560 México D.F. México

Nelson ITP, Australia
102 Dodds Street
South Melbourne
Victoria 3205 Australia

International Thomson Publishing Asia
60 Alberta Street #15-01
Albert Complex
Singapore 189969

Nelson Canada
1120 Birchmount Road
Scarborough, Ontario
Canada M1K 5G4

International Thomson Publishing Japan
Hirakawa-cho Kyowa Building, 3F
2–2–1 Hirakawa-cho, Chiyoda-ku
Tokyo 102, Japan

International Thomson Publishing Southern Africa
Building 18, Constantia Square
138 Sixteenth Road, P.O. Box 2459
Halfway House, 1685 South Africa

Library of Congress Cataloging-in-Publication Data
Nkomo, Stella M.,
        Applications in human resource management: cases, exercises & skill builders /
        Stella M. Nkomo, Myron D. Fottler, R. Bruce McAfee.
    —4th ed.
        p. cm.
    ISBN 0-538-85337-9 (alk. paper)
    1. Personnel management—Case studies. 2. Personnel management—Problems, exercises, etc. I. Fottler, Myron D. II. McAfee, R. Bruce III. Title.
HF5549.N56 1999
658.3—dc21

BK
$31.00

99-23370

This book is printed on acid-free paper.

PREFACE

The purpose of this book is to provide a single source of cases, exercises, incidents, and skill builders to supplement the basic text in human resource management. These materials offer a fresh approach to the management student based on dynamic, "real life" organizational events confronting both human resource managers and line managers who often implement personnel programs and policies. This book's contents are uniquely designed to increase analytical problem-solving skills and may be used in basic courses at the undergraduate and graduate level. Topics range from traditional applications of personnel theory to the more controversial issues of AIDS, telecommuting, the financial impact of human resources, phased retirement, alcohol and drug abuse on the job, new federal legislation on discrimination issues, employment-at-will, work and family, and the human resource aspects of merger activities. The settings cover a wide variety of organizations with an emphasis on the growing service sector.

This book offers opportunities for learning experiences in its seven major sections: (1) Human Resource Management in Perspective: Environment and Legal Issues; (2) Meeting Human Resource Requirements: Job Analysis/Design, Planning, Recruitment, and Selection; (3) Developing Effectiveness in Human Resources: Training, Career Development, and Performance Appraisal; (4) Implementing Compensation and Security: Compensation, Incentives, Benefits, and Safety and Health; (5) Enhancing Employee Relations: Motivation, Employee Rights and Discipline, Labor Relations, and Collective Bargaining; (6) Expanding Human Resources Globally; and (7) Human Resource Audits/Term Assignments. Each of these sections, except Part 7, contains cases, exercises, incidents, and skill builders. Suggestions for group projects and/or term assignments are offered in the final section of the book.

Most cases are based on actual events occurring in private and public sector organizations. All names have been disguised. The first two cases in the introductory section are designed to act as pre- and post-measures of the students' knowledge of human resource management. That is, the two cases in Part 1 can be used at the beginning of the course to pique interest in the material or at the end to test how much students have learned. The student becomes the decision maker in these classroom-tested cases. The instructor may use the skill builders in Part 1 to prepare students to conduct research related to each case, or each case may be considered a class-contained learning tool. Questions are provided at the end of each case and incident to guide discussion, and/or the instructor may ask students to use the case analysis model suggested by the authors.

The exercises include opportunities for students to simulate the human resource work environment through role playing, identifying and solving human resource problems, completing in-baskets, and applying human resource management theories. The role plays and in-basket exercises require students to act just as they might in a real management situation. Virtually all of the exercises can be completed within 45 minutes and all contain a set of detailed procedures to follow.

The incidents are mini-cases composed of critical human resource management events and are designed to help students develop problem-solving skills. They are intended to raise questions around issues that don't have definitive answers and may be used to stimulate class discussions or to introduce students to human resource management topics.

Skill builders are short, individual assignments that can be completed by students outside of class. The skill builders develop the specific technical skills needed by human resource professionals and line managers to effectively manage human resources.

The final section of this book provides a set of suggestions for group projects and/or term assignments: a potpourri of field exercises, class presentations, group projects, and creative exercises to enhance the learning of human resource management. These projects are designed to be challenging and comprehensive by requiring students to draw upon material learned throughout the course.

The instructor's manual includes an analysis of the cases and incidents, solutions to the exercises and skill builders, and alternative approaches for using and presenting the materials in the book. The manual also provides reference sources to aid in the analysis and discussion of the cases and exercises.

Acknowledgments

Many people have assisted in making this book possible. We are grateful to the following case contributors: American Association of Retired Persons, Joyce Beggs, J. Stewart Black, Gerald Calvasina, Susan Corriher, Diana Deadrick, J. Kline Harrison, Sam Holliday, Ed Jennigan, Ronald Karren, Margaret Foegen Karsten, Arno F. Knapper, Gary F. Kohut, Steve Maurer, M. Susan Taylor, and James Wimbush. Special thanks to Juanita Craig,

Ralph Pederson, Jim Bavis, David Abernethy, Diane Marie Eckland, Rusty Rainey, and other friends who shared their professional knowledge and experiences in personnel management with us in developing materials for the book.

The authors wish to acknowledge the contribution of Dorothy Moore of The Citadel and Fraya Andrews of Eastern Michigan University who reviewed the manuscript for the first edition of the book and offered helpful suggestions and comments. We also thank the following reviewers of the first edition: Debra J. Cohen, George Mason University; Jacob Joseph, University of Alaska–Fairbanks; and James C. Wimbush, Indiana University. We are grateful to the reviewers of the second edition: Donald G. Gardner, University of Colorado at Colorado Springs; Cliff Harrison, Concordia College; Joseph Rosse, University of Colorado at Boulder; and Robert C. Schwab, Walla Walla College. We would like to thank the reviewers of the third edition: Matthew Stollak, Mississippi State University; John Ogilvie, University of Hartford; Lois Wise, Indiana University; and Denise Chachere, Saint Louis University.

Stella Nkomo would like to thank her graduate assistants, Debbie Phillips, Sheila Goldbach, Susan Corriher, and Darren Shietze who diligently helped with the research and the seemingly endless day-to-day drudgery of proofreading and verifying details. Thanks to Dean Claude Lilly for his support. Dr. Nkomo is sure that her husband, Mokubung, and her son, Sebenza are relieved to have the book completed. She appreciates their steadfast encouragement and support.

Myron Fottler would like to thank his wife, Carol, for her assistance and input into the book. Her contributions and ideas were particularly important in the development of several cases. Thanks are also due to Dean Robert Holmes of the School of Business, Dean Charles Joiner of the School of Health Professions, and Dr. S. Robert Hernandez, Chair of the Department of Health Services Administration at the University of Alabama at Birmingham for providing support for the preparation of this book. Finally, thanks to Elizabeth Woodard for her research assistance.

Bruce McAfee would like to thank his wife, Chris, for proofreading and Claire Anderson, Diana Deadrick, and Steve Maurer for their help and suggestions on improving the book. Finally, he is grateful to four graduate students who assisted in case development: Stephanie Fox, Kari Miller, Mike King, and Ben Robinette.

This book would have been impossible without the outstanding work of the people at South-Western College Publishing and Ohlinger Publishing Services. We are grateful to Theresa Curtis, who managed the review and revision process.

Finally, we would like to thank our students for their invaluable suggestions for revising and clarifying the materials in this book.

Stella Nkomo
Myron D. Fottler
R. Bruce McAfee

CONTENTS

ix

PART 6   *Expanding Human Resources Globally*   *283*

PART 7   *Human Resource Audits/Term Assignments*   *293*

A MODEL FOR ANALYZING CASES IN HUMAN RESOURCE MANAGEMENT

Purpose of Cases

A case is a written description of events and activities that have taken place in an organization. Cases allow you to experience a different kind of learning—learning by doing. They are intended to give you an opportunity to actively experience the reality and complexity of the issues facing practicing managers and human resource executives. While other disciplines like physical science allow you to test theories in a laboratory, performing a case analysis allows you to apply human resource management theories to specific organizational problems. The cases and other materials in this book will help you develop your analytical and problem-solving skills. Cases enable you to analyze organization problems and to generate solutions based on your understanding of theories and models of effective human resource management (HRM).

Both a "decision-maker" and an "evaluator" approach are used in the cases. In the decision-maker approach, the primary goal is to sort out information given and to propose a viable solution to the problem(s) identified. In the evaluator approach, the human resource management decisions have already been implemented, and the primary goal is to evaluate outcomes and consequences and to propose alternative solutions.

Student Preparation of Written Cases

There are any number of possible approaches to analyzing a case. The most important point to remember is that case analysis involves decision making. There is no absolutely right or wrong solution to a case problem. Your major task as a decision maker is to present a coherent and defensible analysis of the situation based on human resource management concepts and theories. Just as managers in the "real world" must persuade their colleagues and superiors that their proposals are sound, so must you persuade your fellow students and your instructor that your analysis of the case and proposed solution are the best.

You should follow a few preliminary steps before preparing your written analysis. First, give the case a general reading to get an overall sense of the situation. Put it aside for a while, then read it a second time and make notes on the critical facts. Case facts provide information and data on attitudes and values, relative power and influence, the nature and quality of relationships, the organization's objectives and human resource management policies/functions, and other pertinent aspects of the organization. Keep two key questions in mind as you review the facts of the case: First, are there discernible patterns in the facts? Second, what can be inferred about human resource management practices in this organization from the facts presented? You should attempt to classify, sort, and evaluate the information you have identified in this preliminary step. Once you have a clear understanding of the critical facts in the case, you can prepare your written analysis using the five-step model that follows.

Written Case Analysis Model

Step 1. Problem Identification.   The first step in your written analysis is to explicitly identify the major problem(s) in the case in one or two clear and precise sentences. For example, "The major problem in this case is a 15 percent increase in employee turnover compared to last year's rate." Herbert Simon, who received a Nobel Prize for his work on management decision making, has defined a problem as "a deviation from a standard." In other words, one way to identify a problem is to compare some desired state or objective with the actual situation. A problem or series of problems may prevent the organization from reaching its objectives or goals. A key point here is that in order to define a problem, there must be some type of standard for comparison. Possible standards include the organization's stated objectives or goals, objectives or goals of competing organizations, or standards based on normative prescriptions from human resource management theory.

Step 2. Identify the Causes of the Problem.   Before proposing alternative solutions, the decision maker must have a clear understanding of the underlying causes of the problem. HRM problems are usually embedded in a larger context. This means the decision maker must examine internal and external environmental factors over time to isolate causal factors. Causes of problems tend to be historical in nature. To formulate a solid understanding of the specific causes, you should search for root causes and use relevant course concepts and theories to better define them. The "question syndrome" approach may be beneficial here: Why did the problem occur? When did it begin? Where does it occur? Where doesn't it occur? What effective HRM practices should the organization be using? What has the organization failed to do? What are the antecedents of the problem? Posing these questions will help you to probe beyond the symptoms to the root causes of the problem.

The process of identifying the causes of a problem is very much like hypothesis testing. You should set forth possible causes and then test them against the facts in the case. In writing this section, it is important to present a plausible discussion of the causes so as to convince the reader that your analysis is correct.

Step 3. Alternative Solutions. This step involves developing alternative solutions and evaluating their contributions to resolving the problem(s) identified. Proposed alternatives should be consistent with the problem(s) and cause(s) identified. You should attempt to develop at least three possible alternatives. For many cases, you may be able to propose more than three. List each of your alternatives and the advantages and disadvantages associated with each. Keep the following criteria in mind as you evaluate your alternatives: time constraints, feasibility, cost, contribution to meeting the organization's objectives, and possible negative side effects. Developing a list of good alternatives involves creativity and avoiding preconceived attitudes and assumptions. It may be useful to brainstorm possible solutions before weighing their advantages and disadvantages.

Step 4. Select the Best Alternative. Indicate the alternative you have chosen to solve the problem. It is important here to justify why you chose a particular solution and why it will best resolve the problem(s).

Step 5. Implementation Steps. Now that you have a solution, you must develop appropriate action plans to implement it. In this section of your written analysis, you want to specify, as much as possible, what should be done, by whom, when, where, and in what sequence. For example: Who should implement the decision? To whom should it be communicated? What actions need to be taken now? What actions need to be taken later? If you recommend that the organization revise its performance appraisal process, give as much detail as possible on the content of the revisions. Finally, in this section you should also indicate follow-up procedures to monitor the implementation of your solution to ensure that the intended actions are taken and that the problem is corrected.

While these steps have been presented in linear fashion, case analysis does not involve linear thinking. You will probably find yourself thinking about all of the parts of the analysis simultaneously. This is perfectly normal and underscores the complexity of decision making. To present a clear written analysis, however, it is important to write up your report in the analytical form just described. As you gain experience with the case method, you will end the course with a better understanding of both your problem-solving ability and effective human resource management practices.

Pitfalls in Analysis

Amateurs at case analysis often encounter the pitfall of jumping to a conclusion, which in effect bypasses analysis. For example, a student may readily observe some overt behavior, quickly identify it as objectionable and, therefore, assume it is a basic problem. Later, with some dismay, the student may discover that the prescribed action had no effect on the "problem" and that the objectionable behavior was only a symptom and not the actual problem.

Another common mistake is for students to reject a case because they think there is insufficient information. All desirable or useful information is seldom available for analyzing and resolving actual problems in real organizations. Consequently, managers must do the best they can with the information available to them. Furthermore, the main issue in solving the problems of many organizations is to determine what additional and relevant information is available or can be obtained before adequate analysis can be made and appropriate action taken. If additional information is available, the manager must decide whether it is worth getting, whether it is meaningful and relevant, and whether it can be secured in time to be useful. Thus, an apparent lack of information in cases is actually a reflection of reality that students must learn to accept and overcome.

Students occasionally search for the "right" answer or solutions to cases and sometimes they ask their instructor what actually happened in a case. Although some answers or solutions are better than others, there are no "right" answers or solutions. What actually happened in a case is usually irrelevant—the focus of case study should be on the process of analysis, the diagnosis of problems, and the prescription of remedial action rather than on the discovery of answers or results. Many of the cases and incidents in this book were in the process of being studied and resolved at the time the pieces were written. Consequently, the real life outcomes were not always available. Although some of the cases do include what happened, no case is intended to illustrate either right or wrong, effective or ineffective solutions to human resource management problems.

PART 1

HUMAN RESOURCE MANAGEMENT IN PERSPECTIVE: ENVIRONMENT AND LEGAL ISSUES

THE HRM FUNCTION/ENVIRONMENT

1. CASE

The New Director of Human Resources

Mount Ridge Engineering Systems designs, builds, and operates standard-ized, coal-fired utility plants in Kentucky. These small generating plants (35 megawatts and 55 megawatts) are built adjacent to an industrial plant that utilizes steam in its operations. Mount Ridge sells the steam to the industrial plant and electricity to the local utility. Under federal regulations, utilities are required to purchase this independently produced power if it is cost competitive. When Garrett Levinson founded the company he firmly believed that the future of electric generation in the United States would depend upon coal as the primary fuel and standardization as a method of cost control and efficiency. This new technology, known as "cogeneration," is rapidly coming of age as many companies turn to these systems as a way to cut energy costs. Mount Ridge's very efficient plants allowed it to pursue a cost leadership business strategy.

When the firm was formed four years ago, Joyce Newcombe was hired as Director of Human Resources. Newcombe had recently graduated with an M.B.A. degree from a large southeastern university. At the time of its establishment, the company had a total of four employees in addition to Newcombe: the President and founder, a Senior Vice President of Operations, a Vice President for Administration, and a Vice President of Cost and Estimation. From the start, Mount Ridge had both the financing and plans to build seven plants over the next five- to eight-year period. Joyce Newcombe was hired to develop all of the necessary human resource programs, plans, and policies needed to staff the plants once they became operational. She explained, "When I was hired, all we had was a dream and a plan. I had an office with a desk, chair, and telephone. I literally had to develop an entire human resource system." During the first year, Newcombe developed benefit packages for both corporate and plant per-sonnel, an employee handbook, job descriptions, a salary program, a super-visor's manual, and other basic personnel policies. In less than three years the company had built five plants. The size of the work force grew from five to 39 people at corporate headquarters and from zero to 183 employees in the plants (see Exhibit 1.1 for the company's organization structure). The company had been remarkably successful in a short period of time. Newcombe was promoted to vice president. In addition to having two plants currently under construction in the state, Mount Ridge plans to build an additional two to three plants in the Northeast. The demand for cogeneration plants is strong in New Jersey, Connecticut, Maine, and Massachusetts, where state energy regulators are concerned about high electricity prices. Forecasts indicate that the company will grow to a total of nine plants and approximately 650 corporate and plant employees over the next two to three years.

A major constraint faced by the company was the need not to compete for employees with its industrial hosts and the local utility. Benefits and salaries had to be competitive but not too high to attract workers from Mount Ridge's "customers." In addition, since profits were to be put back into the business to finance future plant expansion, a profit-sharing plan was not feasible. Another important goal of the company was to remain nonunion by offering employees a good quality of work life and attractive benefits. Balancing these two goals was often difficult. Low cost production was critical to Mount Ridge's competitive position. The importance of these goals is reflected in the words of Mr. Levinson: "Mount Ridge places great value on its relationship with our industrial and utility clients. Our internal employee relationship has an equally important role in order to maintain an enjoyable and productive work force for the future. Management believes that companies that are good to their employees reap the benefits in terms of increased productivity and loyalty." As part of an effort to build this philosophy into its human resource programs, employee appreciation dinners are held annually at each of the five plants. The president and other corporate officers attend each of the dinners given throughout the state. These dinners have been well received by employees.

Plant Operations

Most of Mount Ridge's plants are scattered throughout the state. Each plant employs approximately 45 workers. The typical plant structure is shown in Exhibit 1.2. Each plant is run by a plant superintendent who reports directly to the manager of plant operations and maintenance. While personnel operations are generally centralized at corporate headquarters, the plant superintendent and shift supervisor of each plant are largely responsible for the day-to-day administration of personnel policies. Newcombe stated that, "One of our biggest problems has been getting management—especially plant management—to understand the legal and governmental regulations affecting human resource procedures." Although Newcombe had developed a detailed employee handbook and supervisor's manual, over the years there had been situations where supervisors had not followed company policy. Newcombe recounted one such incident that occurred in one of the older plants during her third year with the company.

The Termination

One of the first plants built was the Edison plant. It is located in a medium-sized rural community in the eastern region of Kentucky and employs 45 workers. Bud Johnson had worked as an auxiliary operator for the plant for two years and had worked his way to that position after starting as a laborer. An auxiliary operator was responsible for assisting the control room operator and the equipment operator in the basic operations and maintenance of the plant's generating system. Over the years, Johnson had learned quickly and knew a good deal about the equipment operator's job. On many occasions, Johnson was asked to fill in when the equipment operator was absent or when there was a problem no one else could handle. One day Johnson approached the plant superintendent, Larry Braxton, about a promotion to equipment operator:

Johnson: Larry, you know I can handle the equipment operator position, and I'd like to be considered for a promotion.

Braxton: That's not the point. We all know you are capable, but we just don't have any openings right now. Besides, the job qualifications require that you spend sufficient time as an auxiliary operator before moving up to an equipment operator. Just sit tight.

Johnson: Well, I hope some openings will come up soon. I really would like to make more money, and I know that I am qualified. You know I can learn quickly. Look at how fast I moved up from being a laborer.

After this conversation, Johnson was again called on several times to help out with the equipment operator's job and to explain the readings and gauges to Wilma Barker, one of the equipment room operators. When Johnson did not receive a pay increase or promotion after his annual evaluation, he met with Braxton and told him that he was dissatisfied with his pay and felt that since he often performed the equipment operator's job that he ought to be paid at that rate instead of his present rate as an auxiliary operator. Braxton told him he would have to remain at the pay of an auxiliary operator and that he should be satisfied with that for the time being. Johnson became quite upset and stormed out of Braxton's office. The next day Johnson did not report to work and did not call in to report his absence.

Company policy stated that when an employee is absent and fails to notify his or her supervisor, the employee may be terminated. When Johnson returned to work the following day, he told Braxton that he had decided to quit his job because he was very dissatisfied with his pay. Johnson was asked to sign a termination notice form required by company policy and was told by Braxton that he would receive a copy of the form in the mail.

A week later Newcombe received a phone call from Johnson. Johnson told her that the reason given on the copy of the termination form he had just received in the mail was incorrect (see Exhibit 1.3). He had not left to take another job but had left because he was dissatisfied with his pay and lack of promotion at the plant and that he had spoken with the plant superintendent about this several times. Johnson also told her that he wanted his personnel records to be corrected and that he had been asked by Braxton to sign a blank form. He alleged that Braxton had added the incorrect reason after he had signed the form. Johnson also stated that he thought the Department of Labor would have something to say about this whole incident.

Questions

1. Discuss the relationship between corporate human resources' structure and operations at the plant level. What impact, if any, did it have on the situation described by Newcombe?
2. How should Newcombe have handled this situation?
3. What, if any, disciplinary action should have been taken against the plant superintendent at the time of the incident?
4. If Johnson's allegations were true, what are the legal ramifications of Braxton's behavior?
5. Describe Mount Ridge's business strategy. What is the relationship between its business strategy and its human resource practices?
6. What strategic human resource issues will Newcombe likely face as the company expands to the Northeast? How might this expansion affect the structure of the organization and its human resource department?

EXHIBIT 1.1   *Organization Structure*

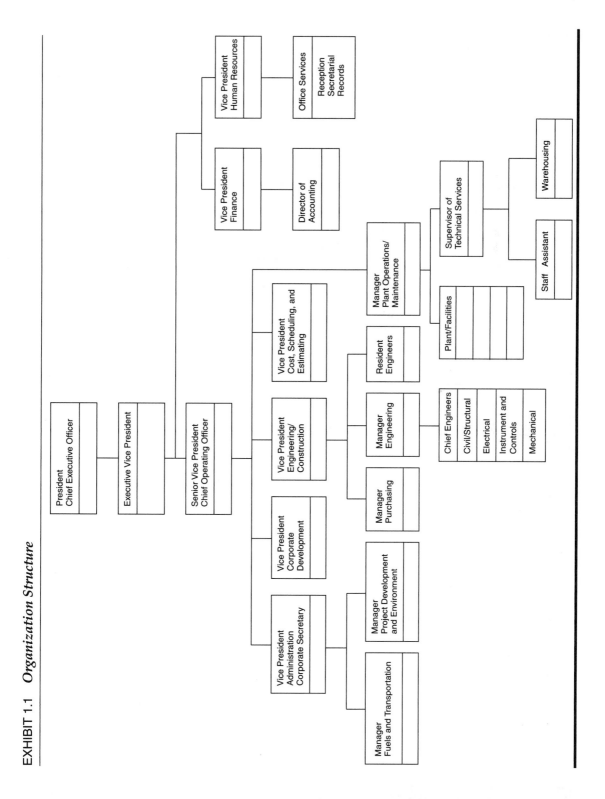

EXHIBIT 1.2   *Typical Plant Structure*

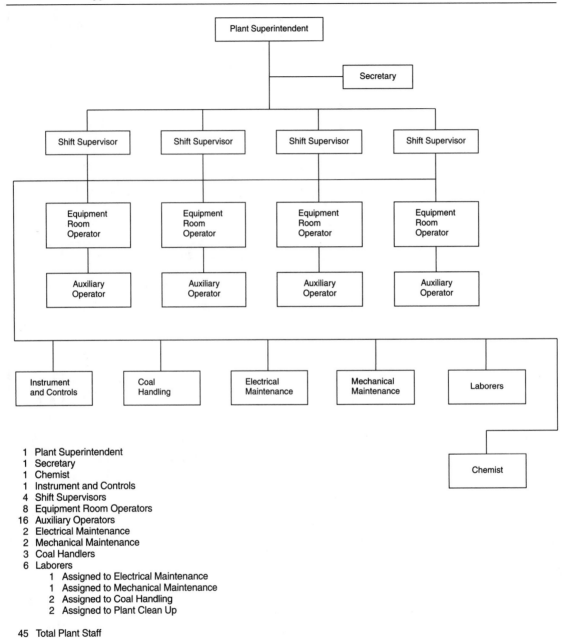

1 Plant Superintendent
1 Secretary
1 Chemist
1 Instrument and Controls
4 Shift Supervisors
8 Equipment Room Operators
16 Auxiliary Operators
2 Electrical Maintenance
2 Mechanical Maintenance
3 Coal Handlers
6 Laborers
    1 Assigned to Electrical Maintenance
    1 Assigned to Mechanical Maintenance
    2 Assigned to Coal Handling
    2 Assigned to Plant Clean Up

45 Total Plant Staff

EXHIBIT 1.3 *Termination Form for Bud Johnson*

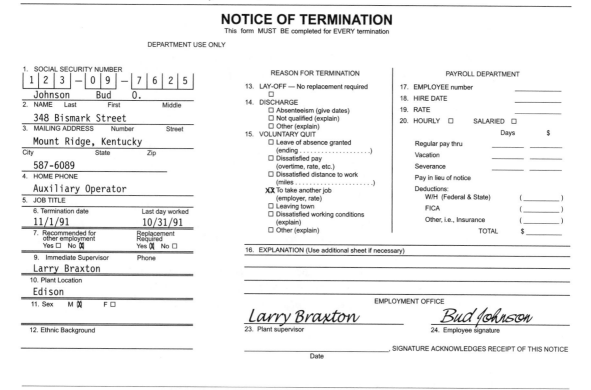

NOTICE OF TERMINATION
This form MUST BE completed for EVERY termination

DEPARTMENT USE ONLY

1. SOCIAL SECURITY NUMBER
1 2 3 – 0 9 – 7 6 2 5

Johnson   Bud   O.
2. NAME   Last   First   Middle

348 Bismark Street
3. MAILING ADDRESS   Number   Street

Mount Ridge, Kentucky
City   State   Zip

587-6089
4. HOME PHONE

Auxiliary Operator
5. JOB TITLE

6. Termination date	Last day worked
11/1/91	10/31/91

7. Recommended for other employment   Replacement Required
Yes ☐ No ☒   Yes ☒ No ☐

9. Immediate Supervisor   Phone
Larry Braxton

10. Plant Location
Edison

11. Sex   M ☒   F ☐

12. Ethnic Background

REASON FOR TERMINATION

13. LAY-OFF — No replacement required
☐
14. DISCHARGE
    ☐ Absenteeism (give dates)
    ☐ Not qualified (explain)
    ☐ Other (explain)
15. VOLUNTARY QUIT
    ☐ Leave of absence granted
       (ending . . . .)
    ☐ Dissatisfied pay
       (overtime, rate, etc.)
    ☐ Dissatisfied distance to work
       (miles . . . .)
    ☒ To take another job
       (employer, rate)
    ☐ Leaving town
    ☐ Dissatisfied working conditions
       (explain)
    ☐ Other (explain)

16. EXPLANATION (Use additional sheet if necessary)

PAYROLL DEPARTMENT

17. EMPLOYEE number   _____
18. HIRE DATE   _____
19. RATE   _____
20. HOURLY ☐   SALARIED ☐

                          Days $
Regular pay thru   _____ _____
Vacation   _____ _____
Severance   _____ _____
Pay in lieu of notice
Deductions:
   W/H (Federal & State)   (_____)
   FICA   (_____)
   Other, i.e., Insurance   (_____)
            TOTAL $ _____

EMPLOYMENT OFFICE

Larry Braxton   *Bud Johnson*
23. Plant supervisor   24. Employee signature

_____, SIGNATURE ACKNOWLEDGES RECEIPT OF THIS NOTICE
              Date

SUPERVISOR'S REPORT OF TERMINATION

WERE WRITTEN WARNING NOTICES OR PERFORMANCE EVALUATION GIVEN?
   ☐ YES (ATTACH COPIES)   ☐ NO
WHAT WAS EMPLOYEE'S REACTION TO COUNSEL, WARNING NOTICES, OR PERFORMANCE EVALUATION?

REASON FOR TERMINATION. (UNEMPLOYMENT INSURANCE CLAIMS ARE A MAJOR COST TO THE COMPANY. WHEN FACTUAL INFORMATION IS LACKING, THE STATE EMPLOYMENT DEVELOPMENT DEPARTMENT GENERALLY FAVORS THE EMPLOYEE'S CLAIM—EVEN THOUGH IT MAY NOT BE MERITED. THEREFORE, THE EXACT REASONS FOR TERMINATION ARE EXTREMELY IMPORTANT. IN ADDITION, THIS INFORMATION CAN BE ESSENTIAL FOR THE RESOLUTION OF UNFAIR LABOR PRACTICE AND EQUAL EMPLOYMENT CASES.)

2. CASE

The Human Resource Function of Harrison Brothers Corporation

Company History

Harrison Brothers Corporation was founded in upstate New York on September 15, 1898 by Aubrey and William Harrison. Harrison's is a multi-line traditional department store which deals mainly with men's, women's, and children's clothing. In recent years, the store has expanded to include household furnishings and other items for the home. The long-term goal of the company is to become the leading chain of department stores in the Northeast selling moderate- to better-priced merchandise to middle-class, fashion-conscious customers. Harrison is one of the largest privately owned retail stores in the United States. A majority of its 20 stores are located in the Northeast. Its largest store is located in a major urban center and has 950 employees. The company is highly decentralized and maintains a very small corporate office.

Industry Challenges

Traditional department stores like Harrison are beginning to experience the effects of a number of changes in the retail industry. Not long ago, major department stores succeeded by being all things to all customers. However, today's customer is looking for both value and specialization. Superstores and giant discounters are also popping up. At the same time, the industry faces the challenge of keeping a well-trained, highly motivated sales staff and management team. James Harrison, who is currently CEO, describes the company's strategic challenges for the next five years: "We can no longer continue to do the same old things that gave us a reputation for fair value. We must reposition ourselves—floor to floor—offering exciting brand names, excellent sales help, and frequent sales. We need sales staff who know the merchandise and understand customer preferences. Buying expertise is also critical because fashions and consumer tastes never stay the same." We have five strategic goals:

1. Convert non-selling space into revenue generating selling space.
2. Build up underdeveloped merchandise categories.
3. Invest aggressively in private brands like Polo, Nautica, and Tommy Hilfiger.
4. Reduce costs through use of advanced computer systems to project sales and manage inventory.
5. Improve productivity of sales associates, buyers, and department heads.

James Harrison took over the business after earning an M.B.A. at a prestigious northeast business school. Unlike previous family members, he wanted to take a much more deliberate approach to charting Harrison's future. To do this he hired a consultant to assist in assessing the company's strengths and weaknesses. Harrison felt their employee quality and performance would be one of the keys to the future. As part of his analysis, the consultant sought to learn more about the human resource function within Harrison Brothers. He decided to interview a few of the HR managers and other key managers at the store level. Both groups were also asked to complete a questionnaire of their perceptions of the responsibilities of the human resource function.

The Westpark Store*

Brenda McCain has been Human Resource Manager at the Westpark store for the past four years. Prior to her employment at Harrison Brothers, Brenda had several years of experience in retail stores and came to Harrison's after being a buyer at one of its major competitors. McCain has a degree in fashion merchandising from a college in New Jersey. Currently there are 950 employees at the Westpark store. The staff includes salespeople, sales support employees (dock, marking room, clerical, and accounting), maintenance, security, and management. The Human Resource Department consists of five people (see Exhibit 1.4). During the peak holiday season a number of people are hired as floating sales staff. These temporary workers may number close to a hundred.

The Human Resource Manager's Job

McCain talked about the Human Resource Department's areas of responsibility: "Our business has really grown in the last two years. We are carrying more specialty and designer clothing lines and have added items we hope will appeal to moderate- to high-income customers. When I came here four years ago, I found too many of the human resource operations being performed by the operations manager, Pat Hartlake, and one of the department heads, Rich Jenkins. Since that time I have attempted to set up procedures and policies to assure proper staffing of the store. I spend most of my time just managing the Human Resource Department. I think it is important to keep abreast of the performance of workers, and I like to observe their work habits regularly. I also spend a good deal of time on selecting applicants for the sales and support jobs. There is heavy turnover on the sales floor in our business and the average salesperson at Harrison Brothers is either part-time, an older employee, or one who is 'in-between jobs'—if a better job came along they would snap it up immediately. For example, of the 119 part-time people hired in the last four months, 65 have left."

*The interview at the Westpark store reflects what the consultant heard throughout the company.

McCain went on to explain their selection procedures: "The main sources of our applicants are newspaper ads and word-of-mouth by present or past employees. We select people based on how well they do in the interview. Right now I conduct about 25 to 30 interviews a week and perhaps more during the holiday rush. I have enough experience in retail to know what it takes to be a good salesperson. We place a lot of weight on their motivation, personality, and drive. Little or no useful information is gained from high school or college records or references. I do check their application forms for an indication of job stability, though."

"The training of new salespeople occurs every two weeks and every week during the holiday season. Now and then we get some employees who cannot effectively complete the cash register training. Our trainer, Joanne Flynn, tries to expose them to selling techniques and how to properly interact with customers. Although we have a trainer, I do spend a good deal of time with her and will help out if the training classes are too large."

"When I came here, discipline was a continual bone of contention between the employees and supervisors. Employees felt the present procedures were inconsistently enforced and applied. Each supervisor was administering punishment depending on his or her own interpretation of the problem. Now, I am totally responsible for all disciplinary actions. I discuss the alleged wrongful act with the employee's supervisor to assess the magnitude of the act. I then talk with the employee before deciding upon the appropriate consequences. In this way, we have better consistency in the application of disciplinary rules. Any employee who receives three disciplinary actions is eligible for dismissal."

"While we hire our salespeople at the minimum wage, we do perform an annual evaluation of their performance to determine merit increases. We use sales productivity as the major criterion. Performance is evaluated on average sales per hour. For example, say an employee works in an eight percent department. The hourly quota would be calculated by dividing the hourly wage by the percent level. This determines how much the sales clerk would have to sell to break even. For any sales above that level, the clerk receives a commission. At evaluation time, if the clerk's sales per hour are above the breakeven point, the new hourly wage is determined by multiplying the sales per hour by the percent level. For example, assume that a salesperson works in an eight percent department and earns $5 per hour. The employee would have to sell $62.50 per hour to break even. Any sales above that level would receive a commission. If sales at evaluation time were actually $95 per hour, hourly pay would increase to $7.60 per hour (95 times .08). We have had moderate success with this system, although I'm not sure how much it helps us to retain good employees."

"For our sales support staff, we have supervisors basically evaluate the employee's quality and quantity of work. Last year, though, we incorporated a form of employee development into the evaluation process. Supervisors are required to discuss the employees' career opportunities and professional development with them. I initiated this as a form of career planning and hopefully as a way to keep good employees. Unfortunately, supervisors have been slack in doing the assessment. They seem to be more anxious to get the performance evaluation completed. Several employees came to me to say they had not received a 'professional assessment' since the program was instituted."

"There is a lot more we need to do here in human resources, but we are somewhat constrained by cost considerations and the realities of the retail industry. The turnover in the sales areas gives me little free time to develop new programs and ideas."

Interview with the Store Manager

Jennifer Daft recently joined Harrison Brothers after being recruited from a major specialty retailer. Jennifer had a number of years of experience in management and retail. During the interview, she talked about her perceptions of the human resource department in her store. "I think they are too internally focused most of the time. Betty and the rest of her staff seem to be struggling to keep up with the day-to-day activities. I don't know if they are understaffed or not. Our store has experienced very high turnover. With the new strategic direction of our company, however, I need human resources to be more of a key player. It's not hard to get the merchandise we want to sell, but we need people who know how to merchandise it and how to sell it to customers. There are a lot of changes going on in the company. It's not going to be a smooth ride for a while. We're all going to have to learn how to do things differently and better to stay competitive. Our human resource people are no exception."

Interview with the Operations Manager

Pat Hartlake, the operations manager, talked about interactions with the Human Resource Department: "I have a good working relationship with the Human Resource Department, but it took some time to develop that relationship. McCain has a good understanding of the retail business, and I am impressed with her knowledge of store operations. They have been somewhat slow in filling the vacant sales positions, and they don't always respond as quickly as they should. They seem terribly understaffed and overworked most of the time."

"Let me give you an example of what I mean. A few weeks ago I was faced with an employee situation which was evolving to the point where I felt termination was necessary. I went to the Human Resource Department to discuss the case to be sure I had covered all bases. With all of the laws today, one needs to be careful in making decisions. They never seem to be able to produce answers to questions without hedging. I had to wait almost two weeks before I got any help from them. In the meantime the situation with the employee continued to deteriorate. I can understand their reluctance to terminate sales staff because of the difficulty in recruiting new people. In a way, however, the old system seemed to be a lot less complicated. Department managers knew how to handle situations that came up in their departments. Don't get me wrong! I know that as we continue to grow we're probably going to need an even larger human resource department."

Questions

1. How does McCain view her role as human resource manager?
2. What is Harrison's business strategy?
3. What is the structure and staffing of HR?
4. Analyze the data in Exhibit 1.5. What are its implications?
5. Given the organization's size and strategic goals, evaluate the development of the human resource function at Harrison Brothers. What problems do you see? How could its major human resource functions be improved?

EXHIBIT 1.4   *Harrison Brothers Organization Chart*

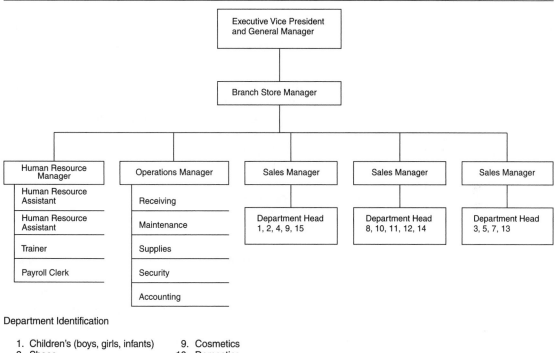

Department Identification

1. Children's (boys, girls, infants)
2. Shoes
3. Dresses
4. Men's
5. Women's coats
6. Fashion accessories
7. Intimate apparel
8. Furniture/Carpet/Bedding
9. Cosmetics
10. Domestics
11. China/etc
12. Housewares
13. Fine Jewelry
14. Sporting Goods
15. Toys

(Each department head supervises several sales clerks)

EXHIBIT 1.5   *Results of Questionnaire Completed by HR Managers and Non-HR Managers*[a]

Human Resource Responsibilities	HR Managers	Store Managers
Staffing	4.5	4.5
Training and Development	3.5	4.5
Performance Management	4.5	4.0
Compensation	3.0	3.5
Safety	2.5	2.5
Knowledge of Business	2.0	4.5
Managing Change	2.0	4.5

[a]Respondents were given a list of human resource responsibilities and asked to rate their importance to store performance using a scale of 1 (not very important) to 5 (very important). The responses were aggregated for all stores. The numbers in the table represent the mean ratings for each item. The questionnaire was completed by all the human resource managers and store managers at each store.

3. EXERCISE

Scanning the Contemporary Work Environment

    I. *Objective:* The purpose of this exercise is to help you understand the potential influence of trends and changes in the external environment on the design and implementation of human resource management practices.

    II. *Out-of-Class Preparation Time:*   None

    III. *In-Class Time Suggested:*   20–30 minutes

    IV. *Procedures:*

        A. This exercise should be done in groups of four to five students.

        B. After completion of the exercise, each group will present its ideas to the rest of the class.

        C. Listed below are some of the major predictions about changes or trends in the labor/employment environment that will take place. Read each trend and list some ideas about the impact of these trends on the major human resource management functions: staffing and placement, training and development, salary administration, performance evaluation, job design, promotions, and career planning. That is, what human resource issues will organizations face because of these changes?

Trend	Impact on HRM
1. Aging of the labor force	
2. Growth of prime-age workers (ages 25–54)	
3. Shift from a manufacturing economy to a service economy	
4. Increasing number of dual-career families	
5. Increasing number of women in the labor force	
6. Increasing number of minority workers in the labor force	

4. EXERCISE

Evaluating the Financial Impact of Human Resource Management Activities

I. *Objectives:*
  A. To provide you with practice in analyzing data and drawing conclusions regarding managerial implications.
  B. To make you aware of the potential costs of controllable, dysfunctional turnover and its impact on net income or profit.
  C. To make you aware of the potential benefits of human resource management activities to an organization's "bottom line."
II. *Out-of-Class Preparation Time:* 2 hours
III. *In-Class Time Suggested:* 45 minutes
IV. *Procedures:* Read the entire exercise, including the "Background" on the Charlotte Health System and the three exhibits. Using the data in the exhibits, do the calculations (on your own, prior to class) requested on Form 3. Then assemble groups of three to five students during the class period and discuss each of the questions. At the end of the class period, have a spokesperson for each group discuss the group's answers and rationale with the entire class.

Background

The health care industry has undergone dramatic change and restructuring during the decade of the 1990s. Mergers, consolidations, and downsizing were the norm as organizations struggled to provide more cost-effective, high-quality services demanded by managed-care organizations and corporate employers. A major response to these pressures has been the development of "integrated delivery systems" which typically combine multiple units of hospitals, physician practices, outpatient facilities, long-term care facilities, and insurance.

While the goal of these systems is to provide "seamless" care through internal referrals, a common medical record, common policies and procedures, etc., the reality has been somewhat less than a total success. Among the problems identified have been differences in values and incentives between the organizational units, lack of top management knowledge of some of the units acquired, and inability to "integrate" the different units clinically and managerially.

The Charlotte (North Carolina) Health System was developed from a base of a public hospital to which various delivery sites were added after Mr. Harry Majors became CEO 15 years ago. Since his arrival, Mr. Majors and his executive team have created the dominant health system in North

Carolina. Despite this success, the system continues to be under pressure from employers and managed-care organizations to further reduce its costs and document both clinical quality and cost-effectiveness.

Almost four years ago, Mr. Majors and the board of directors decided that the time had come to "professionalize" the human resource function since the organizations they had purchased or aligned with exhibited varying degrees of sophistication and vastly different policies and procedures. Ms. Betty Williams was recruited from another health system as the new VP for Human Resources. Ms. Williams came to her job after completion of an M.A. degree in human resources management from the University of Alabama and 16 years of experience in the field. During the three years she has been at Charlotte Health System, she has hired three new HRM staff persons in recruitment, employee benefits, and compensation.

As the board has considered how to reduce the cost of service delivery in the system, the corporate office in general, and the Human Resources Department in particular, have come under increased scrutiny. Ms. Williams has been told she needed to justify the additional budget allocation to her department over the past three years. Exhibit 1.6 shows her department's budget for year one (the year prior to Ms. Williams's arrival) as well as the three years since her arrival. The board has calculated "extra" costs of the Human Resources Department over the past three years (using year one as the base) to be $680,000. The largest percentage cost increases were in "salaries and benefits" and in "equipment and supplies." Most of the latter increases were the result of upgrades in computer hardware and software.

The board has scheduled a meeting for next Monday. One of the agenda items is to examine the costs of the Human Resource Management Department with the possibility of a budget cut for next year. Ms. Williams has been asked to make a presentation to justify her budget and how expansion of her department has contributed to the system's "bottom line." She has considered a *number* of changes she made which she believes *have* improved overall system performance. Among these were the development of system career ladders to increase employee retention, in-house management training programs to improve management competence, development of "model" staffing ratios to reduce employee stress and burnout, quarterly performance reviews to increase employee feedback, absenteeism incentive programs, and initiation of an annual employee survey to identify problem areas.

After some discussion with her staff, she decided that it would be easier to "document" the benefits of increased employee retention. Exhibit 1.7 shows the decline in employee turnover for year one (the year before Ms. Williams's arrival) as well as each of the following three years since her arrival.

Ms. Williams and her staff have calculated the average cost of turnover per employee by personnel category and these calculations are shown in Exhibit 1.8. Most of these calculations can be documented from personnel records. The exception is the "reduced productivity during the learning period." For these calculations, the staff calculated the average monthly productivity for a small sub-sample of the individuals who left and compared it to the average monthly productivity of those who replaced them during their first three months. They then calculated the dollar cost of this lost productivity for a one-year period.

Their assumption is that the lower productivity continues at the same level for a 12-month period and then disappears. More realistically, the lower productivity probably declines over time but continues for longer than a 12-month period. However, they feel their method of calculation is a good approximation of reality since their overestimation of the productivity loss is offset by the shorter time period of their calculations.

Exhibit 1.8 shows that the total cost for each individual who leaves the Charlotte Health System averages $7,049 but this varies from a high of $14,484 for physicians to a low of $3,644 for non-professional employees. These costs are divided into separation costs, replacement costs, training costs, and costs of reduced productivity (for the new employee) during the (assumed) one-year learning period.

Questions

1. Are the calculated benefits of reduced turnover sufficient to justify the $680,000 in increased costs associated with the expansion of the Human Resource Management Department? Would your answer be the same if "reduced productivity during the learning period" was excluded from the analysis?
2. In addition to improved employee retention, what are some other areas of potential economic benefit to the organization from having a Human Resource Department? What calculations would you do to prove such benefits?

EXHIBIT 1.6   *Human Resource Management Department Budget for Years One Through Four*

	Department Budget per Year			
Budget Cost	**One**	**Two**	**Three**	**Four**
Salaries and Benefits	$110,000	$233,000	$288,000	$324,000
Equipment and Supplies	24,000	39,000	48,000	57,000
Communications	41,000	62,000	73,000	81,000
Totals	$175,000	$334,000	$409,000	$462,000

EXHIBIT 1.7   *Annual Turnover Rate by Category for Years One Through Four*

Personnel Categories	Percent Turnover per Year			
	One	Two	Three	Four
Executive (*n* = 127)+	12.8	11.5	9.2	8.3
Physician (*n* = 367)	18.1	17.6	17.9	15.6
Other Professional (*n* = 615)	22.6	22.1	18.3	15.6
Non-Professional (*n* = 804)	29.0	26.3	27.1	24.3
Totals++ (*n* = 19.3)	23.8	22.3	21.3	18.8

+ *n* is the average number of employees in each category over the four-year period.
++ the weighted average turnover rate for all four categories for each of the four years.

EXHIBIT 1.8   *Average Costs of Turnover per Individual Over the Four-Year Period by Personnel Category*

Turnover Costs	Personnel Category				
	All Categories+	Executive	Physician	Other Professional	Non-Professional
	(n = 19.3)	(n = 127)	(n = 367)	(n = 615)	(n = 804)
Separation Costs:					
Exit Interviews	50.73	62.50	73.00	51.00	38.50
Administrative Costs	119.27	127.00	132.50	116.00	114.50
Separation Pay	348.01	2,254.00	1,034.00	—	—
	518.01	2,443.50	1,239.50	167.00	153.00
Replacement Costs:					
Job Advertisements	1,346.49	1,805.00	2,416.50	1,127.50	953.00
Pre-Employment Administration	353.28	405.00	416.50	386.50	291.00
Entrance Interviews	324.86	486.00	724.50	284.00	148.00
Assessment Testing	271.69	382.50	695.00	214.50	105.00
Staff Time	249.00	417.50	522.00	212.00	126.00
Travel/Moving Expenses	293.68	1,215.50	1,110.50	—	—
Processing New Employees	87.50	87.50	87.50	87.50	87.50
Medical Examinations	175.00	175.00	175.00	175.00	175.00
	3,101.50	4,974.00	6,147.50	2,487.00	1,885.50
Training Costs					
Informational Literature	80.00	80.00	80.00	80.00	80.00
Formal Training	147.53	340.00	516.50	35.00	35.00
On-the-Job Training	68.15	—	—	212.00	159.50
	295.68	420.00	596.50	327.00	274.50
Reduced Productivity During Learning Period	3,133.37	4,000.00	6,500.00	3,452.00	1,215.50
Total	$7,048.56	$11,837.50	$14,483.50	$6,433.00	$3,528.50
Tot. Excluding Prod. Svng.	$3,915.19	$7,837.50	$7,983.50	$2,981.00	$2,313.00

+ *weighted average*

FORM 3   *Calculation of Benefits of Higher Employee Retention Using a Base of Year One*

Personnel Category	Savings in Year			Total Savings
	Two	**Three**	**Four**	
Executive				
Physician				
Other Professional				
Non-Professional				
All Categories	_____	_____	_____	_____

Calculation of Savings or Loss:

1. Total Incremental Savings from Higher Employee Retention for all Personnel Categories for Years 2, 3, and 4.

2. Total Incremental Costs of the Human Resource Management Department Budget for Years 2, 3, and 4.   −$680,000

Net Savings or Loss   _____

Benefit/Cost Ratio (1) ÷ (2)   _____

5. SKILL BUILDER

Reference Materials for Human Resource Management

I. *Objectives:*
  A. To familiarize you with practitioner journals, academic journals, and internet sources used by human resource managers.
  B. To allow you to compare and contrast the types of information provided by each of the above sources.

II. *Time Required to Complete:* 4–5 hours

III. *Instructions:* You are to select one of the topics below or another topic approved by your instructor. After you have selected your topic, you should gather information on that topic from two articles taken from one of the practitioner journals and two articles from one of the academic journals. Additionally, you should also find information from two internet sources. The journals and internet sources are listed below. Read the information gathered and prepare a short report in which you: (a) Summarize what you learned about your topic from the sources; (b) Analyze the differences and similarities of the information from the different sources; (c) List the strengths and weaknesses of each source of information. Be sure to include a bibliography that cites the author, article title, journal name, date of publication, web address, etc.

SUGGESTED HUMAN RESOURCE MANAGEMENT TOPICS/AREAS

Changing Role of the Human Resource Manager
Strategic Human Resource Management
Human Resource Planning
Contingent Workers
Affirmative Action
Sexual Harassment
Training Executives and Managers
Dual Career Couples
International Human Resource Management
Skill-Based Pay

Gainsharing
Telecommuting
Managing Diversity
Flexible Employee Benefits
Performance Management Systems
Trends in Unionizing
Executive Compensation
Team-Based Compensation Systems
Merit Pay
On-Line Recruiting
Use of Intranets
Human Resource Information Systems

INFORMATION SOURCES

Academic Journals

Academy of Management Journal
Academy of Management Review

California Management Review
Employee Relations Law Journal

Academic Journals *(continued)*

Administrative Science Quarterly

Human Relations
Human Resource Management
Human Resource Planning
Industrial & Labor Relations Review
Industrial Relations
International Journal of Human Resources
Journal of Applied Psychology
Journal of Collective Negotiation in the Public Sector
Journal of Labor Research

Employee Rights & Responsibilities Journal
Journal of Management
Journal of Organization Behavior
Journal of Occupational Psychology
Journal of Vocational Behavior
Labor Law Journal
Labor Studies Journal
Organization Behavior & Human Decision Processes
Personnel Psychology
Public Personnel Management

Practitioner Journals

Academy of Management Executive
Across the Board
Business Horizons
Harvard Business Review
HR Magazine
HR Focus
Management Review

Organization Dynamics
Personnel
Personnel Journal
Supervisory Management
Training
Training and Development

Internet Sources

Human Resource Issues (from Newspage):
http://www.newspage.com/NEWSPAGE/cgi-bin/walk.cgi/NEWSPAGE/infor/d11/d3/

HR Reporter: *http://www.lrp.com/Human/hrnm.htm*

HR Live: *http://www.hrlive.com*

Institute for International Human Resources:
http://www.shrm.org/docs/IIHR.html

Sierra's Human Resource Information Center:
http://www.sierrasys.com/ie_hr.htm

Society for Human Resource Management: *http://www.shrm.org*

International Personnel Management Association: *http://www.ipmaac.org*

Employment Management Association: *http://www.shrm.org/ema/*

International Foundation of Employee Benefit Plans: *http://www.ifebp.org/*

Human Resource Management Basics:
http://members.aol.com/hrmbasics/index.htm

6. SKILL BUILDER

Using Internet Search Engines to Conduct HR Research

   I. *Objectives:*
      A. To familiarize you with different internet search strategies and search engines.
      B. To acquaint you with some of the human resources web sites available over the Internet.
  II. *Time Required to Complete:* 1–2 hours
 III. *Instructions:* This skill builder has two parts. Your first task is to pick a specific human resource topic and research it using the Internet. In conducting your research, select three of the following search engines:

www.hotbot.com   www.lycos.com
www.altavista.digital.com   www.infoseek.com
www.yahoo.com   www.dogpile.com/
www.excite.com

Then write a 100–200 word report that summarizes your findings. Specifically, the report should answer the following questions:

      A. What *search strategy* did you follow in researching the topic using the three different search engines? Critique your strategy. Was it effective? What would you do differently next time?
      B. Compare the three search engines used in terms of their ease of use and the usefulness of the information each query result provides. Overall, which search engine do you believe was most useful?

The second part of the exercise is designed to familiarize you with different human resource web sites. Search each of the following sites and, in one paragraph, write down the types of information provided by each.

http://www.aflcio.org/
http://www.shrm.org/docs/Hrmagazine.html
http://www.acaonline.org/
http://www.osha.gov/
http://www.trainingnet.com/
http://janweb.icdi.wvu.edu/kinder/
http://www.monster.com/
http://www.dol.gov/

THE LEGAL AND REGULATORY ENVIRONMENT

7. CASE

The Storage Room Massage: A Case of Sexual Harassment?

Background

Standard Valve & Gauge Company manufactures safety relief valves, pressure gauges, thermometers, testing instruments, and spring disks. The company has three small plants scattered throughout the Southeast. Each plant employs approximately 325 workers. Personnel operations are generally centralized at corporate headquarters located in Atlanta, Georgia. However, the plant superintendent of each plant is largely responsible for the day-to-day administration of personnel policies.

The Incident

Bill Winthrop, a Shift Supervisor at the Marshfield plant, had been employed with the company for about six years. On June 11, 1991, Winthrop was terminated by the Plant Superintendent, Jim Hudson, for sexual harassment of a female employee, Mary Harper Jones, on June 9 (see Exhibit 1.9). Jones was employed as a laborer in the Marshfield plant and accused Winthrop of unwanted sexual advances (see Exhibit 1.10).

A few months after Winthrop was terminated, the company received a Notice of Charge of Discrimination from the Equal Employment Opportunity Commission (EEOC), filed by Winthrop alleging that he had been sexually harassed by Jones on three occasions and that her actions unreasonably interfered with his work performance and created a negative work atmosphere. He further alleged that the company failed to take action on his complaints about Ms. Jones and that he had been unduly discharged (see Exhibit 1.11).

The Company's Position

In its reply to the EEOC, the company maintained that Winthrop was terminated for sexual harassment and not on the basis of his race, sex, or any other manner of retaliation. The company also pointed out that after his termination on June 11, Winthrop had applied for unemployment compensation and the Employment Security Commission office hearing his appeal agreed that Winthrop was terminated for just cause. Consequently,

Winthrop was disqualified for unemployment benefits for a period of nine weeks. The commission's report stated, "Winthrop displayed poor judgment in requesting the 'massage' and the employer's discharge of the claimant was for good business reasons to avoid instances of like nature in the future." The company argued that his sexual harassment charges were unsubstantiated and should be dismissed (see Exhibit 1.12). Two weeks after forwarding the letter in Exhibit 1.12 to the EEOC, the Human Resource Director, J. Bevins, received a letter back from the EEOC (Exhibit 1.13) requesting additional information about the charges.

Questions

1. Evaluate the company's handling of Winthrop's termination. Was he terminated for just cause?
2. Under the Title VII guidelines on sexual harassment, what are the legal ramifications of a supervisor accusing an employee of sexual harassment?
3. What alternative actions could Jones have taken in dealing with Winthrop?

EXHIBIT 1.9   *Memo from Plant Superintendent to the Human Resource Director on Winthrop's Termination*

MEMORANDUM

To: J. Bevins, Human Resource Director
From: Jim Hudson, Plant Superintendent
Date: June 11, 1991
Subject: Termination of Bill Winthrop (Shift Supervisor, Marshfield Plant)

Based on allegations substantiated by others (allegations of Miss Mary Harper Jones, black female, who is employed as a laborer at the above plant site), a personal interview was conducted at approximately 11:00 a.m. this date and as a result of the interview Mr. Bill Winthrop was relieved of his duties and terminated effective this date.

Mr. Winthrop admitted he allowed Miss Jones to physically rub his back and allowed such action to take place at the workplace on or about noon on Monday, June 9, and was witnessed by another employee (Mr. Jim Joyner, electrician). Mr. Winthrop disavowed other allegations made by Miss Jones. By his admission of the above contact, Mr. Winthrop was informed that a possible sex discrimination and/or harassment suit could result. Mr. Winthrop stated it was all in jest. I informed Mr. Winthrop of the dire consequences of his actions and the fact that Miss Jones had in fact made it serious as she called his actions to the attention of the plant superintendent and others. A copy of Miss Jones's statement is attached for your information.

Respectfully submitted,

Jim Hudson

Jim Hudson

EXHIBIT 1.10   *Statement from Mary Harper Jones*
Concerning the Events of June 9, 1991

TO WHOM IT MAY CONCERN:

I was cleaning up on the first level of the plant and Bill (Winthrop) came up to me and asked how much I would charge for a massage. I said a professional would charge $35.00 an hour. I said I was not a professional. He asked me if I would meet him in the storage room. I thought he was joking. I smiled and he walked away. He had asked in general if the storage room was locked.

Later, I was on the other end of the plant floor and Bill was in the supervisor's booth motioning for me to come in. I went in and he said, "Sit down and rest; it is hot out there." I sat in J.P.'s chair. Jim Joyner came in at that point. Bill said to me, "Don't sit in that chair; it belongs to J.P. Garnett (Supervisor on shift)." I said it was okay because he is my friend. Bill asked Jim to listen to what I was saying. Jim asked me why I liked J.P., and I told Jim that J.P. has been the same person since the day I met him. Bill then said to me, "I'm going to give you a piece of advice, Mary. Stay away from J.P. because he will get you in trouble." Bill asked Jim what he had done over the weekend. Jim was talking about his weekend, and Bill cut him off saying, "Mary, give me $5.00 worth." Jim looked at me funny, and I had forgotten about the massage. Bill looked at Jim and smiled. Jim left. Bill said, "Mary, come on and stand behind me and massage my shoulders." And then I said, "You told me to come in here and rest and now you are putting me to work." Mr. Hudson (Plant Superintendent) walked in at that point and Bill told me to get over by J.P.'s chair, and I stepped over to it. Mr. Hudson came to where we were, and Bill started talking to him about the shift operations. Mr. Hudson and Bill were talking for a while. Eventually, Mr. Hudson left and went to the plant floor.

Bill told me to go to the storage room and to go one way while he went another way. When I got there he was already there. I walked in and asked him, "What's up?" He sat down on a bucket of cleaning fluid and asked if there was any way to lock the door. I told him there was no way to lock the door. I told him that no one ever came up there except the other laborers and he had sent all three to dump the trash. Then he told me to come on and finish massaging his shoulders. Before I started, I asked him if his wife ever did this and he said she was too puny and did not have the grip that I did. I felt funny because he asked me to do it now and had asked me to stop earlier when Mr. Hudson had walked into the supervisor's booth. After I massaged him 3 or 4 times, I patted him on the shoulder and said, "Okay, Bill, time is up. I am finished." I asked him if something was wrong. He said it was all of the pressure here and his son had gotten hurt over the weekend. He said, "Thanks a lot Mary," and then stood there for a few minutes. I started to leave and he grabbed my arm and pulled me to him and hugged me. I left. When I got downstairs I saw Donald (an engineer) and told him I needed to talk to him. I told him the story and he suggested I go to J.P. Garnett (Supervisor on the shift) and talk to him. Garnett suggested I talk to Joan (secretary). I then went to the office and told the story to Joan.

Mary Harper Jones

Mary Harper Jones

EXHIBIT 1.11 *Charge of Discrimination Filed by Bill Winthrop with the EEOC*

CHARGE OF DISCRIMINATION
This form is affected by the Privacy Act
of 1974; See Privacy Act Statement on
reverse before completing this form.

ENTER CHARGE NUMBER

___ FEPA
_X_ EEOC   1910897654

_____ and EEOC
(State or local Agency, if any)

Name (Indicate Mr., Miss, or Mrs.)		Home Telephone No. & Area Code
Mr. Bill Winthrop		(404) 459-3145

Street Address	City, State and Zip Code	County
229 Hitchcock Street	Marshfield, GA 29768	Macon

NAMED IS THE EMPLOYER, LABOR ORGANIZATION, EMPLOYMENT AGENCY, APPRENTICESHIP
COMMITTEE, STATE OR LOCAL GOVERNMENT AGENCY WHO DISCRIMINATED AGAINST ME (IF
MORE THAN ONE LIST BELOW)

Name	No. of Employees	Telephone No. & Area Code
Standard Valve & Gauge Co.	325	(404) 299-4590

Street Address	City, State and Zip Code
P. O. Box 34517	Atlanta, GA 25843

Cause of Discrimination Based on (Check Appropriate one).   Date most recent or
continuing discri-
mination took place

_X_ Race ___ Color _X_ Sex ___ Religion ___ Age
___ National Origin _X_ Retaliation ___ Other (specify)

June 11, 1991

The particulars are (If additional space is needed, attach extra sheet(s)):

I. On or around April 8, 1991, on or around April 18, 1991, and
    on June 9, 1991, I was sexually harassed. I was initially
    hired in November 1985 and have been employed as a Shift Super-
    visor since my hire. Respondent employs approximately 325
    persons, of whom 300 are males.

II. On or around April 8, 1991, I reported to Jim Hudson (male),
    Plant Superintendent, that I had been sexually harassed by
    Mary Harper Jones (female), laborer.

    I am not aware of Respondent's policy regarding sexual
    harassment.

III. I believe that I have been discriminated against on the basis
     of my sex (male) because:

     A. On or around April 8, 1991, Mary Harper Jones (female),
     laborer, propositioned me. On or around April 18, 1991, Ms.
     Jones made a sexually derogatory statement. On or around
     June 9, 1991, Ms. Jones propositioned me again. Jones'
     sexual advances unreasonably interfered with my work per-
     formance and created a negative work atmosphere.

     B. When I informed Jim Hudson (male), Plant Superintendent,
     about Ms. Jones' sexual advances, he stated that Ms. Jones
     had propositioned him, too. However, no action was taken
     regarding my complaint.

___ I also want this charge filed with
the EEOC. I will advise the agencies
if I change my address or telephone
number and I will cooperate fully with
them in processing my charge in
accordance with their procedures.

I declare under penalty of perjury that
the foregoing is true and correct.

NOTARY - (When necessary to meet
State and Local Requirements).
I swear or affirm that I have read
the above charge and that it is
true to the best of my knowledge,
information and belief.

SIGNATURE OF COMPLAINANT

10-1-91   *Bill Winthrop*

Date   Charging Party (Signature)

SUBSCRIBED AND SWORN TO BEFORE ME
THIS DATE (Day, month, and year)

EXHIBIT 1.11   *continued*

PAGE 2 of 2   CHARGE OF DISCRIMINATION   ENTER CHARGE NUMBER
This form is affected by the Privacy Act of   FEPA
1974; see Privacy Act Statement on reverse   ___ X ___ EEOC   1910897654
before completing this form.

REF: vs.
       BILL WINTHROP   STANDARD VALVE & GAUGE COMPANY

I.   On June 11, 1991, I was discharged from my position as
     Shift Supervisor. Respondent employs approximately 325
     persons, of whom 295 are Caucasians. Similarly, of these
     325 persons, 300 are males.

II. Jim Hudson (Caucasian, male), Plant Superintendent, stated
     I was being discharged because I received a complaint of
     sexual harassment.

     According to the Respondent's employee handbook, I can be
     discharged due to the following reasons: (1) decrease in
     Respondent's business; (2) accepting employment with another
     company; (3) leaving work without properly being relieved;
     (4) reporting to work in a condition not suitable for
     normal performance; (5) gross insubordination; (6) bring-
     ing on-site drugs or alcohol; (7) fighting; (8) bringing
     on-site any type of weapon; (9) failure for any reason
     to perform assigned duties; (10) excessive tardiness or
     absenteeism; and (11) conduct not in the best interest of
     the company.

III. I believe I have been discriminated against on the bases of
     race (Caucasian), sex (male) and in retaliation for com-
     plaining about acts made unlawful by Title VII inasmuch as:

     A. On or around April 8, 1991, I informed Jim Hudson
     (Caucasian, male), Plant Superintendent, that I had been
     sexually harassed by Mary Harper Jones (black, female).
     No action was taken regarding my complaint.

     B. Ms. Jones alleged that I sexually harassed her on June
     9, 1991. Actually, Ms. Jones sexually harassed me on
     that date.

     C. I am not aware of any management employee who received
     a complaint of sexual harassment.

___ I also want this charge filed with the EEOC. I will advise the agencies if I change my address or telephone number and I will cooperate fully with them in processing my charge in accordance with their procedures.	NOTARY - (When necessary to meet State and Local Requirements).
	I swear or affirm that I have read the above charge and that it is true to the best of my knowledge, information and belief.
I declare under penalty of perjury that the foregoing is true and correct.	SIGNATURE OF COMPLAINANT
	SUBSCRIBED AND SWORN TO BEFORE ME THIS DATE (Day, Month, Year)

10-1-91   *Bill Winthrop*
Date   Charging Party (Signature)

EXHIBIT 1.12   *Letter from Company Vice President of Human Resources to EEOC*

October 5, 1991

Atlanta District Office—EEOC
5500 Peachtree Street
Atlanta, Georgia

Attention: Ms. Harriet Burton

RE: EEOC #1910897654
    Bill Winthrop

Dear Ms. Burton:

This letter is to advise your office of our company's position with regard to the above referenced claim. Mr. Bill Winthrop was terminated from our employ June 11, 1991 for sexual harassment. He was not terminated on the basis of his race, his sex, or for any manner of retaliation.

We emphatically deny the sexual harassment charge against our employee. Several unusual circumstances surround this incident. For your information Mr. Winthrop has applied for unemployment compensation and the office hearing his appeal agreed that Mr. Winthrop was terminated for just cause, and he was penalized his unemployment compensation for the appropriate number of weeks. We have interrogated Mr. Jim Hudson, Plant Superintendent, over the phone and he has emphatically denied that Mr. Winthrop had at any time told him he was sexually harassed; and had he done so, Mr. Hudson would have conducted an investigation immediately. It is interesting that the reason for Mr. Winthrop's termination is the same as his charge against his employer.

With reference to Item III, Section B: The superintendent, Mr. Hudson, in our telephone conversation of October 3, 1991, stated that during the last part of April Ms. Mary Harper Jones did come to him and inquire if the company extended employee loans since she needed a down payment for a car. Mr. Hudson told Ms. Jones that the company did not have a Credit Union nor did they give employees loans. She made the comment, "Golly, I would do most anything for a down payment for a car." Mr. Hudson remarked he was sorry he could not help her out. Mr. Hudson did not interpret this as a proposition and neither does our company.

In regard to Item III, Section A: We have reviewed our company records and the dates mentioned in the charge are not documented so we cannot establish the exact date of Mr. Winthrop's allegations and we, therefore, assume he is not being factual.

Because of Mr. Winthrop's position as a Shift Supervisor, we in no way can see how Ms. Jones, a subordinate, could influence Mr. Winthrop's receiving advances, promotions, pay increases, etc. Due to the fact that Mr. Winthrop's allegations were not known by anyone at the plant, we find these charges to be made without fact and that they should be dismissed.

Very truly yours,

J. Bevins, Vice President of Human Resources

JB:tf

cc: Jim Hudson, Marshfield
    Bill Winthrop File

EXHIBIT 1.13 *Request for Additional Information*
from EEOC to Standard Valve & Gauge

REQUEST FOR ADDITIONAL INFORMATION CHARGE #1910897654

1. Please provide a signed statement from Jim Hudson concerning what Charging Party told him about being sexually harassed. Also include whether or not Hudson told Bill Winthrop that Mary Harper Jones had propositioned him.

2. If Charging Party reported being sexually harassed to management, to whom did he report this and what were the specifics?

3. Provide your company's policy on sexual harassment.

4. Please provide the personnel files of Charging Party and Jones.

5. Please provide your company's policy on discipline and discharge.

6. Please explain in detail the reasons for Charging Party's discharge.

7. Please provide a list of employees that were discharged during the last year, indicating their name, race, sex, date of hire, position held, reason for discharge, date of discharge, and prior disciplinary history. Provide the personnel file of a black female employee that was discharged.

8. Please provide a signed statement from Jones concerning whether or not Charging Party sexually harassed her on June 9, 1991.

9. Please provide signed statements from witnesses concerning whether or not Charging Party was sexually harassed or Jones was sexually harassed.

10. Please provide a position statement on every point raised on the face of the charge.

8. CASE

Same Sex Sexual Harassment

Jennifer Perdue, a manager at Perfect Pizzeria, reflected on the events that surrounded the employment of a sixteen-year-old employee, Arthur Green. She wondered whether the decision to hire him was correct and questioned her handling of the events that followed. Just like other fast food restaurants, Jennifer had difficulty staffing the traditional dinner house restaurant. Jennifer hired Arthur to work as a cook and waiter, but what followed was anything but typical for Arthur, his family, or Perfect Pizzeria.

Jennifer hired Arthur to work after school and remembered how young and anxious he looked during the interview. Since this was Arthur's very first job, Jennifer was concerned about how he would fit into the work team. It did not take long to see that there was trouble. Arthur was openly heterosexual; his immediate supervisor, Howard Smith, was an openly homosexual male; and his coworkers included five openly homosexual males and three openly heterosexual males.

According to Arthur, Howard, his supervisor, and the other homosexual coworkers began to sexually harass him and the other heterosexual males. It seemed that after new male employees were hired, the homosexual employees would attempt to learn the new employee's sexual orientation. If the new employee was a male and heterosexual, then the homosexual employees pressured the employee to engage in homosexual sex or to convert them to their sexual orientation. The females and other homosexual males were not harassed. The harassment of Arthur took place on a daily basis for seven months.

During working hours, Howard graphically described his homosexual lifestyle and homosexual sex, made vulgar sexual remarks, called Arthur "honey," embarrassed, and humiliated him. In addition, Howard would run his hands through Arthur's hair, massaged Arthur's buttocks while walking past him, and pulled out Arthur's pants in order to see down into them.

The three other coworkers who were heterosexual also complained of Howard's sexual advances. Among other things, Howard attempted to kiss them, massaged their shoulders, and rubbed up against them. Arthur and the three heterosexual coworkers were not only harassed by Howard but also by the five other homosexual coworkers. Although Arthur and the others were adamant that they were not interested in the sexual advances, they were called at home and asked out on dates.

Arthur and the heterosexual coworkers told Howard and the other homosexual coworkers to stop or to "shut up" each time a sexual comment was made to them. Moreover, they clearly indicated that they were

Contributed by Joyce M. Beggs and Gerald E. Calvasina, Belk College of Business Administration, University of North Carolina Charlotte.

not interested in dates. Despite the objections to their unwelcome advances, the harassment continued.

First, the heterosexual workers complained to Howard about the harassment. Howard laughed and joked about their complaints. Second, Arthur complained to Jennifer and to her assistant about the harassment. Third, Arthur told his mother about the harassment. In fact, Arthur's mother complained directly to Jennifer and the other supervisors about the verbal and physical sexual harassment directed toward her son by employees of Perfect Pizzeria. Jennifer decided to call a meeting to discuss the harassment complaint.

Questions

1. What should Jennifer Perdue do when Arthur Green complains of his treatment?
2. Are individuals who are victims of "same sex" sexual harassment subject to the same legal rights and protection as those who are victims of "opposite sex" sexual harassment? Discuss.
3. What should Jennifer Perdue do at the meeting to inform Howard Smith and others of the sexual harassment complaint? What should she do after the meeting?
4. What should Jennifer do if the behavior continues?

9. CASE

Unfair Promotions at Food Chain Supermarkets

Thomas L. Rutherford, Human Resource Director of Food Chain Supermarkets, Inc., was jolted by the conversation he just had with Walter Jackson, an employee in the company's distribution warehouse. Jackson had complained that black employees were being passed over for promotions in favor of white employees who had less experience and seniority. Jackson had gone on to explain that he had resigned his position in the meat department of the warehouse because, despite his experience and job performance, he felt he would not get promoted. He explained that he had been passed over for promotion three times since he started work with Food Chain.

After Jackson left his office, Rutherford began to immediately investigate his claims. He called in Mark Walters, his personnel assistant, and explained his conversation with Jackson to him. "The last thing I want on my hands is a discrimination suit," Rutherford told Mark. "I want you to get some data on promotions that have occurred in the last couple of years in our warehouse operations. Also, while you're at it, get the same information for our stores. Also, here are the names of three black employees given to me by Jackson. Pull their files and try to get any facts on what happened with their promotion requests." Mark replied, "I don't think it will be too difficult to pull together the information, Tom, now that we have finally gotten our personnel records centralized. But I'll probably have to talk with some of the department managers and supervisors also." Rutherford suggested that he interview the three black employees also. As Mark left his office, Rutherford began to think about the company's human resource practices and Jackson's allegations.

Background

Food Chain Supermarkets, Inc. is a regional chain of supermarkets located in the Midwest. Additionally, the company operates a central warehouse, bakery, and its own transportation system. Its main office, distribution center (warehouse), and a dozen stores are located in Reed County. Presently the company employs over 1,600 people in the county. According to recent census data, Reed County's labor force is about 22 percent black. The company has plans to refurbish its stores and to open four additional stores over the next two years. Rutherford was hired in anticipation of this growth to help better manage the company's personnel needs.

The distribution center has five departments: grocery, meat, frozen food, produce, and transportation. Each department has two shifts. The starting times of various employees on the same shifts are staggered. Both receiving and shipping functions are carried out at the warehouse. Order puller, order selector, order picker, and picker are synonymous terms for the same position. A warehouse crew leader is a working supervisor who assigns duties and performs the same duties as subordinates. Management positions in the stores consist of assistant produce manager, produce manager, grocery manager trainee, relief grocery manager, deli manager, relief assistant manager, assistant manager, head cashier, and assistant head cashier.

Human Resource Practices

When Rutherford was hired four months ago, the President had explained that because of the physical dispersion of the stores, human resource policies were decentralized with a great deal of responsibility placed on the district managers. Promotion recommendations and decisions were made by supervisors of the different departments in the warehouse. In order to be promoted to a warehouse crew leader, an employee had to be on the same shift and in the same department as the opening. The factors utilized in promotion decisions at the warehouse were character, integrity, good sound morals, correct attitude, and initiative. The company felt that the supervisor was in the best position to judge whether or not an employee was promotable. There was no system for employees to apply for promotions. Written performance evaluations were limited to office employees, merchandisers, and store managers. At the retail stores, store supervisors made promotion recommendations to the district manager. Promotions were limited to persons recommended by the store managers. The district managers agreed with the store managers 90 to 95 percent of the time. The district manager decided who would be promoted, transferred, demoted, hired, or terminated for all positions up to the department head. Job vacancies were not routinely posted. Employees could be transferred from store to store as needed.

Rutherford recalled a conversation he recently had with one of the district managers, Joe Perkins: "We really don't need to post jobs since each district manager is usually aware of openings in his or her district and which employees are ready for promotion. Further, an employee doesn't have to ask in order to be considered for a promotion. Although we don't have a written evaluation system, the job performance of an employee is conveyed by word of mouth from one level of supervision to another."

Two Weeks Later

Rutherford had received the reports and data prepared by Mark on promotions within the warehouse and stores for the past two years (see Exhibit 1.14). Mark had also prepared summaries of what had happened to Jackson and the other three black employees mentioned by Jackson. As Rutherford began reading through the report, he wondered what changes would be needed at Food Chain. He certainly did not want to have another conversation like the one he had with Jackson two weeks earlier.

Questions

1. Analyze the table in Exhibit 1.14. What conclusions do you reach? Is there evidence of discrimination in promotion decisions?
2. Do you believe that Gemson, Thompson, LeBlanc, and Jackson were discriminated against?
3. What are some of the potential disadvantages of a "word of mouth" promotion system?
4. What should Rutherford do now?
5. What kinds of policies can the company design to better integrate minorities into management positions?

EXHIBIT 1.14   *Report on Promotion Rates*

TO: T. L. Rutherford, Director of Human Resources
FROM: Mark Walters, Human Resource Assistant
RE: Promotions

I have collected the data you requested on promotion rates at our warehouse and stores for the last two years (see table). I have also summarized what I could learn about the Jackson situation and the other three promotion cases he mentioned.

PROMOTION RATES

Unit	Year	Total Employees White	Total Employees Black	Total Promotions White	Total Promotions Black	Promotion Rates White Rate	Promotion Rates Black Rate
Warehouse/stores	1998	1,603	284	171	21	10.66%	7.39%
Warehouse/stores	1997	1,414	291	122	27	8.62	9.27
Warehouse	1998	411	173	42	13	10.21	7.50
Warehouse	1997	223	192	18	21	8.07	10.90
Stores	1998	1,192	111	129	8	10.80	7.20
Stores	1997	1,191	99	104	6	8.73	6.10

Note: In 1998, blacks represented 5.8% of 137 store promotions and 9% of the work force.
In 1997, 94.6% of the managers were white and in 1998 it was 94.7%.

CLIFFORD GEMSON: Clifford Gemson was hired as a produce clerk in June of 1997. He had originally applied for a management position. He had three years of grocery store management experience including six months in produce management with another company. Gemson worked in two stores between June 1997 and April 1998. On several occasions Gemson asked his district manager (J. Perkins) and his store manager (C. Fagen) about promotion to vacant produce manager positions. The first vacancy was filled on October 8,1997 by Bob Watkins, a white employee. Watkins, a produce clerk, had 18 months of experience with us. Watkins, who had no management experience, was replaced by another white employee, Sheila Wilson, on November 8,1997. Wilson was selected on the basis of her Food Chain experience as a produce clerk and an assistant produce manager for six months. Gemson was not considered for either vacancy.

ROY THOMPSON: Roy Thompson was hired by Food Chain at our warehouse on 9/18/96 as a maintenance (sanitation) employee. His duties included forklift driving, sorting damaged food, and rebuilding pallets. His prior work experience included supervisory duties and self-employment. Thompson trained a white employee of Food Chain (Neal Marcy, hired 5/12/97) who was promoted to crew leader of the maintenance (sanitation) department on 6/16/97. Before Marcy was hired, Thompson asked his supervisor (E. Jones) for the crew leader job to which Marcy was promoted. Jones told Thompson that he would never be a crew leader as long as he was supervisor. Jones denies saying this. According to Thompson, his supervisors had repeatedly told him that he had both excellent attendance and performance. On 8/15/98 a junior white employee, Earl Hanes (with less company experience than Thompson), was promoted to a sanitation crew leader for the same shift and in the same department that Thompson worked. According to Jones, Hanes was better qualified because of his previous work experience.

LESLIE LeBLANC: Leslie LeBlanc was hired by Food Chain on 7/8/96 as a frozen food picker. Her next position was frozen food loader. LeBlanc was trained to act as a "fill-in" crew leader, and in fact did fill in as a crew leader until Ricky Anderson (white) was hired. LeBlanc trained Anderson in the duties of a "fill-in" crew leader. Anderson then assumed LeBlanc's place as "fill-in" crew leader. Anderson was offered a full-time crew leader's position, which he refused. LeBlanc was never offered this job. LeBlanc had previously informed Food Chain management of her prior experience as a shift leader at a textile mill.

WALTER JACKSON: Walter Jackson was employed by Food Chain on 4/14/96 at the warehouse in the meat department. Milk, dairy products, and meat are in the same department. Jackson's job duties prior to April 1998 included milk picking, unloading, and forklift driving. In the spring of 1998 a crew leader told Jackson that he was up for promotion to crew leader in the department. Terry Gibson (a white employee) received the job on 6/7/98. Gibson was initially hired on 1/11/96, resigned 2/5/96 and was rehired 11/3/96. Jackson had more company and departmental experience than Gibson. However, he was never considered for the position. Gibson's prior duties were solely picking meat and Jackson had supervised Gibson when Jackson served as "fill-in" crew leader prior to Gibson's promotion. The supervisor asserted that Gibson had broader departmental experience than Jackson. Since that time two other employees in the meat department with less seniority and experience have been promoted over Jackson.

10. CASE

Managing Diversity: Johnson Chemical International

Jeff Rice, Vice President of Corporate Human Resources at Johnson Chemical International was very anxious about the meeting he was about to have with John Henderson (CEO), Gary Polaski (Secretary and General Counsel), Steven Hong (Vice President of Operations, Haverford Plant, and Matt Beale (Vice President of Public Affairs and Communications). The last two days had been quite tense in the company ever since an e-mail (see Exhibit 1.15) was sent throughout the company's Haverford plant.

Johnson Chemical International is one of the world's leading manufacturers of specialty chemical products. The company was founded in 1902 by Herman Johnson, a MIT trained chemist. Over the years, Johnson Chemical has built a reputation for producing high quality products developed through cutting edge technology and research. As a privately held corporation, Johnson Chemical does not report sales or earning figures. It has plants and operations in 30 countries and manufacturing facilities in 10 countries (Argentina, Canada, Kenya, Indonesia, Greece, United Kingdom, Japan, Taiwan, Malaysia, and Brazil). Johnson Chemical employs more than 14,500 people worldwide. Its headquarters is located in Chicago. Employment in the United States is about one-half of its total workforce worldwide with a majority of those employees in the Chicago area. Because of its need for highly trained scientists and technicians, the company recruits a substantial number of employees with backgrounds and training in the sciences and engineering fields.

U.S. manufacturing operations are conducted at their Haverford plant about 15 miles outside of Chicago. The state-of-the art plant is about three million square feet and is one of the most modern chemical manufacturing facilities in the world. The facility also has state-of-the art laboratories and houses the company's research division. In addition to its hourly employees, the company employs a large number of R&D employees consisting of scientists, technicians, and engineers. Because of its need for highly trained technical employees, the company has extensive recruiting efforts at the major colleges and universities with outstanding science and engineering programs. A majority of its top management has come from the technical ranks of the company. Its current CEO, John Henderson is a Chemical Engineer and the former president of International Operations.

The Meeting

John Henderson: Come on in Jeff. Good morning folks. I want to thank you for meeting with me this morning. We have a major problem on our hands.

A crude e-mail has sent a tidal wave through the company. It's already hit the press. We've had several calls from the media asking for us to comment on what has happened. Matt, how are we handling the calls?

Matt Beale: John, I have issued a press release that basically states that Johnson Chemical does not tolerate any form of racist or sexist jokes and the individual responsible will be dealt with appropriately. Our information systems folks are trying to determine the origins of the e-mail.

Gary Polaski: John, don't worry. We are on firm legal grounds if we fire the individual or individuals responsible for using the company e-mail to send racist and sexist jokes. I think we should take very strong action when we find out who is responsible.

Steven Hong: Well, we better do something fast because it is certainly affecting plant operations. People aren't working but busy talking about the e-mail. I'm afraid that it really has taken people off track for the time. It also seems to be unleashing some grievances that our women and minority employees have about their treatment in the company. The men and white employees seem to be worried that they're going to all be blamed for the e-mail or even worse that they agree with the sentiments in that e-mail. John, I'm worried about the impact of this on employee morale.

Jeff Rice: John, since the e-mail I have had several women and minority employees, especially the African-American employees come to my office to talk about problems and other incidents in the company. To be honest, it has caught me off guard. We have an excellent equal opportunity/affirmative action program in place and have made some strides in hiring women and minorities in the last five years. (See Exhibit 1.16). I am wondering if we've really done enough.

John Henderson: I'm not sure what you mean, Jeff. Our company has enjoyed a good reputation as a leader in the industry when it comes to equal employment opportunity. How could this happen?

Jeff Rice: Well, I was thinking about this last night. You know, John, in the last few years we have begun to have a more diverse group of employees after years of being a company with primarily white male employees. Perhaps, it was only a matter of time before these tensions emerged.

John Henderson: Well, we're going to have to get a handle on the issues. Jeff, I want you and your staff to find out what the issues are and give me a report on your findings in 60 days. After we review your report, we'll have to determine what we need to do.

Get whatever help you need from consultants. I expect a negative media backlash on this thing, and we're going to have to show that we are a company prepared to deal with tough issues. I have prepared a company wide message that will be sent to all employees this afternoon. (See Exhibit 1.17).

Rice's Report

Six months after the meeting, Jeffrey Rice sent John Henderson and the rest of the executive staff a 20 page confidential report of his findings. Excerpts from his report are contained in Exhibits 1.18–1.24. With the assistance of a consulting firm, Rice organized focus groups with African-American employees, women employees, Asian employees, and white male employees. Focus groups were recruited on a volunteer basis and were facilitated by the consultants to assure confidentiality and candidness. (See Exhibit 1.18.) The topics covered in the focus groups are shown in Exhibit 1.19. The views expressed by each group are summarized in Exhibits 1.20–1.23. In addition to the focus groups, an employee attitude survey was also administered to all plant employees. The results of the survey are shown in Exhibit 1.24.

Questions

1. Evaluate Johnson's actions in dealing with the e-mail.
2. Examine the data contained in Exhibits 1.16 and 1.18–1.23. What seem to be the most significant diversity issues at Johnson?
3. What is the cost to the organization of these problems? What will happen if they are not addressed?
4. Where and how do these issues need to be dealt with?
5. What support, skills, and training do managers need to deal with these issues?
6. What human resource management systems or policies need to be examined and possibly modified?

EXHIBIT 1.15   *The E-Mail Message*

The e-mail message

Morning Puzzle: Do you recognize these acronyms?

UFO
IBB
NAACP

Answer: UFO = Ugly ------- Orientals; IBB = Itty bitty breasts; and NAACP = -------, apes, alligators, coons and possums

EXHIBIT 1.16   *Employment Trends*

- There has been a 10 percent increase in employee growth at the Haverford Plant.
- The percent of women employees has increased from 10 to 15 percent.
- The percent of African-American employees has remained at 6 percent.
- The percent of Asian employees has increased from 5 to 10 percent.
- Plant turnover averages 2 percent but is ten times higher for women and African Americans.
- The percent of women in management/supervisory positions increased from 2 to 2.7 percent.
- The percent of African Americans in management/supervisory positions increased from 1.5 to 2.0 percent.
- The percent of Asians in management/supervisory positions increased from 2 to 3.5 percent.
- There has been an 8 percent increase in minority scientists (most of that represents Asians).
- The percentage of women scientists has grown by 2 percent.
- The highest ranking woman in the company is Meredith Jensen, Vice President and Deputy Counsel.
- The highest ranking African-American manager is Vice President for Equal Opportunity and Employee Relations.
- The highest ranking Asian manager is Vice President, Plant Operations.

EXHIBIT 1.17   *Letter to Employees from John Henderson, CEO*

Dear Johnson Employees:

By now, you have heard about the e-mail that was sent through the company's computer system that contained offensive comments. I want to be very clear: We will not tolerate behavior that makes our work environment uncomfortable and hostile for others. The telling of racist, sexist, or offensive comments is not appropriate behavior at Johnson Chemical. It is disrespectful of fellow employees. Using company e-mail to perpetuate offensive views of others violates company policy. Rest assured that we will see that those responsible for sending the e-mail are duly disciplined.

I am counting on you to respect your fellow employees and to commit to ensuring a working climate that is tolerant of our diversity.

John Henderson

EXHIBIT 1.18   *Letter of Invitation to Participate in Focus Group Discussions*

As you know, we continue to be committed to having an equal opportunity work climate at Johnson. In an effort to achieve this goal, we invite you to participate in a focus group to help us collect data around issues of diversity. The focus groups will be organized so that we bring together different categories of employee groups over the next two months.

To assure confidentiality and anonymity, the actual discussion sessions will be facilitated by an outside consultant group we have contracted to assist us in our efforts. Discussion will focus on your experiences and thoughts on topics related to our human resource policies and systems and equal opportunity work climate.

I hope you will be willing to participate in one of the focus groups. Thank you in advance for your help. If you have any questions, please call my office. I'll be happy to provide additional information.

Sincerely,

Jeffrey Rice

Jeffrey Rice, Vice President
Corporate Human Resources

EXHIBIT 1.19   *Focus Group Discussion Areas*

1. Comment on your experience and view of the following areas of the company:

    A. Recruitment and hiring: Sources of recruits; selection criteria; orientation of new employees

    B. Promotion: Fairness of rating system; adequacy of opportunity

    C. Training and career development: Access to training; selection of trainees; adequacy of and availability of career development counseling

    D. Performance management: Pros and cons of the performance appraisal process; supervisor feedback

    E. Benefits: Adequacy; administration of benefits

    F. Affirmative action program: Effectiveness of target of opportunity efforts; attitudes towards

    G. Treatment: Personal experiences of bias or barriers because of one's race, ethnicity or gender, or other areas

EXHIBIT 1.20   *Statements Made by Participants in African-American Employee Focus Group*

- Recruitment of African-Americans scientists and engineers is inadequate.

- African Americans have to be "more qualified" than other groups to get a job in the company.

- African-American students from historically black schools participated in summer intern programs but are rarely hired as full-time employees.

- African Americans do not have access to the same training and development opportunities as white employees. Selection for training and development rests with supervisors. This allows supervisors with negative views of the potential of African Americans to control who gets access to training.

- The promotion system is driven by potential ratings given by supervisors, and African Americans are disproportionately given low potential ratings for promotability.

- White supervisors are not comfortable working with African-American employees, and many do not know how to give helpful performance feedback.

- Most of the African-American employees are pigeonholed into staff positions in management.

- African Americans can't break into the "informal network" and get excluded from many social activities.

- Because there were so few African Americans in higher level positions, there are no mentors and role models.

- African Americans are stereotyped as being non-technical, lazy, and not suitable for management.

- Racial slurs and jokes are often heard on the plant floor.

- There is the "rule of three"—no three African-American employees should be seen together in the cafeteria or other places. If so, majority group employees assume something is going on or ask, "Why are the African-American employees all eating together?"

EXHIBIT 1.21   *Statements Made by Participants in Woman Employee Focus Groups*

- Women are not treated as individuals but subjected to sex role stereotypes. They are viewed as emotional, non-technical, and subordinate. Women who display different behaviors (assertive, good technical skills) are characterized as "pushy or macho."

- A myth persists that many of the women in the company don't need to work.

- Many male supervisors don't know how to work with women as peers or treat female subordinates in condescending ways.

- Women are often made to feel that their ideas are inconsequential. They are cut-off in meetings especially when a woman is the only female in a group meeting.

- There are too few women in management and supervisory positions.

- None of the top women in the company are in line positions.

- There are no women in senior management.

- Women receive lower potential ratings than men in the company.

- Women are excluded from the "old boys" network.

- Women are always being tested with offensive sexual jokes or comments.

- Affirmative action stigmatizes women and make them look like victims rather than leaders.

- Company benefits do not have programs to help women balance work and family.

EXHIBIT 1.22   *Statements Made by Participants in Asian Employee Focus Groups*

- Asian employees are stereotyped as having excellent technical skills but not suitable for management.

- Asian employees are not promoted because supervisors tend to give them low ratings on communication skills.

- Asian employees are stigmatized by affirmative action and shouldn't be lumped with other minority groups in the company.

- There are a very small number of Asian managers in the company relative to their numbers in the company.

- Most employees are ignorant to the diversity among Asian employees (e.g., Chinese, Korean, Japanese, etc.).

EXHIBIT 1.23 *Statements Made by Participants in White Male Employee Focus Groups*

- White men are stereotyped as racist and sexist.
- The company's affirmative action plan has lowered opportunities for white employees.
- White supervisors have to be careful when managing minority employees.
- African-American employees are hostile towards white supervisors.
- The company's focus on equal employment opportunity doesn't include white men.
- Women employees are overly sensitive; plant environments are tough.

EXHIBIT 1.24 *Results of Employee Survey: Percentage of Employees with Favorable Responses*

Question	All Employees	African- Americans	Asian	Women
My department is effectively managed.	75	57	74	60
People in my department have the skills and abilities to be an effective team.	85	79	82	78
I feel proud to work at Johnson.	75	60	70	61
I am satisfied with my opportunity to get a better job.	79	39	65	44
I like the work I do.	85	75	84	74
My manager gives me feedback that helps improve my performance.	52	38	51	35
My department has a climate that respects employee diversity.	65	49	60	48
My manager is sensitive to the relationship between my work life and my personal life.	61	58	59	49
My supervisor applies company policies and rules regardless of race, gender, etc.	77	54	65	55

11. EXERCISE

The Older Worker

I. *Objectives:*
  A. To familiarize you with typical stereotypes toward older workers and the managerial implications of these stereotypes.
  B. To provide you with factual information regarding older workers.
II. *Out-of-Class Preparation Time:*   15 minutes to complete the Older Worker Questionnaire.
III. *In-Class Time Suggested:*   45 minutes for group and class discussion of all items on the Older Worker Questionnaire.
IV. *Procedures:*   Prior to the class meeting in which this exercise will be discussed, you should read any material on older workers assigned by your instructor and complete the Older Worker Questionnaire shown in Exhibit 1.25.

At the start of the exercise, the class will be divided into groups of three to five by your instructor. Your group's task is to discuss each item on the questionnaire and arrive at a consensus regarding the correct answer (20-minute time limit). After all groups have finished, the instructor will present the correct answers along with an explanation. Each group should record these answers alongside the group's own answers and then compare the two to determine the number right and wrong.

EXHIBIT 1.25   *The Older Worker Questionnaire*

Mark the statements "T" for true or "F" for false.

_____ **1.** Younger workers tend to have higher job satisfaction than older ones.

_____ **2.** A worker's creativity peaks between the ages of 55 and 65.

_____ **3.** The life expectancy of the average U.S. citizen has been increasing.

_____ **4.** The proportion of people 65 and over is expected to decline between now and 2030.

_____ **5.** Since 1948, employees have been retiring later in life.

_____ **6.** Job switching (quitting one job and getting another) tends to decline dramatically with age.

(continued)

EXHIBIT 1.25   *continued*

_____ **7.** One's level of education is the major influence affecting the probability of staying in the workforce vs. retiring.

_____ **8.** About 10 percent of all older people work after retirement.

_____ **9.** Older workers generally require less light for performing a task than do younger workers.

_____ **10.** The majority of older employees are set in their ways and are unable to adapt to changing conditions.

_____ **11.** In general, older workers are less healthy than younger ones.

_____ **12.** Older employees experience no more work disabilities than younger workers.

_____ **13.** Older employees usually take a longer period of time to learn something new than do younger employees.

_____ **14.** Studies have universally found that older workers are less productive than younger ones.

_____ **15.** Younger workers have higher injury frequency rates than do older workers.

_____ **16.** Older workers have more serious injuries and lose more time per injury than do younger workers.

_____ **17.** Older workers are increasingly becoming all or nothing employees in the labor market, i.e., they either work full time or not at all.

_____ **18.** Older employees tend to react more slowly than younger employees.

_____ **19.** Less than half of the heads of households stay in career jobs (positions with a single employer) for 15 years or more.

_____ **20.** One's ability to taste and smell tends to improve with age.

12. EXERCISE

Is This Unlawful Discrimination?

I. *Objectives:*
   A. To help you understand the application of the six major federal laws that regulate equal rights in employment. These laws are Title VII of the Civil Rights Acts of 1964 as amended by the Equal Employment Opportunity Act of 1972, the Civil Rights Act of 1991, the Equal Pay Act of 1963, the Age Discrimination in Employment Act of 1967, the Vocational Rehabilitation Act of 1973, and the Americans with Disabilities Act of 1990.
   B. To help you understand the courts' interpretation of these laws.
   C. To help you understand the legal definition of discrimination and the burden of proof placed on defendants and plaintiffs.
II. *Out-of-Class Preparation Time:*   60 minutes
III. *In-Class Time Suggested:*   45 minutes
IV. *Procedures:*
   A. Read the exercise and review the major laws before class.
   B. The class should be divided into groups of four.
   C. Each group should read each of the incidents that follow and answer these questions:
      1. What legal statute(s) apply in this case?
      2. What issue(s) must the court decide in this case?
      3. If you were the judge, how would you rule? Did the employer discriminate unlawfully? Why or why not?

1. Elaine Mobley worked as a social worker with the Virginia Health Department's child abuse program for two years. Mobley was a member of the nonsectarian Unitarian Universalist Church. During her first six months on the job, she divorced her husband of ten years. Her supervisor, a devout Baptist, encouraged her to discuss her marital problems with a Christian psychotherapist. On a number of occasions, the supervisor encouraged other employees in the department who were also Baptists to convert Mobley. Some employees held prayer meetings at her desk while others gave her the silent treatment. Their attempts to convert Mobley did not stop. At one point, the supervisor made her participate in a Christian puppet show. Another time she found a handwritten note on her desk from Jesus that read, "How can you speak of God and reject me? I love you and know all about you." Her attendance at work declined because there were days she didn't want to face the stress in her work environment. Mobley filed a complaint with the director of the division stating that she was being constantly bombarded with efforts to convert her to a Baptist. Shortly thereafter Mobley was fired from her job. Mobley filed a lawsuit claiming that she had been fired because of religious discrimination.

2. Edward Roberts, a black truck driver, applied in person for a tractor trailer driver position at a trucking company on March 31, 1998 in response to a newspaper ad. Roberts' application listed 22 months of prior experience as a road driver. He had an additional 10 years of experience which he did not list on the application due to a lack of space on the form. Roberts was neither interviewed nor contacted by the company about the status of his application. In June of 1998, Roberts saw an identical advertisement for tractor trailer drivers. Upon inquiry, Roberts learned that eight persons (all white) had been hired as truck drivers between April and June of 1998. All of the hirees had less than 22 months of driving experience. The company contended that Roberts was not hired because no opening existed when he applied. Roberts filed a discrimination complaint in district court.

3. Thelma Jones had worked at a large public accounting firm for five years when the partners proposed her as a candidate for partnership. Of the 662 partners in the firm, seven were women. Of the 88 persons proposed that year, Jones was the only woman. Forty-seven were admitted to partnership, 21 were rejected, and 20 including Jones were held for "reconsideration." Thirteen of the 32 partners who submitted comments on Jones' performance supported her candidacy, three recommended holding her application, eight stated that they had insufficient knowledge to comment, and eight recommended denial. While the partners praised her outstanding performance, both supporters and opponents of her candidacy indicated that she was sometimes overly aggressive, unduly harsh, difficult to work with, and impatient with staff. One partner described her as "macho." In a meeting with a senior partner about her candidacy, she was told that to improve her chances for partnership she should "walk more femininely, talk more femininely, dress more femininely, wear make-up, style her hair, and wear jewelry." When the partners refused to repropose her candidacy the following year, she sued the firm charging discrimination.

4. James McFadden was a transsexual who, while still biologically male, announced to his employer (East Coast Airlines) that he intended to dress and act as a woman in preparation for "surgical sex reassignment." Mr. McFadden was subsequently fired from his pilot's job for refusing to comply with its requirement that he continue to dress and act as a man. McFadden subsequently filed a lawsuit in district court alleging that East Coast had conspired to discriminate against him on the basis of sex (now to be female) and that he was treated differently from other women employed by the airline.

5. Andrew Johnson, a black maintenance worker, was constantly referred to as "Chicken Little," "Chicken George," "Sparerib Kid," "Boy," and "Watermelon Man" by his white supervisor. These names were used not

just during private conversations but in the presence of other workers. Despite several complaints to senior management, the name-calling persisted for several months. When management finally investigated Johnson's claims, the supervisor admitted the comments but argued that he was only kidding. The supervisor was instructed to stop both the name-calling and kidding. A fellow employee warned Johnson that his days were probably numbered because he had gone over the head of his supervisor. Shortly thereafter, Johnson was injured on the job. While he was at home recuperating, his supervisor called to say that he accepted his resignation. Johnson denied resigning and wrote asking for his job back. His request was denied. Johnson filed a lawsuit alleging that he had been a victim of harassment because of his race.

6. Paul Martin had worked 12 years for the Department of Transportation when he applied for a promotion to dispatcher. Martin scored 75 on an interview test. Martin sued the county for reverse discrimination when Betty Palmer, another candidate, scored 73 and got the job. The county said that both Martin and Palmer were qualified and that Palmer had gotten the job as part of a voluntary affirmative action plan designed to achieve a work force that reflected the race and gender composition of the county. The county pointed out that none of 238 skilled craft worker jobs in the county were held by women.

7. Elnora Williams, a black female teacher with ten years of classroom experience and partial completion of her doctoral degree in education, applied for several vacant middle and secondary principalships in the Knox County school system. Each time she applied she was told by the superintendent that "the school district believed that a 'male image' is necessary for a middle or secondary school principal." No females had occupied a principal position in the school district. Williams subsequently filed a lawsuit in district court accusing the school system of discrimination.

8. Frank Poole had been teaching hearing-impaired students in the Jackson County schools for six years when he was hospitalized with pneumocystis carinii pneumonia and subsequently was diagnosed as having AIDS. Despite the county medical director's report that Poole's condition did not place his students or others in the school at any risk, the Department of Education reassigned Poole to an administrative position and barred him from teaching in the classroom. Poole filed suit alleging that the Department discriminated against him on the basis of his handicap (AIDS).

9. Harriet Klondike, Cyndy Patton, Helen Waters, and Margaret Double were employed as matrons at the Mailton County Jail. The county also employed male corrections officers and deputy sheriffs. The matrons guarded female inmates and spent the majority of their time on clerical

duties while the corrections officers and deputy sheriffs spent the majority of their time guarding male inmates. The salary of matrons ranged from $525 to $886 per month while the salaries for the male guards ranged from $701 to $940 per month. The four matrons filed suit and alleged that they were paid lower salaries for work that was basically the same and that the pay differential was attributable to intentional discrimination.

10. After working as a title clerk for Harrison and Sons Car Dealership for five years, Donna Skeen resigned. At 62 years of age, Donna had decided that she did not want to put up with the treatment she had received at the dealership. She had demanded an end to the teasing she experienced, but to no avail. In a suit she filed in District Court, Donna alleged that the managers in the dealership referred to her as the "old lady with the sagging boobs." When she forgot something or made an error on a title, she was asked if she had Alzheimer's disease. If she complained about the temperature in the dealership, she was asked if she was suffering from hot flashes. The owner, Frank Harrison, said that there was lots of informal teasing in the dealership among employees and that Skeen often referred to herself as the "Grandma" of the staff.

11. Officials of a city government charged with discrimination signed a consent decree agreeing to an affirmative action plan with specific promotion and hiring goals for increasing the number of minority firefighters in the city's fire department. Four years later, when faced with severe budget problems, the city implemented a layoff plan aimed at protecting minority employees who were recently hired. Jerome Atwood, a white firefighter, was laid off even though he had greater seniority than many of the minority firefighters who retained their jobs. Atwood filed a lawsuit charging reverse discrimination.

12. Herbert Fox worked as an office furniture salesman for 25 years with the same company. In his 25th year with the company he went on leave for clinical depression. When it was time for him to return from leave, he told the company he could not return to work as scheduled. Subsequently, Fox and the company agreed upon a new date for return. However, Fox also requested that he be allowed to miss the first couple of morning sales meetings (a request prompted by the side effects of his antidepressant medicine) or to work on a part-time basis. His request was denied by the company, and they also told Fox that because of increasing financial pressures, the company would be expecting "110" percent from him on his return to work. Fox did not report to work on the agreed upon date and filed for disability benefits. The company subsequently terminated him. Fox filed a discrimination suit against the company alleging that the requirements attached to his return to work caused a relapse of his depression.

13. EXERCISE

What Is Sexual Harassment?

I. *Objectives:*
  A. To familiarize you with the EEOC sexual harassment guidelines.
  B. To teach you the meaning of these guidelines as they relate to the workplace.
  C. To teach you the manager's and organization's role in preventing sexual harassment.
  D. To show you the complexities involved in identifying sexual harassment in the workplace and in interpreting EEOC guidelines.
II. *Out-of-Class Preparation Time:*   20 minutes to read the EEOC guidelines and complete the sexual harassment questionnaire.
III. *In-Class Time Suggested:*   45 minutes for group and class discussion of all items on the sexual harassment questionnaire.
IV. *Procedures:*   Prior to the class meeting in which this exercise will be discussed, you should read the EEOC Sexual Harassment Guidelines in Exhibit 1.26 and any other material related to sexual harassment assigned by your instructor. You also need to complete the 20-item sexual harassment questionnaire in Exhibit 1.27.

At the start of the exercise, the class will be divided into groups of three to five students by your instructor. Your group's task is to discuss each item on the questionnaire and arrive at a consensus regarding whether each item constitutes sexual harassment. More importantly, you need to develop a rationale for your answer (20-minute time limit). After all groups have finished, the class as a whole will discuss the questionnaire items. To facilitate discussion, groups will take turns presenting their analysis, i.e., one group will present its analysis regarding Item 1, another group will present Item 2, another Item 3, etc.

EXHIBIT 1.26   *Excerpts from the EEOC's Interim*
Guidelines on Sexual Harassment

(a) Harassment on the basis of sex is a violation of Sec. 703 of Title VII. Unwelcome sexual advances, requests for sexual favors, and other verbal or physical conduct of a sexual nature constitute sexual harassment when—

   (1) submission to such conduct is made either explicitly or implicitly a term or condition of an individual's employment,
   (2) submission to or rejection of such conduct by an individual is used as the basis for employment decisions affecting such individual, or
   (3) such conduct has the purpose or effect of substantially interfering with an individual's work performance or creating an intimidating, hostile, or offensive working environment.

(b) In determining whether alleged conduct constitutes sexual harassment, the Commission will look at the record as a whole and the totality of the circumstances such as the nature of the sexual advances and the context in which the alleged incidents occurred. The determination of the legality of a particular action will be made from the facts, on a case by case basis.

Source: Equal Employment Opportunity Commission, *1980 Guidelines.* Washington, DC: Government Printing Office, 1980.

EXHIBIT 1.27   *Sexual Harassment Questionnaire*

INSTRUCTIONS: Read each situation and circle your answer.

SITUATION	WOULD IT BE SEXUAL HARASSMENT?		
1. Mr. (Ms.) X (Supervisor) posts cartoons on the bulletin board containing sexually related materials.	Yes	No	Uncertain
2. Mr. (Ms.) X (Supervisor) constantly tells sexually related jokes to female (male) subordinates.	Yes	No	Uncertain
3. Mr. (Ms.) X (Supervisor) asks a female (male) subordinate for a date which she (he) willingly accepts.	Yes	No	Uncertain
4. Mr. (Ms.) X (Supervisor) pats or pinches a female (male) subordinate.	Yes	No	Uncertain
5. Mr. (Ms.) X (Supervisor) terminates a female (male) subordinate for not complying with his (her) request for sexual favors. He (she) has recently given the subordinate a positive performance appraisal.	Yes	No	Uncertain
6. Mr. (Ms.) X (Supervisor) sexually assaults a female (male) subordinate.	Yes	No	Uncertain

(continued)

EXHIBIT 1.27   *continued*

7. Mr. (Ms.) X (Supervisor) denies a raise to a female (male) subordinate for failing to go out on a date.	Yes	No	Uncertain
8. Mr. X (Supervisor) habitually calls all female employees "sweety" or "honey."	Yes	No	Uncertain
9. Mr. (Ms.) X (Supervisor) asks a female (male) employee how she (he) feels about sex education in schools.	Yes	No	Uncertain
10. Mr. X (Supervisor) recommends that a female subordinate wear revealing attire at work.	Yes	No	Uncertain
11. Mr. (Ms.) X (Supervisor) fails to promote a female (male) subordinate for not granting sexual favors.	Yes	No	Uncertain
12. Mr. (Ms.) X (Supervisor) invites a female (male) subordinate to accompany him (her) to a two-day meeting in another city.	Yes	No	Uncertain
13. Mr. X (Supervisor) leans and peers over the back of a female employee when she wears a low-cut dress.	Yes	No	Uncertain
14. Mr. (Ms.) X (Supervisor) tells a female (male) job applicant that she (he) won't be hired unless she (he) agrees to grant sexual favors.	Yes	No	Uncertain
15. Mr. (Ms.) X (Supervisor) invites a female (male) subordinate to meet him (her) at a bar which features female (male) exotic dancers.	Yes	No	Uncertain
16. Mr. (Ms.) X (Supervisor) invites a female (male) subordinate to come over to his (her) apartment for a hot tub party.	Yes	No	Uncertain
17. Male (female) workers whistle every time female (male) employees walk by their work area.	Yes	No	Uncertain
18. A married female employee and a married male employee are having an affair.	Yes	No	Uncertain
19. Male (female) employees repeatedly use vulgar language when talking to each other. Two female (male) employees often overhear what is said and find it offensive.	Yes	No	Uncertain
20. A male (female) repair technician who works for another firm asks female (male) employees for dates whenever he (she) comes to repair equipment.	Yes	No	Uncertain

14. EXERCISE

Understanding the Americans with Disabilities Act

I. *Objectives:*
   A. To help you understand the application of the Americans with Disabilities Act (ADA).
   B. To help you understand the court's interpretation of the ADA.
   C. To help you understand the meaning of the terms "disability," "qualified individual," and "reasonable accommodation."
II. *Out-of-Class Preparation Time:* 45 minutes
III. *In-Class Time Suggested:* 45 minutes
IV. *Procedures:*
   A. Read the exercise and review the Americans with Disabilities Act's definitions of "disability," "qualified individual," and "reasonable accommodation."
   B. The class should be divided into groups of four.
   C. Each group should read each of the case incidents that follow and answer these questions:
      1. What issue(s) must the court decide in this case?
      2. If you were a member of the jury, how would you vote? Did the employer discriminate unlawfully? Why or why not?

1. The Overweight Hospital Attendant

Betty Thomas applied for a position as an attendant for the mentally retarded in a residential facility operated by the Mental Health Retardation Hospital (MHRH). She had previously worked for MHRH in an identical position. She had an excellent work record and left employment with MHRH on good terms. When Thomas reapplied for the position she previously held, she stood 5'2" tall and weighed 320 pounds. During her pre-employment physical, it was determined that although Thomas was morbidly obese, no limitations were found which affected her ability to do the job. MHRH refused to hire Thomas because of her obesity, claiming that her weight compromised her ability to evacuate patients in the event of an emergency and put Thomas at greater risk of developing serious ailments which might lead to higher absenteeism, as well as increasing MHRH's exposure to workers' compensation claims.

2. The Asthmatic's Nightmare

Joanna Deil was promoted to blood bank administrator for a large metropolitan hospital in 1989. Her education and experience were primarily in the

Contributed by Gerald E. Calvasina, The University of North Carolina at Charlotte.

general field of administration. Her work area was in a windowless basement of one of the hospital's facilities, where the blood bank fumes and poor ventilation aggravated her asthma. Deil complained to the hospital and informed the director of safety programs and the medical director about her health problems.

Three months into her new job, Deil's doctor advised her that she should stay away from the blood bank because the location was "an asthmatic's nightmare." Once Deil informed her immediate supervisor of the doctor's conclusion, Deil was allowed to administer the blood bank from an office in another part of the hospital complex. Her health improved rapidly over the next several months.

In 1992, the appointment of a new medical director led to a change in Deil's work routine. The new director requested to meet with Deil on a regular basis at the blood bank facility. When she refused to go to the facility, Deil was discharged. Deil's supervisor had offered to help her find another job either within the hospital or outside of it. Deil filed a complaint with the Equal Employment Opportunity Commission and after receiving her right to sue letter, filed suit against the hospital authority in federal district court alleging discrimination on the basis of her disability.

3. The Ultimatum

Joan, a warehouse worker, was diagnosed with carpal tunnel syndrome. She was subsequently assigned to reduced duties. However, the duties were later multiplied, increasing her arm and wrist pain. When Joan presented her employer with a doctor's note advising her to take a six-week leave of absence, the employer gave her an ultimatum—show up for work or lose her job. Joan decided to sue under the ADA, claiming her carpal tunnel syndrome was a disability worthy of accommodation.

4. The Fainting Technician

Jane Flighty was fired after she fainted on the job, because the company believed she was suffering from an unknown disability. After the fainting episode, she was sent to a physician. The physician's initial diagnosis was that Jane suffered from syncope, a loss of consciousness caused by a temporary deficiency of blood supply to the brain. Later, the physician determined that the employee was within normal limits and that there was no explanation for the fainting. The company discharged Jane without any further medical examination, concluding that she was a safety risk because she was likely to faint again.

5. The Gun-Slinger

John Hitman was fired when he was caught carrying a gun into work. He was hospitalized following the incident and was diagnosed with a mental disorder. His attorney informed the company of his mental status and asked that they delay any decision about his employment status. The company fired John for his clear violation of company rules.

15. INCIDENT

The Employee with AIDS

It was another hectic day for Mary Landschulz, Cafeteria Manager for a department store located in the city of New York. She had just received a call from one of her employees, Cathy, stating that she would not be able to come to work that day. When she asked Cathy why, Cathy reluctantly stated that yesterday her doctor had informed her that she had AIDS (Acquired Immune Deficiency Syndrome). She did not know when she would return to work but knew that it wouldn't be soon. She said she would call next week.

Hanging up the telephone, Mary sat motionless in her office. She was stunned by what she had just heard. Cathy was an excellent employee and had served food on the cafeteria line for five years. Cathy had been sick recently for several days, but Mary had thought Cathy just had the flu or a cold. Now she knew the truth, and it was not a pretty picture. "Oh my gosh!" she exclaimed to herself, "What am I going to do?"

As Mary pondered this question, the alarm on her watch "beeped," reminding her that she had to attend a meeting with her employees. Slowly, she got out of her chair and walked down the hall to the meeting room. When she entered the room she found it buzzing with talk about Cathy. Mary headed for the nearest seat hoping that the topic of discussion would change. As she and the others sat down around the large oval table, one of the cafeteria workers turned to her and asked, "What's wrong with Cathy? She told Frank she might not ever be back to work." Suddenly, a hush fell over the room as everyone awaited Mary's reply.

Questions

1. How should Mary respond to the question?
2. Would it be an invasion of Cathy's privacy if Mary tells the employees that Cathy has AIDS?
3. Assuming that the employees ultimately learn that Cathy has AIDS, how should Mary deal with their fears? What should she do if the employees refuse to work with Cathy when she returns?
4. As a result of the incident, should the company develop a specific AIDS policy?

16. SKILL BUILDER

Data Analysis for Affirmative Action Plans

I. *Objectives:*
   A. To enhance your understanding of how to prepare a utilization/availability analysis for Affirmative Action Plans.
   B. To teach you the data analysis requirements under affirmative action guidelines.

II. *Time Required to Complete:* 2–3 hours.

III. *Instructions:* You work for a manufacturing firm located in Charlotte, North Carolina, and your company has just been awarded its first federal contract of $250,000. This contract is to supply one of your major products over a two-year period to the Department of Defense. You have been asked by your boss, the plant manager, to perform the utilization/availability analyses required under Executive Order 11246 as input in developing an Affirmative Action Plan (AAP) for the Office of Federal Contract Compliance Programs (OFCCP).

You have reviewed the guidelines from the OFCCP on the requirements (see Exhibit 1.28). You have also pulled together labor market data in addition to compiling a detailed breakdown of the company's work force by job category, sex, and race (see Exhibits 1.29, 1.30, 1.31, and 1.32).

Required

Using the relevant data, complete Form 1. You may need to generate additional forms for your use. It is easier to set this up in a spreadsheet form. This is the first step towards developing an Affirmative Action Plan. Be sure to list any assumptions you make about the relevant labor market for each job category. Also be sure to indicate the job categories where women and minorities are underutilized. Make any other recommendations you deem necessary to the plant manager.

EXHIBIT 1.28 *OFCCP/AAP Guidelines*

DEFINITION

An Affirmative Action Plan is a set of specific and result-oriented procedures to which a contractor commits to supply every good-faith effort. The objective of those procedures plus such efforts is equal employment opportunity. An acceptable Affirmative Action Plan must include an analysis of areas within which the contractor is deficient in the utilization of minority groups and women, and further, goals and timetables to which the contractor's good-faith efforts must be directed to correct the deficiencies and thus to increase materially the utilization of minorities and women at all levels and in all segments of the workforce where deficiencies exist.

UTILIZATION ANALYSIS

An AAP must contain a utilization analysis—a comparison of the percentages of women and minorities in each job category (workforce analysis) with the percentages available in the relevant labor market (availability analysis). The workforce analysis is a listing of the number of employees in the organization by job categories. For each job category, the total number of male and female incumbents in each of these groups (blacks, Hispanics, American Indians, and Asians) is assessed (see Exhibit 1.29).

An analysis of all major job groups and the extent to which minorities or women are underutilized is also requested. Underutilization is having fewer minorities or women in a particular job category than would reasonably be expected, according to their availability in the relevant labor market. When making the utilization analysis, eight points must be considered:

1. Minority population in the labor area around the organization.
2. Size of minority and female unemployment force in the area.
3. Percentage of minority and female workforce as compared with the total work force in the immediate labor area.
4. Availability of minorities and women with requisite skills in immediate area.
5. Availability of promotable and transferable minorities and women within the employer's work force.
6. Existence of training institutions capable of training in the required skills.
7. Availability of minorities and women with skills in areas where the employer can recruit.
8. Degree of training the employer is able to undertake as an avenue for making all job classes available to minorities and women.

Based on 41 C.F.R. Chapter 60, Office of Federal Contract Compliance Programs, Department of Labor.

EXHIBIT 1.29 *Workforce Analysis*

Job Categories	Overall Totals (Sums of Columns B thru K) A	Number of Male Employees					Number of Female Employees				
		White (Not of Hispanic Origin) B	Black (Not of Hispanic Origin) C	Hispanic D	Asian or Pacific Islander E	American Indian or Alaskan Native F	White (Not of Hispanic Origin) G	Black (Not of Hispanic Origin) H	Hispanic I	Asian or Pacific Islander J	American Indian or Alaskan Native K
Officials and managers*	154	138	2	0	0	0	13	1	0	0	0
Professionals	137	126	1	0	0	0	10	0	0	0	0
Technicians	76	61	2	1	1	0	6	2	0	3	0
Sales workers	77	65	4	0	0	0	7	1	0	0	0
Office and clerical	188	21	3	0	1	0	144	17	2	0	0
Craft workers (skilled)	150	120	15	1	2	0	9	3	0	0	0
Operatives (semiskilled)	294	200	58	2	10	2	16	4	0	2	0
Laborers (unskilled)	655	504	82	5	10	1	38	10	3	2	0
Service workers	89	17	49	5	1	2	2	9	2	0	2
TOTALS	1,820	1,252	216	14	25	5	245	47	7	7	2

*Includes supervisors

EXHIBIT 1.30   *Civilian Labor Force by Sex and Race,*
Charlotte, Gastonia, Rock Hill, NC-SC, SMSA, 1986[1]

Sex and Race	Civilian Labor Force	Employed	Unemployed
Both Sexes			
TOTAL	514,796	489,574	25,222
White	417,540	400,260	17,280
Black	90,270	82,710	7,560
American Indian, Eskimo, and Aleut	1,093	1,048	45
Asian and Pacific Islander	2,193	2,066	127
Hispanic	3,700	3,490	210
Female			
TOTAL	233,298	220,545	12,753
White	184,190	175,420	8,770
Black	45,970	42,150	3,820
American Indian, Eskimo, and Aleut	495	467	28
Asian and Pacific Islander	993	938	55
Hispanic	1,650	1,570	80

[1]Based on 1980 census proportions. North Carolina Only.
Source: Employment Security Commission of North Carolina, Labor Market Division.

EXHIBIT 1.31   *Occupations of the Civilian Labor Force by Sex and Race, 1980, Charlotte, Gastonia, Rock Hill, NC-SC SMSA*[1]

Occupation	Total[2]	Total White	Total Black	American Indian	Asians	Hispanic	White Not Hispanic	Black Not Hispanic	Total Minority
TOTAL									
All industries	447,254	364,832	78,955	1,348	1,837	3,165	362,595	78,302	84,659
Managerial and professional specialty	87,018	77,673	8,482	119	689	589	77,211	8,410	9,807
Technicians	10,077	8,557	1,415	20	80	53	8,517	1,407	1,561
Sales occupations	45,837	42,341	3,241	84	141	287	42,115	3,203	3,772
Administrative support including clerical	72,927	62,762	9,857	115	173	387	62,438	9,814	10,489
Service workers	47,097	29,970	16,627	225	249	429	29,765	16,429	17,332
Farming, forestry, and fishing	5,483	4,301	1,103	53	19	26	4,282	1,103	1,201
Precision production and craft	59,987	51,716	7,830	282	130	477	51,341	7,757	8,646
Operators and fabricators	92,707	69,331	22,678	344	251	713	68,884	22,515	23,823
Handlers, equipment cleaners, helpers, and laborers	26,121	18,181	7,722	106	105	204	18,042	7,664	8,079

[1]North Carolina portion only.
[2]Racial and ethnic group columns may not be additive to total due to "race or ethnic group not classified" in census response.
Source: 1980 Census.

EXHIBIT 1.32 *Occupations of the Female Civilian Labor Force by Sex and Race, 1980, Charlotte, Gastonia, Rock Hill, NC-SC SMSA[1]*

Occupation	Total[2]	Total White	Total Black	American Indian	Asians	Hispanic	White Not Hispanic	Black Not Hispanic	Total Minority
TOTAL									
All industries	202,039	160,509	40,184	524	702	1,436	159,524	39,821	42,490
Managerial and professional specialty	36,447	30,864	5,346	48	167	260	30,682	5,290	5,765
Technicians	4,667	3,716	923	7	16	23	3,706	915	961
Sales occupations	20,006	17,652	2,211	53	71	170	17,524	2,181	2,482
Administrative support including clerical	55,628	48,504	6,928	86	95	280	48,269	6,898	7,359
Service workers	28,122	17,269	10,557	134	143	261	17,159	10,425	10,963
Farming, forestry, and fishing	1,166	877	278	6	5	0	877	278	289
Precision production and craft	5,778	4,488	1,256	13	14	51	4,450	1,250	1,328
Operators and fabricators	43,556	32,601	10,588	169	165	344	32,375	10,503	11,181
Handlers, equipment cleaners, helpers, and laborers	6,669	4,538	2,097	9	26	47	4,507	2,081	2,162

[1]North Carolina portion only.
[2]Racial and ethnic group columns may not be additive to total due to "race or ethnic group not classified" in census response.
Source: 1980 Census.

FORM 1   *Utilization/Availability Analysis*

Job Category	Sex		Race				
	Male	Female	White	Black	Hispanic	Asian	American Indian
Number of employees							
Percentage of employees (utilization)							
Percent available							
Underutilized:							

Note: A table will be needed for each job category.

MEETING HUMAN RESOURCE REQUIREMENTS: JOB ANALYSIS/ DESIGN, PLANNING, RECRUITMENT, AND SELECTION

JOB ANALYSIS/PLANNING

17. CASE

Employee Layoffs at St. Mary's Hospital

St. Mary's Hospital is a medium-sized, 400-bed hospital in a northwestern city. It was established in 1908 by the Sisters of the Sacred Heart, an order of Catholic sisters. The facility has grown gradually over the years and is now the third largest hospital in the city. It is entirely nonunion and has never experienced an employee layoff since its inception.

Sister Mary Josephine has been the Chief Executive Officer of the hospital for 11 years. Eight years ago she hired Ms. Sharon Osgood as Director of Personnel. Ms. Osgood has an M.A. in Human Resource Management and has been instrumental in formalizing the institution's human resources' policies and procedures.

Occupancy rates in the hospital had run between 76 and 82 percent from 1970 to 1982. However, since then, occupancy has fallen to 57 percent. Such declines have not been unusual for this industry during this time period as a result of changing reimbursement policies, emphasis on outpatient services, and increasing competition. However, the declining occupancy rate has affected this hospital's revenues to such an extent that it ran a deficit for the first time last year. The only response to these changes thus far has been a tightening of requirements for equipment or supply purchases.

At the most recent quarterly meeting of the Board of Directors, Sister Mary Josephine presented the rather bleak financial picture. The projected deficit for the coming year was $3,865,000 unless some additional revenue sources were identified or some additional savings were found. The Board's recommendation, based on the immediate crisis and need to generate short-term savings, was that employee layoffs were the only realistic alternative. They recommended that Sister Mary Josephine consider laying off up to 10 percent of the hospital's employees with an emphasis on those in "nonessential" areas.

Sister Mary Josephine responded that the hospital's employees had never been laid off in the history of the institution. Moreover, she viewed the employees as part of the "family" and would have great difficulty in implementing such a layoff. Nevertheless, since she had no realistic short-term alternative for closing the "revenue gap," she reluctantly agreed to implement a layoff policy which would be as fair as possible to all employees, with a guarantee of reemployment for those laid off, and to find additional revenue sources so that layoffs would be unnecessary in the future.

Sister Mary Josephine called Sharon Osgood into her office the next morning, shared her concerns, and asked her to prepare both a short-term plan to save $3 million over the next year through employee layoffs as well as a long-term plan to avoid layoffs in the future. Her concerns were that the layoffs themselves might be costly in terms of lost investment in some of the laid-off employees, lost efficiency, potential lawsuits, and lower morale. She was concerned that the criteria for the layoffs not only *be* equitable, but also *appear* to be equitable to the employees. She also wanted to make sure that those being laid off received "adequate" notice so they could make alternative plans or so that the hospital could assist them with finding alternative employment. Since the hospital had no previous experience with employee layoffs and no union contract constraints, her feeling was that both seniority and job performance should be considered in determining who would be laid off.

Sharon knew the hospital's performance appraisal system was inadequate and needed to be revamped. While this task was high on her "to do" list, she also knew she had to move ahead with her recommendations on layoffs immediately. The present performance appraisal system uses a traditional checklist rating scale with a summary rating. Since there is no forced distribution, the average ratings of employees in different departments varies widely.

Exhibit 2.1 shows the summary ratings of employees in each department. Most supervisors in all departments rate most of their subordinates either "satisfactory" or "outstanding." Sharon has done a quick review of those employees whose overall ratings were "unsatisfactory" or "questionable." Most are employees with less than three years of seniority, whereas the "satisfactory" employee has worked for St. Mary's approximately seven years. Sharon is preparing to submit her recommendations to Sister Mary Josephine and has come to you for advice. Exhibit 2.2 provides a summary of the distribution of employees and payroll expense by department for the most recent year.

Questions

1. Identify the major problem or problems and their causes.
2. What are some alternatives for dealing with these problems? For example, is it possible to avoid layoffs through the use of attrition?
3. Develop a plan for implementing employee layoffs over the next year which will generate $3 million in savings. Give specific details concerning departments affected, the use of seniority versus merit, the amount of notice, and out-placement activities. What additional information (if any) will you need? Provide a rationale for each recommendation, together with reasons why other alternatives were not chosen.
4. What might be the effects of a layoff plan on "survivors" in terms of morale, job security, organizational commitment, productivity, and career planning? How could you avoid or minimize any potential problems in these areas?

5. What long-term solutions do you see for the hospital once it gets its cash flow problems under control and eliminates its deficit? What can it do to increase revenue so that future layoffs will not be necessary?
6. What difficulties exist in using "performance" as a criterion for layoffs? How can such difficulties be overcome?

EXHIBIT 2.1 *Percentage Distribution of Performance Appraisal Summary Ratings by Department at St. Mary's Hospital*

Department	Unsatisfactory: Needs to Improve Substantially	Questionable: Needs Some Improvement	Satisfactory: Meets Normal Expectations	Outstanding: Substantially Exceeds Norms
Nursing	6.4	6.4	54.2	33.0
Allied Health	5.7	6.2	47.8	40.3
Central Administration	2.7	3.1	67.5	26.7
Dietetics/ Nutrition	2.1	6.2	68.3	23.4
Housekeeping/ Maintenance	7.8	12.4	54.6	25.2
Medical Staff	1.1	6.2	63.8	28.9

EXHIBIT 2.2 *The Distribution of Employment and Payroll Expenditures at St. Mary's Hospital*

Department	Number of Employees	Payroll ($)	Annual Turnover Rates (%)
Nursing	602	$15,050,000	12.2
Allied Health Departments	261	5,742,000	8.7
Central Administration	154	6,160,000	3.5
Dietetics/Nutrition	65	1,430,000	7.3
Housekeeping and Maintenance	36	540,000	8.4
Medical Staff	32	1,680,000	2.1
TOTAL	1,150	$30,602,000	9.5*

*Represents weighted average turnover for all employees.

18. CASE

Strategic Human Resource Management

The College of Business Administration at Old State University is one of 12 state-supported collegiate business schools in a midwestern state. It is located in a city with a population of 400,000 with a diversified industrial base. Old State is the only state-supported institution in town. One small private college provides competition to the college.

Recently, the college has experienced leadership transition. Dr. George Barnes, Dean of the college since 1978, retired. During his administration, the enrollment had increased from 1,202 undergraduates and 76 M.B.A. students in the 1978–79 academic year to 2,089 undergraduates and 218 M.B.A. students in the most recent academic year.

Dean Barnes was well liked by students, faculty, and the central administration of Old State. However, he had not led the college in any new directions and had basically concentrated on "doing the same things better." The "same things" meant an emphasis on traditional programs (accounting, marketing, finance, etc.), teaching undergraduate students in the age range of 18–22 in daytime programs, and teaching a small number of full-time M.B.A. students. The latter have been mostly graduates of the college's undergraduate program who decided they were willing to spend two more years on campus to obtain the second degree.

Dean Barnes had also been successful in upgrading the proportion of faculty with terminal degrees from 56 percent in 1978 to 85 percent in the most recent year. Exhibit 2.3 provides faculty and student enrollment data for the college for selected years during Barnes' tenure.

During the most recent academic year, the Dean's Search Committee (consisting of faculty, students, alumni, central administration, and local business representatives) met frequently, screened over 100 applicants, and personally interviewed six. While the committee arrived at no consensus, the majority supported Mr. Jack Blake for the Deanship. An offer was made and after several weeks of negotiation, Blake accepted the Deanship. His background was an M.B.A. from a prestigious Ivy League business school and executive leadership positions in a variety of U.S. corporations in marketing. He left the position of Vice President of Marketing at one of the "Fortune 500" companies to accept the Deanship.

During the screening interviews with the Search Committee, Mr. Blake had made it clear that, if he were selected, the college would be "moving in new directions and exploring new markets." It was very clear Blake did not want to be a "paper pusher," but did want to be an innovator and an entrepreneur. When pressed for specifics, he had indicated he "would have to study the situation in more detail."

When the new Dean arrived on campus in the fall, he immediately convened a Strategic Planning Committee to (1) evaluate the college's external environment, opportunities, constraints, competitive advantages, and internal environment and (2) recommend a new set of long-term missions, goals, objectives, and programs. The committee consisted of two senior professors, the university's Vice President for Academic Affairs, one graduate student, one undergraduate student, two prominent alumni, and two local business leaders.

The committee recommended that the college focus on the adult learner since demographic analysis suggested the age group 18–22 was shrinking and would be a declining market over the next decade. Specific recommendations included (1) more evening courses for both undergraduate and graduate students; (2) structuring the schedule so that both degrees could be earned entirely in the evening; (3) offering credit courses in some suburban locations; (4) offering requested noncredit practitioner courses at the college, at the employer's work site, and in various underserved small cities around the state; (5) exploring the possibility of offering degree programs at these locations; (6) offering new M.B.A. degree concentrations in such areas as management of the arts, health care management, and public sector management, and (7) offering a new "executive" M.B.A.

The new Dean enthusiastically endorsed the report and distributed copies at the last faculty meeting of the fall semester. Several questions were raised, but it didn't appear serious opposition existed. However, at a following meeting of department Chairs, the Dean indicated that his top priority for the next academic year was to fill the five vacant positions with new faculty who would be supportive of the new directions in which the college was moving. Specifically, he asked them to keep several criteria in mind while recruiting and selecting new faculty. These included previous managerial work experience, a willingness to teach night courses, a willingness to travel to other cities to offer coursework, an ability to work with management practitioners on special projects, and previous experience in teaching executives.

In addition, he suggested that the Chairs consider those criteria when evaluating the performance of existing faculty and recommending salary increases. Finally, he indicated that one of the faculty positions would be used to recruit a new Assistant Dean for External Affairs who would be his link to the practitioner community. The latter would be involved with helping practicing managers identify their needs, working with faculty to meet these needs, and negotiating contracts for these services.

When word of the Dean's faculty recommendations spread through the "rumor mill," the reaction was swift and negative. Many of the "old guard" faculty felt they were hired primarily to teach full-time students on campus during the day. Consequently, they were threatened by the new evaluation criteria. They were also concerned that the Dean was interjecting nonacademic criteria into their departmental faculty recruitment processes and diverting resources to nonacademic activities. These faculty felt the inevitable result would be a declining quality of education in the college.

A group of these faculty have asked to meet with the Dean to discuss his proposals. The Dean is preparing a justification for both his strategy and his human resource management (faculty) recommendations.

Questions

1. How and why do strategic decisions affect human resource management policies? Can human resource policies or constraints ever affect strategy? Why or why not?
2. Identify the problem and causes of the problem in this case.
3. Evaluate Dean Blake's strategy and human resource policies. Did the strategy make sense in terms of the internal and external environment of the college? Do the human resource strategies support and reinforce the organizational strategy? Why or why not?
4. Evaluate the process by which Dean Blake implemented the strategic and human resources changes. Can you suggest any improvements?
5. How can resistance to his plans and strategies be overcome?

EXHIBIT 2.3   *Faculty and Student Enrollment Data for the College of Business Administration in Selected Years, 1978–1999*

Academic Year	Faculty	Faculty with Ph.D.	Student Enrollment		
			B.S.	M.B.A.	Total
1978–79	54	30	1,202	76	1,278
1980–81	58	36	1,289	98	1,387
1985–86	66	46	1,654	134	1,788
1990–91	74	57	1,913	154	2,067
1995–96	78	66	2,065	221	2,286
1999–00	80	68	2,089	218	2,307

19. CASE

The Bank Merger

Jack Duncan Ramsey, Senior Vice President of Human Resources at Northeastern Bank & Trust Company, reread the memo calling a meeting of top management to discuss the merger agreement signed with First Bank & Trust Company. First Bank & Trust Company was one of the largest commercial banks in Connecticut (see Exhibit 2.4) and this would be one of the largest mergers they had ever undertaken. First Bank & Trust enjoyed a strong market position throughout the state and over the years had exhibited above-average profitability. First Bank & Trust Company was a heavy personal and real estate lender. About 45 percent of its earning assets represented personal and real estate loans while about 10 percent were commercial and industrial loans.

In contrast, Northeastern is a big commercial lender offering a diversified range of financial services, with about 35 percent of its earning assets in corporate loans. Although Northeastern Bank & Trust Company had been basically put together through mergers, usually the mergers were with much smaller banks, and most involved converting the acquired bank's operational procedures for loans and deposits to their system. Most of the banks that were purchased did not have centralized operating or administrative functions. The major personnel actions involved putting employees of the acquired bank on the payroll and conducting a short orientation program to inform them about benefits and bank policies and procedures. Typically, no employees lost jobs because of the merger and any adjustments needed were handled through normal turnover and attrition.

Ramsey felt that this merger would be quite different and would require a more complex process to implement. First Bank & Trust Company was a statewide bank with over 80 branches in 38 cities and over 1,800 employees. As is often the case in banks of this size, First Bank & Trust Company had centralized support functions such as operations, personnel, audit, and accounting. Ramsey knew that consolidating the support functions and, in some cases, the line functions would be a major challenge in this merger.

The Planning Meeting

Larry McDonald, Chairman and Chief Executive Officer of Northeastern Bank & Trust Company, opened the meeting with the top officers, Jack Ramsey, Pat Stevenson (Senior Vice President of Operations), and Thomas "Buddy" Kent (President):

McDonald: Our merger with First Bank & Trust Company is a natural fit. We are located in sister states with very similar social,

	cultural, and political heritages. We already have a large corporate customer base in Connecticut and our advertising has covered many of its markets for years. I called this meeting today because we want this to be one of the smoothest mergers in our history. We need to come up with a plan to complete and implement the merger. I think we need to start now even though the merger is still pending board and shareholder approval.
Ramsey:	Larry, from the personnel side I can already anticipate some concern from First Bank & Trust about protecting their employees. There are probably already all kinds of rumors circulating and a lot of anxiety about what this merger is going to mean in terms of job security for their employees. We may have very few changes in personnel on the line side of the bank but some problems may crop up if there are major changes on the staff side.
Stevenson:	I also think we're going to have to make some decisions about consolidating computer systems and getting their people up to speed on using our equipment and technology. The economies of scale here are a real plus and we should definitely keep that in the forefront of our thinking and planning.
Kent:	We also probably need to come up with a combined business plan which should help us in getting First Bank & Trust Company management committed to our goals. We need to capitalize on our geographical proximity and similar cultures in developing a business plan.
McDonald:	We must remain true to our own corporate philosophy. We have recognized for years that our customers will be treated well if our employees are treated well. This strategy has worked for us and we want to carry it over to all our bank employees. We can't guarantee them a job because we are going to take advantage of the economies of scale and consolidate many positions, but we should at least try to do everything possible to absorb and maintain as many good people as possible.
Ramsey:	I agree with you, Larry. I think our hardest task is going to be managing the people side of this merger, especially the communication part. We've done the operations part many times before and have had good results. I really believe a successful merger is 10 percent planning and 90 percent communication.

The Steering Committees

Shortly after the meeting, three steering committees were formed to guide the merger process over the next year to 18 months. The Business Planning

Committee consisted of the President of Northeastern Bank Corporation, the President of First Bank & Trust Company, and the top managers from the operations, human resources, and line functions of each bank. The committee compared bank products, decided how to handle the transition period, made pricing decisions, and decided how to phase in the merger. The committee developed a one-year profit plan and a three-year business plan for the combined banks. The business plan spelled out the bank's objectives for each of its major activities and an overall market strategy. The planned strategy was around the theme "Your Southern New England Bank." A major outcome of this planning was a decision to consolidate most of the bank's support functions at the headquarters of Northeastern Bank in Boston. These and other projected consolidations would save about $16 to $18 million a year. Once the overall business plans were formulated, the postmerger organization structure was developed for each major division of First Bank & Trust to reflect which jobs would remain. For example, the pre- and post-merger organization chart developed for the Connecticut Trust Center is shown in Exhibit 2.5. A profile of the employees in that division is given in Exhibit 2.6.

The Operations Committee developed detailed work plans to operationally merge the banks. These plans included procedures for the conversion of loans, deposits, check processing, and other operational activities. The committee included managers from every major unit in the Operations Group of each bank as well as managers from support functions throughout both banks.

The Human Resource Steering Committee, headed by Jack Ramsey, consisted of human resource staff from both banks. The committee was charged with developing a strategy for implementing human resource policies, practices, and procedures for placing employees whose jobs might be eliminated in other positions. During initial meetings, differences in philosophy emerged. First Bank & Trust Company traditionally had taken a more conservative, by-the-book approach to applying human resource policies. Northeastern Bank tended to be more flexible and would often consider the particular employee's circumstances and situation before making personnel decisions. At the time of the merger, First Bank & Trust Company did not have formal job descriptions and because of its smaller size did not have the same level of employee benefits as Northeastern. The turnover rate at First Bank & Trust was around 10 percent annually, somewhat higher than Northeastern's. One of the first things done by the committee was to draw up a list of major human resource issues to be managed over the next year or so:

1. Staff reductions and transfers.
2. Maintaining employee productivity during the merger transition period.
3. Communication flow to employees to minimize unwarranted rumors.
4. Socializing employees to Northeastern's "culture and philosophy."
5. Designing appropriate training programs.
6. Balancing EEO/Affirmative Action goals.

Two months after the merger announcement, Ramsey received a memorandum (see Exhibit 2.7) from the Business Planning Committee requesting that a plan of action be developed to deal with expected staff displacement. Ramsey was somewhat alarmed at the number of employees who were being displaced—almost 20 percent of First Bank & Trust's workforce. He also learned that there were a number of officer positions in the total.

Two days after receiving the memo, Ramsey's assistant, Ed Flanders, burst into his office with news that he had received several phone calls from employees of First Bank & Trust. The callers had heard that a big layoff was about to occur, and they wanted to know how they could keep their jobs. Flanders wanted to know how he should respond to the employees. Ramsey simply said, "I knew this one would be different."

Questions

1. Evaluate the bank's approach to implementing the merger.
2. Are there human resource issues other than those listed by the Human Resource Steering Committee that emerge when two companies merge?
3. Do you agree with Ramsey's comment that a successful merger is 10 percent planning and 90 percent communication? Why or why not?
4. Develop a plan of action for handling the projected labor surplus. What factors need to be considered?
5. How should the Human Resource Steering Committee handle the needed staff reduction in the Trust Center?

EXHIBIT 2.4   *Profile of Northeastern Bank and First Bank & Trust Company*

	Northeastern	First Bank & Trust
Net income	$101.3 million	$18.7 million
Return on assets	0.71%	1.08%
Return on equity	13.92%	15.09%
Total assets	$13.5 billion	$1.6 billion
Total deposits	$9.6 billion	$1.2 billion
Number of employees	7,560	1,857
Number of branches	201	83

EXHIBIT 2.5   *Trust Center, First Bank & Trust Company, Pre- and Postmerger Organization Chart*

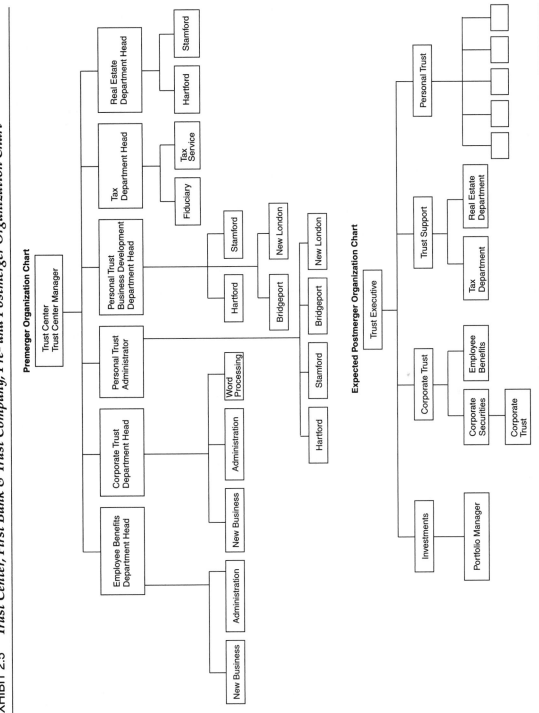

EXHIBIT 2.6   *First Bank & Trust Company, Employee Profile (Trust Center)*

Name	Position	Sex	Race	Age	Tenure	Last Performance Rating[a]
Douglas Reid	Trust Center Manager	M	W	52	20	5
Harriet Jones	Employee Benefits Department Head	F	W	40	18	4
Bryan Dinkins	Employee Benefits New Business	M	W	37	8	4
Diva Brown	Employee Benefits Administration	F	B	32	5	3
Carol Cushman	Employee Benefits Administration	F	B	28	4	4
Diane Reeves	Employee Benefits Administration	F	W	41	7	3
Kathy Neel	Employee Benefits Administration	F	W	50	17	3
Bob Watson	Corporate Trust Department Head	M	W	54	19	5
Henry Jeffrey	Corporate Trust New Business	M	W	44	10	4
Margaret Neale	Corporate Trust Administration	F	W	29	3	4
Barbara Westin	Corporate Trust Word Processing	F	W	31	2	3
Vivian Hawkins	Personal Trust Administrator	F	B	37	10	4
Victor Dale	Personal Trust Hartford	M	B	49	12	4
William Devoe	Personal Trust Stamford	M	W	39	7	5
Leslie Hill	Personal Trust Bridgeport	F	W	33	4	4
Donald Phillips	Personal Trust New London	M	W	59	23	4
Arthur Barnett	Personal Trust Business Development Head	M	W	62	25	5
Alonzo Alvarez	Personal Trust Business Development Hartford	M	H[b]	35	8	4
Kendrith Hanks	Personal Trust Business Development Stamford	M	W	27	4	3
Robert Davidson	Personal Trust Business Development New London	M	W	28	5	5
Jennifer Degen	Personal Trust Business Development Bridgeport	F	W	47	9	5
Cynthia Fuchs	Tax Department Head	F	W	38	10	5
Michael Gridley	Fiduciary	M	W	34	4	3
Rosalind Smith	Tax Services	F	B	26	3	4
Leonard Clay	Real Estate Department Head	M	W	57	15	4
Katherine Stern	Real Estate Hartford	F	W	27	2	3
Betty Henderson	Read Estate Stamford	M	B	40	9	5

[a]The company uses a rating scale of 1 (poor) to 5 (outstanding).
[b]Hispanic

EXHIBIT 2.7   *Memorandum on Postmerger Staffing*

MEMORANDUM

DATE: September 15, 19xx
TO: Jack Duncan Ramsey, Chair
          Human Resource Steering Committee
FROM: Buddy Kent
          Business Planning Committee
RE: Postmerger Staffing

Approximately 375 individuals will be displaced in the next 6 to 12 months—almost all of these in Hartford. We will be unable to deal with this total number via reassignments and normal turnover. A plan of action must be developed to handle this situation. One such reduction needs to occur in the Trust Center where we must cut that staff from 27 to 19. In addition to a general plan of action, we would also like to see a run-through on a proposal for handling the situation in the Trust Center. I believe your committee has the necessary data.

20. EXERCISE

Which Employee Should Be Terminated?

I. *Objectives:*
   A. To make you aware of the difficulties involved in making termination decisions.
   B. To familiarize you with possible criteria a manager can use in making termination decisions.
   C. To give you practice in conducting termination interviews.
II. *Out-of-Class Preparation Time:* 10 minutes to read exercise and decide which employee should be terminated.
III. *In-Class Time Suggested:* 40–50 minutes
IV. *Procedures:* Either at the beginning of or before class you should read the exercise and determine which title examiner should be fired.

   To start the exercise, the instructor will ask five students to play the role of title examiners. One of you will play the role of Rick Feinberg, another the role of Jeff Simon, and so on. These individuals will be asked to leave the classroom and prepare to play their role. They should study carefully the material contained in this exercise and determine how to respond if in fact they are the one chosen to be terminated.

   The instructor will divide the remaining students into groups of four to six. Each group should develop a list of criteria for layoffs, and rank the title examiners from first to go to last to go. After the group has reached a consensus, it should select one spokesperson to communicate the decision to the title examiner who is to be terminated.

After all groups have finished performing the preceding tasks, the role play begins. One at a time, each group's spokesperson announces to the class which title examiner his or her group believes should be terminated. The instructor then brings that person into the room and asks him or her to sit down in the front. The spokesperson sits down opposite the title examiner, tells that person that he or she is terminated, and gives the rationale behind the decision. The title examiner then responds in any realistic way which he or she deems appropriate. This process continues until all groups' spokespersons have had an opportunity to present their decision. A critique of the role plays and a discussion of the difficulties involved in terminating an employee should then follow.

Situation

The Stanton Title Insurance Company was founded in 1964 by Harvey Stanton to sell title insurance policies to buyers of real estate. The company works closely with a group of about 35 lawyers who, although they do not actually buy the title insurance policies, encourage their clients (the property purchasers) to do so. When the company was originally established, Mr. Stanton was its only employee. As company sales increased, new employees were hired, and now 23 individuals are working in various capacities for the firm. Mr. Stanton has always followed the policy of making all major decisions himself. This includes making all personnel decisions such as determining who should be hired and how much they should be paid.

Five of the employees work primarily on examining titles at local government offices. In recent weeks, Harvey has noticed that the workload of these five employees has declined considerably. In part this is due to the recent election of three "no-growth" candidates to the city council. In addition, a competing firm has recently opened an office in town and is successfully taking business away. Harvey has reluctantly decided that he must terminate the employment of one of the title examiners. He cannot simply transfer one of them to a new position. His only question is, which one?

A summary of Harvey's evaluation of each title examiner is in Exhibit 2.8; a profile of each of the five title examiners appears below:

Rick Feinberg: Forty-five years old; white; married with three children; 20 years with the company; graduated from a community college; knows how to resolve difficult title policies due to his extensive experience; is difficult to get along with; antagonizes other employees at main office; hates to fill out company reports not related to title examination and refuses to do so on occasion; will not work overtime under any condition, which puts a burden on others.

Jeff Simon: Twenty-three years old; black; married; attending college; one year with the company; wife works at main office as a computer programmer; works very hard and is eager to learn; well liked by all employees and is highly dependable; is never absent and will gladly work overtime to meet emergencies; with more experience he should be an outstanding title examiner; is highly loyal and dedicated; moved recently to a new apartment across the street from the government office where he works.

Kathy Wallace: Twenty-four years old; single; college degree; black; working on M.B.A. at night; three years with company; well liked by employees; very active in community affairs; capable of moving up to a top management position with the company; often misses work due to school and community activities.

Doris Matthews: Thirty-six years old; married; white; attended community college but did not graduate; ten years with company; niece of Harvey Stanton; has had eye problems and headaches which affected work quality this year and may continue to do so; has been very helpful in getting new business for the company; is well known and highly respected by law firms.

Anthony Pope: Sixty-three years old; white; 15 years with company; no college; hard working and well liked by employees; three children in college; a solid, stable employee who is able to remain calm and solve problems in crisis situations; excellent at resolving conflicts between employees; well known to local government officials; very slow but highly accurate worker.

EXHIBIT 2.8 *Harvey's Evaluation of Individual Job Performance for Title Examiners for Last Year*

Title Examiner	Current Salary	Work Quality	Work Quantity	Knowledge of Job	Dependability	Cooperativeness
Rick Feinberg	$27,500	Excellent	Good	Excellent	Good	Poor
Jeff Simon	$22,000	Good	Good	Fair	Excellent	Excellent
Kathy Wallace	$26,500	Good	Fair	Good	Fair	Excellent
Doris Matthews	$24,000	Poor	Good	Excellent	Good	Good
Anthony Pope	$25,000	Good	Poor	Excellent	Excellent	Excellent

21. EXERCISE

Writing Job Descriptions

    I. *Objectives:*
        A. To familiarize you with the job analysis process and with job descriptions.
        B. To give you practice in writing job descriptions.
   II. *Out-of-Class Preparation Time:* 30 minutes
  III. *In-Class Time Suggested:* 45 minutes
  IV. *Procedures:*
        A. Before beginning this exercise, you should (a) review carefully, if you have not already done so, the different methods organizations use to conduct job analyses and (b) review the Job Analysis Questionnaire (in Exhibit 2.9).
        B. Students should be divided into pairs. Each person should then interview his or her partner with reference to a job about which the partner is very familiar. Use the Job Analysis Questionnaire for the interview. The questionnaire can be used to help determine the major responsibilities and tasks of the job and the required knowledge, skills, abilities, and personal characteristics needed to perform the job.
        C. After each of you has interviewed his or her partner and vice versa, write a job description covering your partner's job. Remember to use action verbs when describing the employee's tasks, duties, and responsibilities. It is also important that specific duties be grouped and arranged in descending order of importance. The completed job description should follow the format shown in Exhibit 2.10. The completed job description should be shown to the partner to determine whether additional information is required or whether changes need to be made. Your instructor may require that you turn in a final copy of the completed job description at the next class period.
        D. If time permits, the entire class discusses the various uses of job descriptions and the effectiveness of the interview as a method of job analysis.

EXHIBIT 2.9 *Job Analysis Questionnaire*

A. Job Responsibilities and Duties
  1. Job title
  2. Department title and/or division title
  3. Title of immediate supervisor
  4. Description of duties (Describe the duties in enough detail to provide a complete and accurate description of the work.)
    a. Provide a general overall summary of the purpose of your job.
    b. What are the major results or outputs of your job?
    c. Describe the duties and tasks you perform daily; weekly; monthly.
    d. Describe duties you perform irregularly.
  5. List any machines, instruments, tools, equipment, materials, and work aids used in your job. Indicate percent of time used.
  6. Describe the nature of your responsibility for nonhuman resources (money, machinery, equipment, etc.). What monetary loss can occur through an error?
  7. What reports and records do you prepare as part of your job? When are they prepared?
  8. What is the source of instructions for performing your job (e.g., oral or written specifications)?
  9. Describe the nature and frequency of supervision received.
  10. How is your work reviewed, checked, or verified?

B. Reporting Relationships
  11. How many employees are directly under your supervision? What are their job titles?
  12. Do you have full authority to hire, terminate, evaluate, and transfer employees under your supervision? Explain.
  13. What contacts are required with other departments or persons other than your immediate department in performing your job? Describe the nature and extent of these contacts.

C. Working Conditions
  14. Describe the working conditions present in the location and environment of your work such as cold/heat, noise, fumes, dust, etc. Indicate frequency and degree of exposure.
  15. Describe any dangers or hazards present in your job.

D. Job Qualifications (Be certain not to list the incumbent's qualifications, but what is required for performance by a new employee.)
  16. Describe the kind of previous work experience necessary for satisfactory performance of this job.
  17. What is the amount of experience required?
  18. What kinds of knowledge, skills, and abilities (KSAs) are needed to perform the job?
  19. What is the minimal level of education (grammar, high school, two-year college, four-year college, etc.) required?
  20. Are any special physical skills and/or manual dexterity skills required to perform the job?
  21. Are there any special certification, registration, license, or training requirements?

EXHIBIT 2.10   *Sample Job Description*

JOB TITLE: Shift Supervisor

POSITION PURPOSE: The purpose of this position is to maintain a safe and efficient plant operation through directing the activities of the operation's personnel and providing a management support function for the plant superintendent.

TYPICAL JOB DUTIES:

1. Directs the activities of the operations personnel and coordinates the activities of the maintenance personnel.
2. Issues written communication to employees concerning personnel policies and operational concerns.
3. Administers maintenance request program through collecting requests, scheduling, and recording maintenance activities.
4. Administers the plant tagging procedure.
5. Conducts the training and safety programs for shift employees.
6. Schedules shift assignments to reflect workload and vacation schedules.
7. Performs administrative tasks such as recording workers' time, maintaining records concerning operational activities, and updating written procedures.
8. Prepares annual budget for assigned plant area and maintains the inventory level on these items.
9. Appraises performance of shift employees annually.
10. Counsels employees on disciplinary problems and job-related performance.
11. Assumes plant superintendent's duties when assigned.

PHYSICAL REQUIREMENTS: Walking and climbing stairs

WORKING CONDITIONS: Good, some noise

EQUIPMENT AND MACHINES USED: CRT, spectrometer, PH meter, conductivity meter

REPORTING RELATIONSHIPS: The shift supervisor reports directly to the plant superintendent. The shift supervisor directs the control room operator, two or more utility operators, trainees, and other assigned personnel and coordinates the activities of the maintenance personnel present on shift.

QUALIFICATIONS:

Education: Associate degree or equivalent training (e.g., management training classes) OR five (5) years of management experience.
Related Experience: minimum of three (3) years as a control room operator for a coal-fired boiler operation.

JOB KNOWLEDGE/SKILLS REQUIRED:

1. Comprehensive understanding of plant systems.
2. Fundamental understanding of electrical systems and motor control centers.
3. Thorough knowledge of boiler chemistry.
4. Comprehension of flow, logic, and electrical prints.
5. Ability to perform elementary mathematical and algebraic calculations.
6. Communication and human relations skills.
7. Ability to operate CRT, Spectrometer, PH meter, and conductivity meter.
8. Managerial skills.

22. EXERCISE

Work and Family Issues

    I. *Objectives:*
        A. To understand the conflicts that sometimes arise between the individual's work and family responsibilities.
        B. To analyze the advantages and disadvantages of alternative policies and programs that attempt to reconcile the sometimes conflicting demands of work and family.
   II. *Out-of-Class Preparation Time:*   2 hours
  III. *In-Class Time Suggested:*   45 minutes
  IV. *Procedures:*
        A. Read the entire exercise before class. Students may want to conduct research on the topic prior to class.
        B. Develop a list of possible policies and programs for this company to better reconcile work and family life.
        C. Form groups of two to five students and either choose one of the three options below or you will be assigned one of the three options by the instructor.
            1. Option 1—Use Form 1
                Prepare specific recommendations for the Task Force regarding policies and programs they should consider to help their employees better reconcile their work and family responsibilities. List these recommendations on Form 1 together with your estimate of how much time will be required for each recommendation to be implemented. The time frame for implementation will depend upon how high a priority the group assigns to a particular recommendation and how much time will be required to work out the details of the proposal. In preparing your recommendations, consider the pros and cons of responding to the needs of workers with small children.
            2. Option 2—Use Form 2
                Develop new policy statements for the *Employee Handbook* in the areas of absence, employee benefits, leave without pay, and sick leave. These new policy statements should modify the present policy statements shown in Exhibit 2.12. The revised policies are then written on Form 2.
            3. Option 3—Use Form 3
                Examine the four day-care service options recommended by the Task Force. For each option, list their expected advantages or benefits and their expected disadvantages or costs on Form 3. Circle your recommended option on Form 3.
        D. Share your group's recommendations with the rest of the class.

Background

Anderson's Department Stores are a regional retail chain based in Seattle, Washington. Over the past ten years Anderson's Department Stores have been very successful in providing high-quality merchandise to upper-middle class customers primarily in the Pacific Northwest. It presently has 84 stores employing 11,100 employees as well as a corporate headquarters with 154 employees. (See Exhibit 2.11 for a demographic profile of the current workforce). Anderson's Department Stores' rate of return on sales and growth rate in sales have been the highest in the retail industry over the past decade. While the shares of company stock are publicly traded on the American Stock Exchange, the Anderson family currently controls about 40 percent of this stock.

Anderson's Department Stores built its reputation and its success on customer service. It has the highest ratio of salespersons to customers in the retail industry and each salesperson is highly trained in products and customer service. In addition, the sales commissions are among the highest in the industry. Company publications indicate that the company views its employees as "family members." This is reinforced by company dinners, picnics, and other social events. These approaches to customers and employees seem to have worked well. Not only are the financial results excellent, but there are 7.5 applications for each position in the company. This allows the company to be very selective in its hiring policies.

The company also has taken the position that the individual's family and work life are and should be separate. Both require time and effort, but should never interfere with each other. The company's philosophy has been that each individual has a responsibility to hire or otherwise provide child care service or whatever other services are necessary for the proper functioning of the family. The company's responsibility has been only to provide jobs for employees while serving customer needs.

Recently, that philosophy has been challenged by several employees who claim the company is "insensitive" to employees who have family responsibilities. In particular, they cite the lack of any child-care facilities and family-leave policies. They argue that uniform personnel policies applied rigidly to all employees (irrespective of their family situation) are inherently unfair. If the company really viewed their employees as "family members," it would be more flexible in accommodating the employee's family responsibilities. Exhibit 2.12 provides excerpts from the Anderson's Department Stores' *Employee Handbook.* The sick leave policy, for example, indicates that the company does not provide any sick leave to care for a sick child or family member or to care for elderly relatives.

The board of directors consists of the major stockholders in the Anderson family, several non-family top executives, and outside directors from other companies. At its most recent meeting, the board discussed its current philosophy regarding the work/family life separation, the charge of "insensitivity," and possible modifications. The major concern expressed was that the company's image as "a good place to work" was being threatened and that, in turn, could adversely affect the company's ability to recruit and retain the highest quality personnel. If the quality of personnel (particularly salespersons) were to decline, this would jeopardize the business strategy of differentiating their product based on excellent customer service.

In addition, Mr. Peter Anderson, the company CEO, recently read an article in *Business Week* identifying the "best companies for women." This article identified a number of family-oriented policies and programs followed by 24 leading companies. Among the most significant of these were modifications in the company culture, executive development to enhance "sensitivity," child care, sick-child care, women on the board, career development policies, family-leave policies, maternity leave with partial pay, modified work and family benefits, flexible benefits, hiring a "pluralistic" workforce, job sharing, mentoring programs, and part-time professional and/or executive positions. Some of the 24 corporations identified in the *Business Week* article were in retail trade.

The Task Force

In response to employee criticism and the potential for negative publicity, the board of trustees made a decision to establish a "Task Force on the Work/Family Interface." The mission of the Task Force was to make recommendations on possible additions and modifications to company policies and programs that will better accommodate the family responsibilities of its employees. Members of this Task Force included company executives, exempt and nonexempt employees, and members of the board of trustees. Members of the Task Force reviewed newspaper, magazine, and journal articles and discussed options with others in the community prior to making their recommendations.

The Task Force made recommendations in a large number of areas including health insurance coverage, absence with pay, leave without pay, sick leave, promotion criteria and policies, training programs, family leave, job sharing, flextime, and child care. The latter recommendation on child care provided several options from which the company could choose. These are listed in Exhibit 2.13.

The Task Force recognized that each of the four day care options has advantages and disadvantages. The benefits will be both economic and noneconomic, but the noneconomic benefits may be translated into economic terms by estimating the expected reductions in employee turnover and then calculating the expected savings in recruitment and training costs. The present annual turnover rate for female employees is 18.6 percent compared to 15.8 percent for male employees. However, the female rate is higher for nonexempt positions, for married females, for those under 35, for those with children, and for those with children under six years old. All of these subgroups have turnover rates of 20 to 30 percent. The Human Resource

Department has calculated that the recruitment/training costs of replacing an "average" employee is $1,750. These costs are higher for exempt positions and full-time positions (these positions average $2,000–2,500 for each employee replaced). Even these costs may be understated, since the average employee leaving Anderson's Department Store is estimated to be more productive than the average employee retained.

The disadvantages or costs may also be economic or noneconomic. The economic costs can be estimated by gathering data on the direct costs of providing each particular program or service. For example, the Human Resource Department has determined that the average daily cost of child care per child is $23.84 in the cities where their department stores are located. Since the typical employee works 240 days per year, the yearly cost per child would be $5,722 ($23.84 × 240 days). The total yearly cost of the service would be that figure times the estimated number of individuals using the service.

EXHIBIT 2.11   *Percentage Distribution of Anderson's Department Stores Workforce by Demographic Category*

	Demographic Category	
	Exempt % (n = 2846)	Nonexempt % (n = 8254)
Sex		
Male	45.9	20.5
Female	54.1	79.5
Job Status		
Part-time	0	38.3
Full-time	100	61.7
Marital Status		
Single	32.1	33.1
Married	52.2	54.9
Divorced	15.7	12.0
Age		
18 and under	0	.3
19–25	10.1	27.8
25–35	15.2	43.2
36–50	47.1	19.6
51–59	18.6	5.1
60 and over	90.0	4.0
Number of Children		
None	10.1	8.1
1–2	60.9	58.3
3–4	18.0	23.7

(continued)

EXHIBIT 2.11   *continued*

5–6	5.0	7.5
6 or more	6.0	2.4
Age of Children		
0–2 years	3.1	15.1
3–5 years	4.9	31.9
6–12 years	15.0	25.0
13–18 years	57.0	18.0
Over 18	20.0	10.0
Race		
White	89.1	70.1
Black	4.0	13.2
Asian	1.0	2.0
Hispanic	5.9	14.7
Spouse Employed	43.7	79.6

EXHIBIT 2.12   *Excerpts from Anderson's Department Stores Policy Manual*

AUTHORIZED ABSENCE WITH PAY

You will be excused with pay at the discretion of your department supervisor as follows: (1) in the case of death in your immediate family; (2) to serve on jury duty; and (3) leave required for active duty or for annual training as a member of the military reserves.

EMPLOYEE BENEFITS

The company offers broad insurance for you and your dependents.

Medical Coverage: Your individual medical coverage is paid for by the company. If you insure your spouse and dependents, the company will pay half of the costs and make deductions from your paycheck for the other part.

Dental Coverage: Coverage may be purchased from an inexpensive group plan that emphasizes diagnostic and preventive care.

Life Insurance: The employee's life insurance is paid for by the company. You may purchase insurance for your qualified dependents.

LEAVE WITHOUT PAY

Each employee is eligible for up to five days of unpaid leave per year with the written permission of your immediate supervisor.

(continued)

EXHIBIT 2.12 *continued*

SICK LEAVE

You are eligible to take sick leave with pay in case of personal illness or disability.

Full-time employees accrue sick leave at the rate of one working day of sick leave for each full month of service.

Permanent part-time employees accrue sick leave as follows: 20 hours but less than 30 hours per week = 6 days annually; 30 hours but less than 40 hours per week = 9 days annually.

Sick leave may be used subject to the following: If the absence is caused by: (1) personal illness or physical incapacity resulting from causes beyond your control; or (2) physical disability. Other uses are prohibited and will be subject to disciplinary action.

EXHIBIT 2.13   *Child-Care Options Recommended by Anderson's Department Stores Task Force on the Work/Family Interface*

1. *Alternative One: Establish and operate a daycare center in each department store.*
   Estimated capital investment required for this option will be $58,000 per store or a total corporate investment of $4,872,000. Then the annual operating costs will average $108,000 per store or $9,072,000.
2. *Alternative Two: Contract out daycare services to Child Care Services of America, a private corporation.*
   The rates average about $3.25 an hour per child for an eight-hour day and $3.75 per hour for shorter periods in their own facilities. They also are willing to provide the service in the department stores for $3.50 and $4.00 per hour, respectively.
3. *Alternative Three: Contract out daycare services to public schools in the local communities.*
   The rates average about $3.00 an hour per child, but the service is typically available for limited hours.
4. *Alternative Four: Provide a voucher system whereby parents may choose their own daycare services and use redeemable vouchers to pay for this service.*
   Vouchers would limit reimbursement to $3.50 an hour per child.

FORM 1   *Recommendations for the Task Force on*
Work/Family Interface, Anderson's Department Stores

Policy or Program	Time Frame for Implementation*
1.	
2.	
3.	
4.	
5.	
6.	
7.	
8.	
9.	
10.	
11.	
12.	

*short-term = within the next year
intermediate term = one to two years
long-term = more than two years

FORM 2   *Revised Policies for Anderson's*
         Department Stores Employee Handbook

Authorized Absence With Pay

Employee Benefits

Leave Without Pay

Sick Leave

FORM 3   *Task Force Recommendations Regarding*
           Daycare Services, Anderson's Department Stores

Daycare Options	Expected Advantages or Benefits	Expected Disadvantages or Costs
1. Establish and operate daycare center		
2. Contract with private corporation		
3. Contract with public schools		
4. Establish voucher system		

23. SKILL BUILDER

Human Resource Forecasting Assignment

I. *Objectives:*
   A. To give you practice in forecasting an organization's human resource needs.
   B. To familiarize you with some of the factors which affect an organization's future human resource needs (growth, automation, turnover).
   C. To familiarize you with the complexities involved in making human resource forecasts.
   D. To point out that all human resource forecasting is based on assumptions and that these assumptions are critical to the accuracy of the forecast. Incorrect assumptions lead to erroneous forecasts.
II. *Time Required to Complete Assignment:* 1–2 hours.
III. *Instructions:* You have been given the assignment of forecasting the human resource needs of the National Bank And Trust Company which currently employs approximately 1,100 employees. The bank presently has 50 branch offices located throughout the metropolitan area, each of which employs approximately 14 individuals. The bank expects to add 38 branches during the next three years. Branches within the bank differ considerably in size so the figures given represent averages.

   During the past month, the bank has placed an order for 30 automated teller machines that will be placed in its old branch offices. These machines are scheduled to be in operation December 31, one year from now. The bank has found that for each new machine purchased, one less teller is needed, on the average.

   A breakdown of the bank's current staffing is shown in Table 1 below:

TABLE 1   *Present Staffing*

Total Employees	1,100
Number of Branches	50
Supervisors per Branch	4
Number of Supervisors	200
Tellers per Branch	10
Number of Tellers	500
Branch Employees	700
Main Office Employees	400

The bank has asked you to perform three human resource forecasting tasks. First, based on the assumptions given below, you are required to determine employee turnover for the main office, the old branches, and for the new branches. Your boss would like to know this information for each of the next three years and for each of the major personnel categories (i.e., supervisors, tellers/clerical, and main office). Your job is to complete Table 2 shown below:

TABLE 2   *Turnover*

Employee Category	Year 1	Year 2	Year 3
Old Branch Supervisors			
Old Branch Tellers			
Main Office			
New Branch Supervisors			
New Branch Tellers			
Totals			

Second, your boss would like to know the number of new employees the bank will need to hire for each major personnel category for each of the next three years. Your job is to complete Table 3 shown below:

TABLE 3   *Number of Employees to Be Hired*

Employee Category	Year 1	Year 2	Year 3
Old Branch Supervisors			
Old Branch Tellers			
Main Office			
New Branch Supervisors			
New Branch Tellers			
Totals			

Finally, your boss would like to know the total number of employees who will be working for the bank as of the end of each of the next three years. Your job is to complete Table 4 shown on the following page:

TABLE 4   *Year End Employment*

Employee Category	Year 1	Year 2	Year 3
Old Branch Supervisors			
Old Branch Tellers			
Main Office			
New Branch Supervisors			
New Branch Tellers			
Totals			

In order to complete your assignment, your boss has told you to make a number of assumptions. They are:

A. You are making all projections in December for subsequent years ending December 31.

B. With regard to old branches, assume
1. The 50 old branches employ 4 supervisors and 10 clerical personnel/tellers each.
2. 30 teller machines are placed in operation on December 31 (one year hence) and replace 30 tellers.
3. The bank does not terminate any employees because of the new teller machines. Rather, as tellers quit throughout the year, 30 are not replaced.
4. Turnover is 30 percent for tellers/clerical personnel and 20 percent for supervisors.

C. With regard to new branches, assume
1. New branches are added as follows: 10 in year one, 12 in year two, and 16 in year three.
2. Each new branch employs 14 individuals (4 supervisors and 10 tellers/clerical).
3. New branches are added evenly throughout the year. Thus, for the purpose of calculating turnover, on average, there are 5 new branches in year one (50% × 10); 16 in year two [10 in year one plus 6 (50% × 12)]; and 30 in year three [22 plus 8 (50% × 16)].
4. Turnover is 30 percent for tellers/clerical personnel and 20 percent for supervisors.

D. With regard to the main office, assume that turnover will be 10 percent per year.

24. SKILL BUILDER

From Welfare to Work

I. *Objectives:*
   A. To give you practice in using the Internet to generate information relevant to solving human resource problems.
   B. To familiarize you with the challenges and complexities of moving individuals and families from welfare to work.
II. *Time Required to Complete:* 2 hours.
III. *Instructions:* Read the "Situation" below and then search the web sites outlined in the Internet skill builder (or others you may prefer) to identify at least one strategy or tactic proposed or currently being successfully implemented elsewhere for each of the problems identified on Form 1. In addition, describe a comprehensive strategy they might use to avoid or minimize the potential problems of this initiative and describe this at the bottom of Form 1. Among the most useful web sites for this search might be the following:

http://www.hbs.htv.ac.uk/staff/1yerj/list/hromt.htm
http://webcrawler.com
http://www.excite.com

Write your suggestions in the spaces provided on Form 1 prior to class. Your instructor will then assign teams of three to five students who will discuss their recommendations for 20 to 30 minutes during class. The teams will then share their recommendations with the class.

Situation

There has been an increased interest in hiring welfare recipients since President Clinton signed the Personal Responsibility and Welfare Reconciliation Act of 1996. In essence, the act required one million people to be placed in jobs in one year with an additional million being placed over the following five-year period. To entice businesses to develop programs to hire and train welfare recipients, the government offered tax credits to businesses. The Work Opportunity Tax Credit provides up to $2,100 per employee hired off the welfare rolls.

By September 1998, just under 8 million people remained on welfare nationally, down 44 percent from 14.3 million in 1994. While the decline in the welfare rolls has generally been a positive development, nearly all the people who can move off welfare with relative ease have already done so. Those who remain have deeper problems than simply a lack of a job including homelessness, substance abuse, domestic violence, learning disabilities, lack of transportation, and lack of understanding of workplace discipline (i.e., attendance and punctuality).

The Jefferson (Alabama) County Department of Human Resources has been successful in reducing their welfare rolls from 8,180 welfare recipients two years ago to 4,500 this year. Now the Department is faced with the challenge of how to further reduce their rolls while moving "hard-core" welfare recipients from welfare to work. On the positive side, they have the good fortune of operating in a labor market with a 3.1 percent unemployment rate and high demand for entry-level workers, particularly in restaurants, hotels, and security firms.

On the negative side, some employers have criticized the lack of "job-readiness" of the trainees previously sent to them. This complaint was not surprising since the previous approach was "work first" whereby the Department focused on helping recipients look for work and then pushed them to take any job offered. The Department reasoned that work experience, in or of itself, would help the former recipients move up the economic ladder. It didn't try to solve their problems or provide the education (training) they may have needed.

At this point, the Department has called on your student team to advise them on a comprehensive program to prepare the remaining 4,500 welfare recipients for work. Their goal is to place 1,000 people a year over the next three years. Despite the above complaints, they already have commitments from several restaurants, hotels, and security firms to employ graduates of the program in entry-level positions with the possibility of upward mobility later on. However, they are also concerned that negative experience and resultant negative "word-of-mouth" or publicity may derail achievement of their goals.

FORM 1   *Challenges Facing the Jefferson County*
         Department of Human Resources

Problem	Strategies/Tactics
1. Client homelessness	**1.**
2. Client substance abuse	**1.**
3. Client victim of domestic violence	**1.**
4. Client learning disabilities	**1.**
5. Client lack of transportation to job site	**1.**
6. Client lack of understanding of workforce discipline	**1.**

Comprehensive Strategy:

25. SKILL BUILDER

Phased Retirement Options

   I. *Objectives:*
   A. To give you practice in using the Internet to generate information relevant to solving human resource problems.
   B. To familiarize you with the various options to traditional employee retirement.
   II. *Time Required to Complete:* 1–2 hours
   III. *Instructions:* Read the "Situation" below and then search the Internet for the following: (1) phased retirement options; (2) advantages or benefits of each option for employees and the employer; and (3) disadvantages or costs of options for each.

   Possible web sites are as follows:

   http://www.magicnet.net/benefits.index.html
   http://ebn.communications.com
   http://www.vcn.bc.ca/timework.worksite.htm
   http://www.insword.com/newsletter/index.html

   Then fill in Form 1 (provide at least one advantage and disadvantage for each of the listed options) and be prepared to present your findings and recommendations to the class.

Situation

The Owens Engineering Company provides a full range of engineering services to a wide variety of governmental and private organizations in the Denver metropolitan area. Ron Owens, the company President, has become increasingly concerned about his company's demographics. Two-thirds of their 82 engineers are in the age range from 50 to 67. The company's current retirement policy is to offer retirement to all employees who reach age 55 or more with 25 or more years of service.

Within the next few years, Mr. Owens has determined that 42 percent of the engineers will be eligible for retirement, and, based on past company data, 70 percent *will* retire within two years of their actual eligibility. This means he expects to lose 29 of 82 engineers to retirement over the next four years. In addition, the "normal" annual turnover rate among engineers has been 8 percent per year. This would reduce the company's "pool" of engineers by another seven per year or 28 over the next four years.

After discussing the situation with Susan Barber, the Human Resources Manager, Mr. Owens concluded most voluntary turnover was "unavoidable." While the company provides competitive salaries and benefits for the Denver area, the local unemployment rate is extremely low (averaging 2.8 percent), and there are virtually no unemployed engineers in the area. Future forecasts are for a continued "tight" labor market for engineers in Denver.

Mr. Owens and Ms. Barber determined that the best way to deal with their potential engineer shortage was to retain older engineers as they become eligible for retirement. This decision was not only based on the numbers, but also on the qualities and qualifications they anticipated losing. For example, when four senior civil engineers retired during the past year, the company lost their contacts and influence, their knowledge of their customers, special requirements in the contract bidding process, and their knowledge about who to see and how to get things done internally.

Ms. Barber is a friend of your instructor in "Human Resource Management" this term. Your instructor has assigned your student team the term project of assisting Owens Engineering in assessing its options for retaining its older engineers.

FORM 1   *Phased Retirement Options*

Option 1:

Advantages/Benefits to the Company	Advantages/Benefits to the Employee
1.	1.
2.	2.
3.	3.

Disadvantages/Costs to the Company	Disadvantages/Costs to the Employee
1.	1.
2.	2.
3.	3.

Option 2:

Advantages/Benefits to the Company	Advantages/Benefits to the Employee
1.	1.
2.	2.
3.	3.

Disadvantages/Costs to the Company	Disadvantages/Costs to the Employee
1.	1.
2.	2.
3.	3.

Option 3:

Advantages/Benefits to the Company	Advantages/Benefits to the Employee
1.	1.
2.	2
3.	3.

Disadvantages/Costs to the Company	Disadvantages/Costs to the Employee
1.	1.
2.	2.
3.	3.

RECRUITING AND SELECTION

26. CASE

Recruiting Recreational Vehicle Surveyors

Liberty Engineering Co. is located in a large suburb of Cleveland, Ohio. The company was founded during the 1940s and does a considerable amount of drafting and design work for the major automotive companies and their suppliers. When sales in the auto industry are high, Liberty Engineering experiences a significant volume of work. However, when recessions hit the automotive marketplace, work at Liberty also sharply decreases.

In an attempt to stabilize revenues, the President of Liberty Engineering decided it would be prudent to diversify the company by bidding on government contracts. The company had little experience in these areas, but the President felt that this would not preclude it from bidding on contracts and obtaining them.

Within a six-month period the company had bid on and lost two contracts. However, a third bid pertaining to the safety and use of recreational vehicles proved to be successful. The contract was for several hundred thousand dollars and was granted on a cost-plus basis. The government was interested in obtaining information regarding how people actually use recreational vehicles such as pick-up truck campers, motor homes, and various kinds of recreational trailers. Ultimately, the purpose of the study was to determine what additional safety rules, if any, should be established relating to the manufacture and use of recreational vehicles. Among the pieces of information desired by the government were how much weight citizens place in their recreational vehicles, what kinds of trailer hitches are in use, whether recreational vehicles have proper suspension systems, and to what extent citizens are aware of the safety features of their recreational vehicles.

In Liberty's proposal to the government, the company stated that it would recruit, select, and train qualified individuals to survey over 1,000 recreational vehicles. The surveying would be done at three different sites: a desert location, a seashore site, and a mountainous locale. At a meeting with government officials, three locations were selected: Cape Hatteras, North Carolina; Smoky Mountains National Park, Tennessee; and Lake Mead, Nevada. Two other important decisions were also made at the meeting. First, to ensure consistency of data collection, all surveyors would be trained together at a campground at Smoky Mountains National Park. Second, the employees would then be divided and sent to their respective job sites. It was also decided that each survey crew would consist of one leader and four surveyors and that two crews would be sent to each data collection site.

All responsibility for recruiting and training the 30 employees (6 leaders and 24 surveyors) fell on the shoulders of Bob Getz, the new Human Resource Director. Bob had worked as a designer for Liberty for 20 years before being transferred to Human Resources. At the same time a project Bob had been working on for two years ended, the former Human Resource Director quit, so Bob was a logical choice. In addition, Bob was well liked by most of Liberty's older employees and knew a great deal about the company's policies and procedures. Bob's major shortcoming was that he knew little about staffing activities.

Before recruiting potential job applicants, Bob knew that he would first need to develop a set of job descriptions for all 30 employees. Since crews would be doing essentially similar jobs, albeit at different locations, Bob needed only to develop job descriptions for each of four survey positions and that of the leader. Hence, Bob obtained the list of data which was to be collected on each vehicle, determined the tasks required to collect the data, and divided the task into four job positions. Bob realized that the job duties of each surveyor would ultimatley need to be changed based on actual experience. Nontheless, he roughed out the following job descriptions:

Surveyor I: Take pictures of recreational vehicle with a camera. Interview driver and record information received.

Surveyor II: Read and record scale weights for each recreational vehicle tire. Take tire pressures and measure tread depth. Record make, size, and air capacity of each tire.

Surveyor III: Unhook trailer hitch, if present, and record make of hitch, ball diameter, and whether levelers are present. Determine type of suspension on recreational vehicle and count number of leaf springs if present.

Surveyor IV: Stop recreational vehicle as it enters campground, explain to driver the purpose of the study, ask the driver to participate in study. When survey of recreational vehicle is complete, discuss the findings with the driver.

The leader's responsibilities would be to plan daily work activities, motivate the employees to do the surveying, complete all forms, and do occasional troubleshooting.

With job descriptions in hand, Bob met with Norm Larson, Vice President of Liberty, and the one ultimately responsible for conducting the recreational vehicle surveys. During the meeting Bob learned that all 30 employees were to meet at Smoky Mountains National Park on June 10. They were to be trained on the job for four days, and the company would provide them with lodging and food while they were there. All employees were to provide their own transportation to the park and to their subsequent job sites and ultimately back home. The company would pay them for travel time but would not provide any mileage allowance, lodging, or food. Upon arrival at the job site, employees would need to find accommodations for July and August and would receive no lodging or food allowance from the company during their stay. Once work commenced at each job site, employees would be responsible for providing their own transportation to and from the campground.

All employees were to be paid $7.45 per hour. No vacation benefits, sick days, or other major benefits would be provided. The company would, however, provide benefits mandated by law such as social security and workers' compensation. No one under the age of 18 would be hired because of safety reasons.

After the meeting with Norm, Bob decided he should check with the campground management at the different job sites. He learned that most recreational vehicles leave campgrounds early in the morning and enter late in the afternoon. Few arrive or depart between 10 A.M. and 4 P.M. In order to survey a maximum number of vehicles, therefore, crews would need to work from 6 A.M. to 11 A.M. and from 3 P.M. to 8 P.M., a total of 10 hours a day. Therefore, each crew could work a four-day-on and a four-day-off schedule. Bob was told that temperatures at Cape Hatteras would range between 65 and 95 degrees, while at Lake Mead they would range between 85 and 115 degrees. Neither of these locations would provide employees with any shade; hence employees at these sites would need to work in the sun and wear uniforms, including hats. The Smoky Mountains National Park location would be cooler than the others and surveying could be done in shaded areas. When Bob asked the campground managers whether they knew of any people who would be interested in working on the survey project, their response was, "You've got to be kidding." The manager at Lake Mead campground flatly told Bob that he couldn't conceive of any person being willing to drive from Lake Mead to Tennessee and back under the conditions Bob outlined. He suggested that Bob put a want ad in the Cleveland newspaper.

After talking with the campground managers, Bob was quite depressed. He knew that he had to hire 30 employees within the next few weeks. He knew that six of them had to have sufficient leadership skills to get the job done while not antagonizing the employees so much that they would quit. He further realized that the 24 surveyors would have to enjoy the outdoors and be willing to tolerate extreme heat. He realized, too, that the ideal surveyor would be one who had above-average knowledge of auto mechanics, legible handwriting, reasonable communication skills, and an ability to work well with others under adverse conditions. What Bob didn't know was how he could recruit and hire 30 people who fit these descriptions.

Questions

1. If you were Bob, how would you recruit the needed employees?
2. Evaluate the Lake Mead campground manager's suggestion that Bob recruit employees by placing a want ad in the Cleveland newspaper.
3. What should the firm do if they are unable to recruit sufficient employees for the job?

27. CASE

Selecting Patient Escorts

City Hospital is located in the heart of a large midwestern city. It is one of five major hospitals in the area and has recently built a small addition for treating well-known patients such as professional football players, top company executives, and singing stars. Visiting or local celebrities always choose City Hospital if they need treatment.

City Hospital has about 1,200 hospital beds and employs 4,500 individuals, including about 40 patient escorts. The job of patient escort is a rather simple one, requiring only minimal training and no special physical talents. When patients need to be moved from one location to another, patient escorts are summoned to assist in the move. If the move is only a short distance, however, a nurse or orderly can move the patient. Of particular importance is the fact that patient escorts almost always take patients who are being discharged from their hospital room to the front door of the hospital. A wheelchair is always used, even if the patient is able to walk unassisted. Thus, the typical procedure is for the nurse to call for a patient escort; the escort gets a wheelchair and goes to the patient's room, assists the patient into the wheelchair, picks up the patient's belongings, wheels the patient down to the hospital's front door or to his or her car in the parking lot, and returns to the work station.

The job of patient escort is critical to the hospital since the escort is always the last hospital representative the patient sees, and hence has a considerable influence on the patient's perception of the hospital. Of the approximately 40 escorts, about three-fourths are men, and one-fourth are women. Most are high school graduates in their early twenties. Some, particularly those on the early morning shift, are attending college at night and working for the hospital to earn money to pay college expenses. Four of the escorts are older women who had previously served as hospital volunteers and then decided to become full-time employees instead. Turnover among patient escorts is quite high and has averaged 25 percent in recent years. In addition, upward mobility in the hospital is quite good, and as a result, another 25 percent of the escorts typically transfer to other jobs in the hospital each year. Thus about half of the patient escorts need to be replaced annually.

The hospital follows a standard procedure when hiring patient escorts. When a vacancy occurs, the Personnel Department reviews the file of applications of individuals who have applied for the patient escort job. Usually the file contains at least 20 applications because the pay for the job is good, the work easy, and few skills are required. The top two or three applicants are asked to come to the hospital for interviews. Typically, the applicants are interviewed first by Personnel and then by the patient escort supervisor. The majority of those interviewed know some other employees of the hospital, so the only reference check is a call to these employees. Before being hired, applicants are required to take physical exams given by hospital doctors.

Every new escort attends an orientation program the first day on the job. This is conducted by a member of the hospital's Personnel Department. The program consists of a complete tour of the hospital, a review of all the hospital's personnel policies, including a description of its promotion, compensation, and disciplinary policies, and a presentation of the hospital's mission and philosophy. During this orientation session, employees are told that the hospital's image in the community is of major importance and that all employees should strive to maintain and enhance this image by their conduct. After orientation, all patient escorts receive on-the-job training by their immediate supervisor.

During the last two-year period the hospital has experienced a number of problems with patient escorts that have had an adverse effect on the hospital's image. Several patients have complained to the hospital administration that they have been treated rudely, or in some cases roughly, by one or more patient escorts. Some complained that they had been ordered around or scolded by an escort during the discharge process. Others stated that the escort had been careless when wheeling them out of the hospital to their cars. One person, in fact, reported that an escort had carelessly tipped him over. All escorts are required to wear identification tags, but patients usually can't remember the escort's name when complaining to the hospital. Additionally, the hospital usually has difficulty determining which escort served which patient because escorts often trade patients. Finally, even when the hospital can identify the offending escort, the employee can easily deny any wrongdoing. He or she often counters that patients are generally irritable as a result of their illness and hence are prone to complain at even the slightest provocation.

At the hospital administrator's request, the Personnel Manager asked the Chief Supervisor of Patient Escorts, the head of the Staffing Section within the Personnel Department, and the Assistant Personnel Director to meet with her to review the entire procedure used to select patient escorts. It was hoped that a new procedure could be devised that would eliminate the hiring of rude, insulting, or careless patient escorts.

During the meeting a number of suggestions were made as to how the selection procedure might be improved. Criticisms of the present system were also voiced. The chief supervisor of patient escorts argued that the problem with the hospital's present system is that the application blank is void of any really useful information. He stated that the questions that really give insights into the employee's personality were no longer on the application blank. He suggested that applicants be asked about their hobbies, outside activities, and their personal likes and dislikes on the application blank. He also suggested that each applicant be asked to submit three letters of recommendation from people who know the applicant well. He wanted these letters to focus on the prospective employee's personality, particularly the applicant's ability to remain friendly and polite at all times.

The Assistant Personnel Director contended that the hospital's interviewing procedure should be modified. He observed that during the typical interview little attempt is made to determine how the applicant reacts under stress. He suggested that, if applicants were asked four or five stress-producing questions, the hospital might be in a better position to judge their ability to work with irritable patients.

The head of the Staffing Section noted that patient escorts require little mental or physical talent and agreed that the crucial attribute escorts need is the ability always to be courteous and polite. He wondered whether an "attitude" test could be developed that would measure the applicant's predisposition toward being friendly, etc. He suggested that a job analysis could be done on the patient escort position to determine those attitudes that are critical to being a successful patient escort. Once the job analysis was complete, questions could be developed that would measure these critical attributes. The test questions could be given to the hospital's present patient escorts to determine whether the test accurately distinguishes the best from worst escorts. The staffing head realized that many of the questions might need to be eliminated or changed, and that, if the test appeared to show promise, it would probably need to be revalidated in order to meet government requirements. He felt, however, that a well-designed test might be worth the effort and should at least be tried.

The meeting ended with all four participants agreeing that the suggestion of trying to develop an "attitude test" was probably the most promising. The Assistant Manager and Chief Supervisor of Patient Escorts stated that they would conduct a thorough job analysis covering the patient escort position and develop a list of attitudes that are critical to its success. A second meeting would then be held to prepare the actual test questions.

Questions

1. Critique each of the alternative approaches suggested for solving the problem of selecting patient escorts.
2. Recommend a procedure for recruiting and hiring patient escorts.
3. Besides improving its selection procedures, what other actions could the hospital potentially take to improve the behavior of the patient escorts?

28. CASE

A Solution for Adverse Impact

A federal government agency was in need of assistance regarding its staffing practices. Recently, some of the job applicants had complained that the selection procedures for one of the entry-level law enforcement jobs were discriminatory. The personnel specialists, who had previously ignored this possibility, were now alerted to the potential problem of adverse impact against women and minorities.

Bob Santa was a personnel specialist for the agency and had been employed with the staffing division for almost three years. He had kept up with the laws and regulations on discrimination and equal employment opportunity. About two months ago, he had attended a training seminar on the *Uniform Guidelines on Employee Selection Procedures*. Upon returning to the agency, Bob decided that an evaluation of their current staffing practices was necessary as they had been developed over ten years ago and prior to the adoption of the *Uniform Guidelines* in 1978. These guidelines were designed to provide a proper framework for determining the proper use of selection procedures. They indicated how organizations should evaluate their selection rates using the four-fifths rule and also specified the standards that organizations should use to validate their procedures.

The Selection Process

The selection of entry-level agents for the law enforcement job involved a two-step multiple-hurdle process. Applicants were first required to pass a cognitive ability test, a similar but somewhat easier test than the Scholastic Aptitude Test (SAT). The exam was made up of 25 verbal items and 25 quantitative items. A candidate was required to receive a passing score of 70 (35 of the items correct) in order to be eligible for the second step of the selection process, an interview. A three-member panel of supervisors asked each applicant questions on how they would deal with various hypothetical job situations. After an initial period of questions regarding the applicant's education and experience, the applicant was given a situation and then asked to respond to the situation. Typically, after each candidate's initial response, further questioning would ensue from the panel to determine the full response of the candidate. The interview would last about a half hour. At the end of the interview, the three interviewers would rate the candidate on ten dimensions such as attitude, motivation, communication, etc. Candidates receiving high scores on most of the dimensions would pass the interview.

This case was prepared by Ronald J. Karren, School of Management, University of Massachusetts at Amherst.

After a physical examination and a security check, the candidate was hired and asked to report to training.

The Determination of Adverse Impact

Bob knew that the guidelines required employers to make adverse impact determinations at least once a year. Although records had been kept, the agency had not calculated the selection rates over the past three years. Bob thought that it was long overdue and decided to have this done as soon as possible. A week later the selection rates were tabulated. The data are presented in Exhibit 2.14.

After calculating the adverse impact for both the test and the interview, Bob decided that a discussion with the Personnel Psychologist in the agency would be necessary. A meeting was arranged between Bob, his supervisor and head of the staffing division, and the Personnel Psychologist for the agency, Ron Burden. A discussion ensued regarding the validation requirements of the *Uniform Guidelines*. It was decided that the original job analysis was poorly done and that very little documentation had been retained by the agency. Although there was a task inventory, the major tasks or job duties had not been rated for importance, frequency, difficulty, and trainability. Ron pointed out that this documentation would be critical if they ever needed to defend the selection procedures in court. At the end of the meeting it was decided that it would probably be a good idea to do another job analysis that was in accordance with the new *Uniform Guidelines*. Ron felt that the selection procedures would have to be modified to fit the results of the job analysis. Ron was asked to determine how the job analysis would be done while Bob would coordinate the project in the field.

Job Analysis

The *Uniform Guidelines* recognize that there is no one best way of analyzing the job. Since there was little documentation available, Ron had to decide on a method or technique that would generate from the agents and supervisors the important work responsibilities and the tasks associated with them. After much deliberation, he decided to use the critical-incident technique. Ron knew that if the agency wanted to continue using situational questions in the interview, the critical-incident job-analysis technique readily lends itself to the development of this type of question. The method involves collecting reports of behaviors that are "critical," in that they distinguished between successful and unsuccessful work performance. Instructions to the agents and supervisors were to include (1) the circumstances that preceded the incident, (2) the setting in which the incident occurred, (3) what the agent did that was effective or ineffective, and (4) the consequences of the incident.

Ron asked a sample of agents to develop three critical incidents and to indicate the task associated with each critical incident. Upon receipt of the critical incidents, Ron and Bob derived an inventory of work behaviors. This list of work behaviors was then sent back to the agents, and they were asked to rate the importance of the behavior, how frequently it was performed, and the amount of training that was required to learn that behavior.

When this information was collected, Ron and Bob generated a list of major job tasks or job duties. They then assigned all the important work behaviors to their associated tasks. This list of tasks and work behaviors was then sent out to a group of supervisors who were asked to review the list. This same group of supervisors were also asked to meet for a two-day conference later in the month. This group of experts was to determine the important knowledge, skills, abilities, and other characteristics (KSAOs) required to perform these work behaviors. Ron also planned for these experts to select the critical incidents to be used for the new interview.

Supervisory Conference

At the conference the supervisors were given the inventory of tasks and their corresponding work behaviors. They were asked to derive the KSAOs and then to rate how important the skill or ability was for the performance of the work behaviors. The most important knowledge, skills, abilities, and other characteristics are shown in Exhibit 2.15.

The job experts were asked to evaluate the current staffing practices in light of this list of KSAOs. Ron, Bob, and the supervisors agreed that the content of the exam would have to be changed to reflect the first three KSAOs. Ron proposed a reading comprehension exam in which the content would be a small sample of the procedures, laws, and regulations that are taught at the training academy. Applicants would read a section and then answer questions regarding the laws and regulations taught in that section. This type of test has been called a miniature training and evaluation test. All the parties agreed that this would be a very job-related procedure and a good way of assessing the first three KSAOs.

The job experts wanted to retain the interview. Ron and Bob thought that this was fine as long as the following conditions were met:

1. All the questions in the interview would have to be job-related.
2. Critical incidents from the job analysis would be selected to assess the last five KSAOs.
3. Sample answers to each critical incident would be determined in advance. Interviewee responses would be rated on a five-point scale defined explicitly in advance.
4. The same scoring method would be used for each applicant. All procedures would be consistently used for each applicant so that all applicants had the same chance of being selected.
5. All interviewers would be required to attend a training session to learn how to administer and assess the structured interview.

The supervisors agreed to these conditions. However, they did not want the interview to be completely structured. They felt that the interview should begin with a few questions regarding the applicant's past education and experience. Bob and Ron agreed to this with the stipulation that this information should not bias how the candidate would be assessed and scored at the end of the interview.

When Bob and Ron returned to the agency, they were happy about what had transpired at the supervisory conference. The question that remained was the type of validation to be used on the newly developed selection procedures. Ron felt that they should validate the selection procedures with a criterion-related validity strategy. They would collect the scores for both the interview and the test and later compare them to either success in training or their performance appraisal at the end of the first year. Since Ron was familiar with these procedures, he felt that this was a preferred strategy over a content validity strategy. On the other hand, Bob felt that a predictive validity study was too costly and unnecessary. Since their newly developed procedures were job-related, a content validity approach was sufficient. Instead of arguing over which type of validation strategy to use, they decided to discuss the matter with Bob's supervisor and meet again later in the week.

Questions

1. Is there any evidence of adverse impact against any race, sex, or ethnic groups?
2. If the total selection process for a job has no adverse impact, should the individual components of the selection process be evaluated for adverse impact?
3. Which type of validation would you use? Why? What are the differences between content and criterion-related validity studies?
4. Evaluate the job-analysis procedures used in this case. Is it necessary to do such a thorough analysis?
5. If you are doing a criterion-related validity study, should your criterion be success in training or on-the-job performance?

EXHIBIT 2.14   *Tabulation of Selection Rates*

Pass Rates for the Test

Group	Number Who Took Test	Number Who Passed	Pass Rate %
Whites	282	134	47.5
Blacks	36	10	27.8
Hispanics	102	44	43.1
Asians	0	0	0
American Indians	0	0	0
Men	385	170	44.2
Women	35	18	51.4
TOTAL	420	188	44.8

Pass Rates for the Interview

Group	Number Interviewed	Number Who Passed	Pass Rate %
Whites	112	87	77.7
Blacks	8	5	62.5
Hispanics	40	22	55.0
Men	148	109	73.6
Women	12	5	41.7
TOTAL	160	114	71.2

Note: The number interviewed for each group is less than the number who passed the test. The difference represents individuals who did not wish to continue through the second part of the selection process.

EXHIBIT 2.15   *KSAOs Derived from the Task/Behavior Inventory*

1. Knowledge of federal law
2. Knowledge of procedures and regulations
3. Reading and verbal comprehension
4. Ability to perform effectively in dangerous situations
5. Ability to communicate effectively
6. Skill in interpersonal relations
7. Judgment ability
8. Ability to solve problems quickly and effectively

29. EXERCISE

Evaluating the Recruiting Function

I. *Objectives:*
  A. To make you aware of the necessity of evaluating the efficiency and effectiveness of various recruitment sources.
  B. To provide you with practice analyzing data, drawing conclusions, and planning a strategy to remedy identified problems or deficiencies.
  C. To make you aware of the linkages among staff turnover, recruitment sources, recruitment methods, and adequate staffing.
II. *Out-of-Class Preparation Time:*   2 hours
III. *In-Class Time Suggested:*   45 minutes
IV. *Procedures:* Read the entire exercise, including the "Background" on St. Vincent's Hospital. Then, using the data provided in Exhibit 2.16, do the calculations on Form 1. A yield ratio is the number of applicants necessary to fill vacancies with qualified people. It is the relationship of applicant inputs to outputs at various decision points. For example, the yield ratio for all recruitment sources in Exhibit 2.16 shows that 273 nurse applicants were generated over the three-year period from 1992 to 1995. Since only 221 were classified as potentially qualified, the yield ratio is 273/221 or 1.24 to 1. The yield ratio for "potentially qualified" among "walk-ins" is 1.26 (53 ÷ 42). The average cost per nurse hired among "walk-ins" is $119.23 ($1,550 ÷ 13). Yield ratios at other steps in the process are also shown for all recruitment sources on Form 1. These data show that the hospital needs to start with more than five times as many applicants as it needs to fill job openings and more than 13 times as many applicants as it hopes to have as "above average" performers.

Do the calculations for Form 1 on your own prior to class. Think about the implications of these data for future recruitment at the hospital. Then look at Exhibit 2.17 in conjunction with the background description and think about the implications for the recruiting process. During the class period, form groups of three to five, which will act as a consulting team for the hospital. Discuss and answer the "Questions" in your group. At the end of the class period have a spokesperson for each group discuss the group's answers and rationale with the entire class.

Background

St. Vincent's Hospital is a 260-bed hospital in a northeastern city affiliated with the Roman Catholic church. The administrator is Sister Claire, a 56-year-old member of the Daughters of Charity religious order.

During the last decade the hospital operated with a nursing staff of approximately 450 registered nurses and experienced a nursing turnover rate of about 25 percent per year. The turnover rate was average for that city during the time period. However, it has accelerated to an average of 35 percent over the past three years.

These higher turnover rates have put additional pressure on the recruiting process to provide larger numbers of qualified candidates. However, Sam Barnett, Director of Human Resources, has reported more and more difficulty locating qualified nurse candidates over the last three years. Barnett's office has prepared the recruitment data shown in Exhibit 2.16. The data show that 273 applicants (from all sources) had to be screened to produce 52 qualified candidates who accepted a job offer. One year later 19 of these 52 had left the hospital. The last column shows the direct and indirect costs of recruitment by source, including clerical time, supervisor time, and direct costs such as travel and postage. The Human Resource Department has also conducted a telephone survey of all the nurses they could locate who did *not* accept a job offer from the hospital during the most recent three-year period. Reasons for such rejections are shown in Exhibit 2.17.

Sister Mary Louise, the 62-year-old Director of Nursing Service, has been conducting all the off-site recruitment for many years. This includes both the nursing Job Fair and the State Nursing Association meeting. She has begun to feel "burned out" because of all her external recruiting and internal evaluation of candidates over the years.

At a recent meeting, she suggested that an outside group (your group) be brought in to analyze the whole recruiting process, identify problems and opportunities, and suggest improvements. Sister Claire and Barnett both readily agreed to an outside consultant because they are aware of current severe nursing shortages due to declining nursing school enrollments. St. Vincent's itself contributed to this enrollment decline by closing its own School of Nursing due to fewer applications and the high cost of operation.

Since recruitment of new nurses has begun to fall behind turnover of nurses employed at St. Vincent's, the vacancy rate has begun to increase. In the middle of the past decade only 11 percent of staff nursing positions were unfilled. Now, this percentage has increased to 23 percent. One result has been an increasing workload on the existing nursing staff. In addition to increased turnover, the symptoms of staff burnout (i.e., stress, conflict, absenteeism) are becoming more evident.

Questions

1. How would you evaluate the nurse recruiting strategy currently being used by the hospital? Is the hospital using too few or too many recruiting sources? Why?

2. If you presently feel the hospital is using too many recruitment sources, which ones would you eliminate and why?

3. What stage or stages in the recruitment process seem to be most amenable to improvements? What specific improvements would you suggest to decrease the yield ratios? Why?

EXHIBIT 2.16   *Data on Recruitment Sources for Registered Nurses at St. Vincent's Hospital, 1996–1999*

Recruitment Source	Number of Applicants	Potentially Qualified	Invitation for Interview	Qualified and Offered Job	Accepted Job	One-Year Survival	Above-Average Rating	Total Recruitment Cost
1. Direct applications								
write-ins	53	42	30	20	13	8	4	$ 1,550
walk-ins	64	47	38	24	11	5	2	1,500
2. Employee referrals	13	12	7	5	4	3	2	400
3. Newspaper ads	24	16	8	4	2	1	0	750
4. Journal ads	19	18	10	8	4	2	2	450
5. Educational institutions								
junior colleges	16	13	11	6	2	2	1	1,200
hospital-based schools	8	8	3	2	1	0	0	800
university programs	24	24	16	14	10	8	7	1,300
6. Private employment agency	9	9	8	5	2	2	1	4,000
7. Public employment agency	8	4	2	1	1	0	0	300
8. Direct mail	15	14	4	3	1	0	0	450
9. Job fair	13	7	5	3	1	1	1	900
10. State Nursing Association meeting	7	7	4	3	0	0	0	1,150
TOTALS	273	221	146	98	52	33	20	$14,750

FORM 1   *Yield Ratios at Each Step in the Recruitment Process and Recruitment Cost per Nurse Hired, St. Vincent's Hospital, 1996–1999*

Recruitment Sources	Yield Rates						Average Cost Per Nurse Hired
	Potentially Qualified	Accepted Interview	Offered Job	Accepted Job	One-Year Survival	Above-Average Rating	

1. Direct applications
    write-ins
    walk-ins							

2. Employee referrals							
3. Newspaper ads							
4. Journal ads							

5. Educational institutions
    junior colleges
    hospital-based schools
    university programs							

6. Private employment agency							
7. Public employment agency							
8. Direct mail							
9. Job fair							
10. State Nursing Association meeting							
Averages for all sources	1.24	1.87	2.79	5.25	8.27	13.65	

EXHIBIT 2.17   *Reasons for Nurse Rejection of a Job Offer from St. Vincent's Hospital, 1996–1999*

Reason	Number	Percent
Recruitment Processes		
Job attributes not communicated	2	4.3
Negative perception of recruiter	12	26.1
Negative perception of hospital	2	4.3
Lack of timely follow-up	13	28.3
Perceived lack of honesty in recruitment process	1	2.2
Negative information from recruiter	1	2.2
Job Attributes		
Location of hospital	3	6.5
Salary offer	2	4.3
Hours of work	2	4.3
Promotional opportunities	0	0.0
Fringe benefits	0	0.0
Working conditions	3	6.5
Perceived poor job "match"	5	10.9
TOTALS	46	100.0

30. EXERCISE

Selection Decisions

I. *Objectives:*
   A. To make you aware of the complex criteria often used to select candidates for administrative positions.
   B. To help you develop skills in planning and implementing semistructured interviews.
   C. To give you practice in preparing for, participating in, or evaluating the selection interview.
II. *Out-of-Class Preparation Time:* 2 hours
III. *In-Class Time Suggested:* 45 minutes
IV. *Procedures:*
   A. Read the entire exercise including the "Background," "Questions for the Semistructured Interview," and the various forms. During the previous class period, the instructor should have divided students in the class into groups of seven: four executive committee members, two applicants, and one observer.

B. Prior to class, prepare for your role in the group. Committee members should fill in the first two columns of Form 1 and the interviewer questions on Form 2 in pencil or on a separate sheet of paper. This will facilitate committee discussion, reduce the amount of class time needed for interview preparation, and save the forms themselves for the *final* list of criteria (Form 1) and interview questions (Form 2). Committee members should be prepared to play their roles (Form 2) as they would expect the described individuals to behave in real life. The observer for each group should read Form 3 in advance. Then he or she should fill it out during the interview and be prepared to discuss it at the end of the class period.

The two applicants in each group should review their résumés in either Exhibit 2.18 or Exhibit 2.19 and be prepared to elaborate on any of the data in the résumé as well as to provide supplementary information not on the résumé to the committee. An alternative to using two class members as job applicants is to use two individuals from *outside* the class.

C. During the class period, each committee should spend 10 to 15 minutes comparing notes and designing a *final* set of criteria and weighting system for Form 1 and interview questions for Form 2. An option is to have the different committees come together and agree to a given set of selection criteria and their weight.

Neither the applicants nor the observers should be present during these discussions. When the committee is ready, the applicants should be called from outside the room one at a time. In the meantime, the applicants should be doing final preparations for their interviews, including consideration of how they will respond to hypothetical questions that may be asked.

Possible selection criteria the committee may want to consider are: previous experience as a hospital CEO, educational background, ability to "fit" into the organization in terms of personal views and goals, knowledge of Brookdale Hospital and its problems, ideas for solving the hospital's problems, interpersonal skills, communication skills, and administrative skills.

D. Each candidate is then interviewed for 10 to 15 minutes. After each interview, board members fill out the remainder of Form 1 including the rating of each candidate on each criterion, the total score for each, and any additional comments. The observer will take notes and make an evaluation on Form 3 during the interviews. At the conclusion of these interviews, the committee compares notes and makes a decision concerning which candidate should be recommended for the position and why.

E. When all the groups have finished the interview and assessment process, the instructor asks each group to report to the entire class in the following order: the committee decision and rationale, the performance of the two applicants, and the observer's report. Lessons concerning the selection interview process are presented by both interviewers and interviewees. Depending on class size, this "wrap-up" phase should take 10 to 15 minutes.

Background

Brookdale Hospital is a 420-bed proprietary (for-profit) hospital located in a large midwestern city. The hospital was originally founded by a group of local physicians in 1948. In 1982, they sold out to one of the national hospital chains and are now part of a large system of hospitals involving 49 hospitals with about 12,000 beds in 18 states (mostly in the Midwest). The corporation follows a policy of decentralization. Consequently, while corporate support services have been provided, the hospital has continued to operate with a great deal of autonomy.

Recently, the hospital has begun to experience declines in occupancy rates and increased annual deficits. John Rhodes has been the Chief Executive Officer for the past eight years. Two months ago he suffered a stroke and, at the advice of his physician, has decided to retire at age 55.

The Board of Trustees has appointed the Associate Administrator, Terry Bradford, as the Acting Administrator and Chief Executive Officer while a search for Rhodes' replacement is made. The Executive Committee of the Board has advertised the position widely over the past six weeks in a variety of professional publications, including *The Wall Street Journal*.

As a result of the résumés generated through this recruitment process, the Board has selected the two top candidates for the position: Terry Bradford and Chris Smith, an administrator of a small 60-bed hospital in a nearby city. Résumés for each are shown in Exhibits 2.18 and 2.19. The committee has also developed a job description for the position as shown in Exhibit 2.20.

The process for hiring a new CEO requires a formal vote by the entire Board as well as concurrence by the President of the corporation. However, the latter two steps have always been formalities. The critical decision is the recommendation of the Executive Committee. This committee consists of the following four individuals: Sam Gordon, Amanda Simpson, Steve Bailey, and Jane Sears.

Gordon is a physician and the Chief of the Medical Staff (salaried position) and has been with the hospital for 13 years. He is 58 years old and has a specialty in general surgery. He has been concerned about what he views as the eroding power of physicians vis-a-vis administrators and outside regulators over the past few years. Consequently, he would like the committee to recommend someone who can work well with physicians, understand their needs, and generally support their desires to provide high-quality patient care.

Simpson is President of the City Council and was selected for both the Board and the Executive Committee because of her political contacts. Her goals are to make sure the hospital survives, keeps its costs under control, and continues to provide some care for indigents. Since Brookdale is one of the major hospitals in the city serving her constituents, Simpson naturally is concerned that the corporation may shut its doors due to the deficits it has been experiencing. She feels the hospital has to be more innovative in developing and marketing new services to off-set the declines in inpatient services.

Bailey is President and Chief Executive Officer of Applied Electronics, a very successful company which he founded 18 years ago. He admits he still doesn't know much about health care, but has been a member of the Board for 12 years due to his entrepreneurial talents and his business contacts. His view is that the hospital needs to become more "businesslike" and focus on services which are profitable. He also believes that the hospital has not done enough to raise funds through private philanthropy.

Sears is the president of a local bank. She has an M.B.A. from the Wharton School and has been in banking for 22 years. Her major concern is the deteriorating financial position of the hospital. In her view, the new CEO should have excellent financial management skills as well as an ability to work well with physicians. She views the previous CEO (Rhodes) as deficient in these areas.

The committee has invited both Bradford and Smith to interview for the position of CEO. The outline for the selection process is shown on Form 1 and the form for questions to be developed by the committee is Form 2.

Questions for the Semistructured Interview

In its purest form, a structured interview occurs when the interviewers bring to the interview a list of predetermined questions to ask the interviewee. The advantage is that the interviewers have previously discussed and agreed upon the relevant criteria. During the interview, all interviewers focus upon these criteria. Weighting of these criteria is often used as well. This systematic process usually results in higher levels of consistency among interviewers than is the case with unstructured interviews.

However, structured interviews do not allow the interviewee to discuss a topic of his or her choice or to provide additional information on areas that require further explanation. An unstructured interview emphasizes creating a supportive climate and helping the interviewees discuss values, goals, objectives, and career plans.

A compromise that retains the benefits of a structured interview while also creating the openness of the unstructured interview is the semistructured interview. Here the interviewers not only develop a set of structured questions to evaluate the candidate based on the agreed-upon criteria but also ask open-ended questions, such as "What are your long-term career goals?" and "Why is that important to you?"

Develop a list of up to ten questions to ask the two applicants and decide which committee members should ask which questions. Be sure to consider the criteria identified on Form 1 as well as some open-ended questions designed to learn more about the applicant. Write these questions on Form 2.

EXHIBIT 2.18   *Résumé 1*

TERRY A. BRADFORD
119 Brook Hollow Lane
Columbus, Ohio

JOB OBJECTIVE

To secure a position as Chief Executive Officer for a large proprietary hospital in the Midwest.

EDUCATION

<u>1972–1976:</u>   Oberlin College, Oberlin, Ohio
                    Major: Sociology
                    Degree: B.A., June 1966, <u>Cum laude</u>, GPA 3.52

<u>1982–1983:</u>   Ohio State University, Columbus, Ohio
                    Major: Business Administration
                    Emphasis: Organization Behavior
                    Degree: M.B.A., June 1973, GPA 3.86
                    Member: Beta Gamma Sigma (national scholastic
                    honorary in Business)

<u>Other:</u>   After completing my M.B.A. degree, I have taken two additional graduate courses in accounting and one additional course in finance at Ohio State University.

EMPLOYMENT HISTORY

<u>February 1995–Present:</u>   Associate Administrator; Brookdale Hospital, Columbus, Ohio
        Duties: liaison between the CEO and the medical staff, nursing staff, and other major hospital departments; represents administrator at various functions; strategic planning and marketing; reviews financial and occupancy data.

<u>June 1988–February 1995:</u>   Assistant Administrator; Oakland Hospital, Oakland, Ohio
        Duties: worked with the Administrator and Associate Administrator on a variety of administrative functions in finance, personnel, marketing, and public relations.

<u>August 1983–June 1988</u>   Personnel Assistant; Bayview Municipal Hospital, Bayview, Ohio
        Duties: designed personnel appraisal form, conducted selection interviews, designed and taught courses for supervisors, and designed advertisements for positions.

(continued)

EXHIBIT 2.18   *continued*

June 1976 - September 1982:   Various sales and administrative positions in
                                   a variety of organizations.

PERSONAL

Date of Birth:	September 6, 1954
Height:	5'8" Weight: 150 lbs.
Marital Status:	Divorced, no children
Hobbies:	Music, travel, and swimming

EXHIBIT 2.19   *Résumé 2*

CHRIS A. SMITH

Home Address	Office Address
2057 Hickory Street	Administrator
Anytown, Ohio	Morningside Hospital
	204 Jefferson Street
	Tiffin, Ohio

Personal: Married, two children

Educational Background:
B.S.—Heidelberg College, Tiffin, Ohio (1977)
M.B.A.—Cleveland State University, Cleveland, Ohio (1982)

Experience:

Morningside Hospital, Tiffin, Ohio	November 1991–Present
Acting Administrator	June 1999–Present
Associate Administrator	June 1993–June 1999
Assistant Administrator	November 1991–June 1993
Eastside Hospital, Tiffin, Ohio	
Financial Manager	June 1988–November 1991
McLains Department Store, Tiffin, Ohio	
Financial Manager	January 1986–June 1988
Financial Trainee	June 1982–January 1986
City of Tiffin, Ohio	
City Planner	July 1977–August 1981

Member: Rotary Club and First Baptist Church

Interests: Snow skiing and politics

EXHIBIT 2.20   *Job Description: Chief Executive Officer, Brookdale Hospital*

DESCRIPTION OF WORK *General Statement of Duties:* Supervises and coordinates administrative work of a complex nature involving the entire hospital and all its components; represents the hospital to outside stakeholders.
Supervision Required: Implements policies developed by the Board of Directors.
Supervision Exercised: Plans, organizes, motivates, coordinates, and directs a staff of administrative and clerical personnel. Total direct supervision involves over 15 individuals.

EXAMPLE OF DUTIES

1. Initiates and coordinates activities related to long-range planning and marketing of the hospital's services.
2. Develops and enforces policies and procedures related to administrative functions.
3. Coordinates major staff services, including budget, personnel, medical services, nursing services, dietetics, and housekeeping.
4. Develops and compiles administrative reports as required by the Board or external regulatory agencies.
5. Performs related work as required.

REQUIRED KNOWLEDGE, SKILLS, AND ABILITIES Extensive and broad knowledge of complex management systems (internal and external) in a health-care environment. Skill and ability in planning, personnel management, and budgetary control. Ability to relate to external stakeholders, including the Board of Directors.

QUALIFICATIONS FOR APPOINTMENT *Education:* Graduation from a college or university with major coursework in business administration, public administration, or health administration.
Experience: Ten years or more of progressively responsible experience in administration or management.

FORM 1   *Criteria for Selecting a Chief Executive Officer and Ratings of Applicants Based on These Criteria*

Criteria: Major dimension of the CEO job based upon the job description and personal characteristics desired	Weight of the Criteria (1-5)	Job Applicant Rating on the Criteria (1-10)		Total Score (Weight x Rating)		Comments About Each
		Bradford	Smith	Bradford	Smith	
1.						
2.						
3.						
4.						
5.						
6.						
7.						
8.						
9.						
10.						
Total Scores						

FORM 2   *Questions for Interview**

1.

2.

3.

4.

5.

6.

7.

8.

9.

10.

---

*Develop interview questions that are not biased or illegal, but which relate to the performance dimensions developed in Form 1.

FORM 3 *Observation Sheet*

1. How well did the committee establish rapport with each applicant?

2. How well did each of the candidates respond to the committee's questions? What improvements would you suggest? Why?

3. Approximately what percentage of the 15 minutes interview time was spent listening to the applicant and what percentage consisted of committee questions and/or comment? How appropriate was this breakdown?

4. Did the committee overemphasize negative information, ask illegal questions, show bias based on irrelevant factors, or otherwise treat either applicant unfairly?

5. Did the committee probe unclear areas, or did it allow short answers which did not provide necessary information?

6. What is your overall assessment of the success of the committee in eliciting relevant information for making this selection decision? Why?

31. EXERCISE

Selection Interview Role Play

I. *Objectives:*
   A. To help you develop skills in conducting selection interviews.
   B. To provide you with practice in applying the basic principles of effective interviewing.
II. *Out-of-Class Preparation Time:* 30–90 minutes, depending on role played (students who play the applicant will need to prepare a résumé).
III. *In-Class Time:* 45 minutes
IV. *Procedures:* The class should be divided into groups of three: an interviewer, applicant, and observer. Roles should be assigned ahead of time so you will have time to prepare your role. This is especially important for those of you who will play the role of interviewee since you are to use your own résumé and qualifications during the role play. The interviewer should prepare a set of interview questions. Read the scenario

that follows and the role description provided by the instructor. Participants should assume that the interview is taking place in a campus placement office. The role play begins when the applicant arrives for the interview and ends when both individuals have accomplished their objectives. At the end of the role play the interviewer completes the interviewer's report (Form 1) and shares it with the applicant. Next, the observer provides feedback on his or her observations to the group (Form 2). The group then identifies and discusses the hardest part of the interview from both the interviewer's point of view and the applicant's perspective. If time permits, the entire class then discusses the reliability and validity of the interview as a method of selecting applicants for jobs.

Scenario

The director of college recruiting for Duro Insurance Company is presently recruiting college students for its administrative trainee program. The one-year training program involves a combination of on-the-job training and formal classroom training. Upon successful completion of the training a candidate is assigned a position as assistant department supervisor.

Duro Insurance Company ranks in the top 15 percent of life insurance companies nationally with in-force insurance in excess of $6 billion. Duro markets all forms of insurance, bonds, and pension products on an individual and group basis. More recently, the company added diversified financial services, including discount brokerage services, real estate financing, and mutual funds. The company is divided into six major divisions (Employee Benefits, Commercial Insurance, Individual Life, Automobile, Homeowners, and Diversified Financial Services) and functionally into several major operating departments: Sales, Underwriting, Administrative, Loss Prevention, Actuarial, Claims, Legal, Financial and Investments, Advertising and Public Relations, Personnel, and Research and Policy Development. Duro has over 25,000 employees and more than 300 field offices throughout the country. Management at each field office consists of a manager, several department heads, and their assistants. The company has enjoyed a pattern of steady growth and expansion over the years.

Job Description for Administrative Trainee

1. Handle day-to-day administration of field office, including direct supervision of office clerks.
2. Plan and oversee the use of space, furniture, and equipment on a continuing basis and recommend changes as necessary.
3. Supervise computer processing operations for issuing and servicing insurance policies, including claims.
4. Implement and maintain accounting and collection procedures.

The trainee works closely with the department head in learning these duties.

Job Qualifications

1. B.S./B.A.with business management background (knowledge of accounting desired).
2. Ability to communicate effectively.
3. Ability to handle detail.
4. Ability to plan and direct activities of subordinate personnel.
5. Demonstrated leadership potential.
6. Knowledge of computers and software packages including Lotus 1-2-3 and dBase.

Additional Job Data

1. The trainee position reports directly to a department head.
2. Expected career progression is to assistant department supervisor (1–2 years) and, with continued development, to department head (4–5 years after supervisory assignment).
3. The position requires relocation.
4. The company offers competitive salaries and benefits, including a tuition repayment plan and in-house career planning and development.

FORM 1   *Interviewer's Report*

APPLICANT_____ **POSITION** _____

DATE_____ **INTERVIEWER**_____

Rate the applicant's background and behavior, taking into consideration the factors listed for each area. Circle a rating for each factor. Give an overall rating also.

1. Presentation (appearance, manner, oral communication skills, interest, motivation):

    Poor 1   2   3   4   5   Excellent

2. Education (major, intellectual abilities, academic achievement, knowledge of field):

    Poor 1   2   3   4   5   Excellent

3. Work experience (related experience, skill and competence, job performance, interpersonal skills, leadership):

    Poor 1   2   3   4   5   Excellent

4. Summarize candidate's strengths:

(continued)

FORM 1   *continued*

5.   Summarize candidate's weaknesses:

6.   Overall evaluation and recommendation:

Poor 1   2   3   4   5   Excellent

Recommendation: (   ) Invite for field visit (   ) Do not invite

Comments:

FORM 2   *Observation Sheet*

1.   What was the quality of the interaction between the interviewer and applicant?

2.   What type of interview did the interviewer use (structured, semi-structured or nonstructured)? How well did it work?

3.   Were the questions job-related?

(continued)

FORM 2   *continued*

4.   What did the interviewer do to put the applicant at ease?

5.   Did the interviewer listen? Did the interviewer spend too much time talking?

6.   Did the interviewer follow up on questions not completely answered?

7.   Did the interviewer gain enough information to make a decision about the applicant?

8.   General observations.

32. EXERCISE

Which Selection Procedure Is Most Effective?

I. *Objectives:*
   A. To examine the strengths and weaknesses of four different methods for selecting new employees.
   B. To enhance your oral communication skills.
II. *Out-of-Class Preparation Time:* 30 minutes to prepare for the debate
III. *In-Class Time Suggested:* 50–75 minutes
IV. *Procedures:* Your instructor will divide the class into five groups at the end of class prior to conducting this exercise. There will be four debating groups consisting of three to five members each and one or more groups of "judges" that consist of the remaining class members. Debaters will be assigned one of four positions and told to prepare to argue in favor of

that position. Judges will be told to read the textbook chapter pages that cover those positions. The issue to be debated is: Which approach to selecting employees is most effective in selecting new employees? The positions are: (1) the structured interview; (2) the unstructured interview; (3) ability and personality tests; and (4) obtaining application blanks and résumés and talking to and getting letters from references.

At the start of the next class, your instructor will announce that a four-way debate will be held. The judges' role in the debate is to "search for the truth." They are to listen to the different sides presented and then, after the debate is over, to tell the class what they believe is the "correct" answer to the debate question, not who "won" the debate.

The debate consists of two rounds. The purpose of Round One (15–20 minutes) is for each team to learn the position of the other debating teams. Hence, each team has up to five minutes to explain their position as comprehensively as possible. At the completion of Round One, the debating teams are given up to ten minutes to prepare criticisms of each of the other three teams for Round Two. During this intermission, judges are to discuss what they have heard and begin to formulate their own position.

In Round Two (15–20 minutes), each debating team is given up to five minutes to criticize the position of each of the other teams. Unlike a traditional debate, teams are not allowed to rebut the criticisms made by others. They must simply listen to them. Round Two ends when Team Four has finished criticizing the position of the other three teams.

After the debate has ended, the judges have five minutes to discuss the case among themselves and to arrive at a consensus, if possible. The judging team(s) then explains its decision to the debaters.

33. INCIDENT

The Ethical Selection Dilemma at Integrity Motors

Background

Integrity Motors is a ten year old retailer of quality used cars and trucks. It is located in a large midwestern city, and has become the largest and most successful used car dealership in the region. Integrity Motors employs 11 full-time salespersons. Timmy Blackburn, the owner, wants to maintain a policy of having a lean, yet highly productive staff, which means that the employees have to be dependable, highly competent, and willing to work at a high level of productivity for long hours each day.

Contributed by James C. Wimbush, Indiana University

After ten years at Integrity Motors, the sales manager was resigning to start his own business. Timmy felt he needed the same type of employee he had had in the position—someone who had considerable experience as a sales manager, was creative, a good motivator, who had good communication and management skills, and someone who would be committed to the dealership for a long time. Although Timmy felt it prudent to take the necessary time to carefully select a new sales manager, time was of the essence because the end of the year was approaching and the inventory needed to be drastically reduced.

Seemingly, applications for the job started pouring in almost immediately. After a week, 45 applicants had expressed interest in the job, of which ten potentially suitable candidates were invited for interviews. A panel comprised of the office manager, Helen, the service manager, Joe, and Timmy interviewed the ten applicants. Based upon the interviews, it was clear that one candidate, Gladys Morrison, was outstanding compared to all other applicants. Gladys had recently moved to the area from a metropolitan city where she was a sales manager for 15 years. Everyone agreed that she was the perfect candidate. The next morning an offer would be extended to Gladys. Everyone left the meeting feeling satisfied that they had made an excellent choice.

A New Development

The next morning when Timmy arrived at the dealership he was met by Helen and Joe, who seemed troubled. Apparently, after the meeting the prior evening, Helen happened to meet an old friend at a convenience store. The friend told Helen she was four months pregnant and that, coincidentally, her new neighbor was also four months pregnant. To Helen's surprise, the pregnant neighbor was Gladys Morrison, the person to whom the dealership would extend a job offer the next morning. Helen said absolutely nothing to her friend about Gladys' employment inquiry or pending job offer, yet throughout the night, Helen pondered about the potential hire.

The next morning, as Helen shared this development with Timmy and Joe before Gladys was contacted, all three discussed the potential consequences of hiring Gladys. Joe was astounded that Gladys had not informed them of her pregnancy. Timmy quickly told him that legally she did not have to tell them about it, and furthermore, an employment decision could not be based on her pregnancy. Helen observed that though legally this was true, from a practical standpoint the dealership could not afford to be without a sales manager for an extended period of time. Timmy agreed. He, too, was concerned about her potential absence as well as her potential inability to work for long periods under intense pressure, especially when they needed to reduce inventory. Helen also reminded them that although Gladys was clearly the best applicant, there were at least nine other applicants who would be suitable sales managers.

Questions

1. What are the legal and ethical issues involved in this case? Was it ethical for Gladys to have applied for the position in the first place?
2. Should the owner hire Gladys or some other applicant? Should the information about the pregnancy be considered?
3. If Gladys is hired, how could Integrity Motors accommodate her pregnancy?

34. INCIDENT

The Exit Interviews

Mr. William James has recently been hired as the Director of Human Resources for an academic medical center located in the northeast. While he was interviewing for the position, several administrators and physicians told him there was a severe employee morale problem, particularly among registered nurses. Mr. James later learned that the average annual turnover rate of nurses at this facility has averaged 18.4 percent as compared to 11.6 percent in the metropolitan area over the past three years.

Mr. James was aware that all exiting employees are required to complete an exit interview questionnaire and interview prior to receiving their final pay check. He then asked his assistant to pull the files for all exit interviews of departing nurses and prepare a summary of the major reasons for leaving and specific suggestions for how the facility could increase its retention of nurses.

When the results were compiled, Mr. James was disappointed. The utility of these data was very low. Most of the respondents indicated they were leaving for "personal reasons," "family responsibilities," or "job offer." Very few volunteered recommendations for how the facility could improve nurse retention even when asked directly on both the questionnaire and during the interview. The recommendation mentioned most frequently was "better parking."

The prevailing opinion of individuals with whom Mr. James spoke was that departing employees are reluctant to discuss any "sensitive" issues or concerns for fear of alienating the interviewer or supervisor. He was told no one wanted to possibly jeopardize their recommendation to other employers due to anything they might say during the exit interview. Through his informal conversations with nurses and nurse supervisors he knew there were many problems and concerns shared by many nurses including inadequate staffing, lack of respect and support from supervisors and top management, favoritism in salary increases and promotions, and high stress levels due to all of the above. Yet he was unable to document these problems and others with the current exit interview data.

Mr. James is now attempting to determine the best methods of identifying employee problems and assessing employee reaction to the organization, its various components, and various human resource policies and programs. He is also interested in determining factors which cause many of the long-tenured nurses to stay.

Questions

1. Discuss the nature and causes of the problem.
2. Should Mr. James attempt to improve the exit interview process? If so, how should this be done?
3. What other assessment alternatives should he consider in addition to or rather than exit interviews?
4. How can Mr. James use the information generated about why nurses stay or leave to improve nurse retention?

35. SKILL BUILDER

Evaluating Job Application Forms

I. *Objectives:*
   A. To familiarize you with the criteria for selecting questions to put on an application form.
   B. To give you practice in evaluating the questions on an application blank.
II. *Time Required to Complete:* 1 hour
III. *Instructions:* Review the application form that appears in Exhibit 2.21. This form is used by United Holy Radio Network for their administrative and clerical employees. You should thoroughly review the legal requirements for preemployment inquiries and other relevant information on application forms found in your text. Use the guide below to evaluate the questions that appear on the application. Prepare a short write-up summarizing your findings and make specific recommendations for improving the questions.

Source: Adapted from Robert D. Gatewood and Hubert S. Feild, *Human Resource Selection* (New York: Dryden Press, 1987), 279.

Questions to Be Asked in Evaluating Appropriateness of Application Blank Items

1. Is this question job-related?
2. Will answers to this question have an adverse impact in screening out members of protected groups (i.e., disqualify a significantly larger percentage of members of one particular group than of others)?
3. Is this question really needed to judge an applicant's qualifications and suitability for the job?
4. Does the question constitute an invasion of privacy?
5. Can the applicant's response to this question be verified?

EXHIBIT 2.21   *Job Application Form*

UNITED HOLY RADIO NETWORK
APPLICATION FOR EMPLOYMENT

Name
_____
(Last)   (Middle initial) (First)

Address
_____
(Street)   (City)   (State)

PHOTO

Sex: Male   Female   Age:_____

Own home: Yes   No   How long?_____Rent: Yes   No   How long?_____

Phone No. (____) _____

Marital Status: Married   Divorced   Never Married   Widowed   (circle one)

If married indicate name of spouse:_____

Of what country are you a citizen?: _____

Indicate languages spoken fluently:_____

List all physical disabilities: _____

Religion:_____

Church membership: _____

Name of Minister:_____

How often do you attend church?_____

List church activities: _____

Do you smoke?: Yes   No   Do you consume alcoholic beverages?:   Yes   No

Have you ever been arrested?: Yes   No   Indicate offenses: _____

Military experience: _____Type of discharge _____

(continued)

EXHIBIT 2.21   *continued*

EDUCATION

High school name:_____ Date of graduation_____

Business or technical school name:_____ Degree_____

Attended:_____ Date of graduation:_____

Junior/community college name:_____ Degree_____

Attended:_____ Date of graduation:_____

College name:_____ Degree_____

Attended:_____ Date of graduation:_____

WORK EXPERIENCE

Name of employer _____ Job title _____ No. of years _____

Reason for leaving: _____

Name of employer _____ Job title _____ No. of years _____

Reason for leaving: _____

Name of employer _____ Job title _____ No. of years _____

Reason for leaving: _____

Name of employer _____ Job title _____ No. of years _____

Reason for leaving: _____

I certify that all the information which I have given in this application is true, accurate, and complete. I understand that any misstatement or omission of a material fact may be a cause for dismissal.

Date _____ Signature_____

36. SKILL BUILDER

Staffing for a Telecommuting Job

I. *Objectives:*
   A. To give you practice in revising a job description for a telecommuting job.
   B. To enhance your understanding of how to prepare a staffing plan for a telecommuting job.
   C. To familiarize you with some of the differences between staffing for telecommuting job environments versus staffing for traditional job (office) environments.

II. *Time Required to Complete:* 1–2 hours

III. *Instructions:* A large pharmaceutical company, located in the northeast, is one of the leading pharmaceutical manufacturers in the U.S. Because of the intense competition in the industry and the heightened competition for highly skilled personnel, the company believes that quality-of-work-life (QWL) is a key factor for achieving competitive advantage. In support of this belief, the company is considering the adoption of a telecommuting work arrangement for selected jobs.

   The job of Public Relations Specialist has been identified as an appropriate job for telecommuting due to the fact that the job responsibilities are mostly information-related activities that require independent mental effort with no supervisory responsibilities. Exhibit 1 contains the current job description for the P.R. Specialist, which reflects the primary job activities and qualifications for a full-time, in-office P.R. Specialist. There is currently only one job incumbent, and that person has resigned.

   You have been asked to develop a plan for recruiting and hiring a replacement who will telecommute from home.
   A. What method of job analysis do you recommend to determine the job requirements and job specifications for a telecommuting job? Is the method you recommend different than the method you would use if the job were performed in a traditional office environment?
   B. What procedures do you recommend for recruiting and hiring a telecommuter? Are the procedures you recommend different than the procedures you would use if the job were performed in a traditional office environment?
   C. What changes would you make to the job description in Exhibit 1 to reflect the telecommuting nature of the job?
   D. What other recommendations would you make in order to ensure the successful implementation of a telecommuting work arrangement?

Contributed by Diana Deadrick, Old Dominion University.

EXHIBIT 1

Job Title: Public Relations Specialist

Department: Public Relations

Reports To: Director of Public Relations

General Summary: Serves as a writer on numerous firm publications; coordinates materials; writes, edits, and proofs articles, public relations publications and advertising copy using WordPerfect software.

Essential Job Functions:

1. Writes, edits, and proofs public relations articles, newspaper copy, and human interest stories.
2. Writes advertising copy in conjunction with the marketing department.
3. Writes, edits, and coordinates printing and layout of company newsletter.
4. Meets with executives to determine PR needs.
5. Meets with media officials and the public to publicize firm's accomplishments.
6. Attends information meetings at the main office on an as-needed basis.
7. Gives presentations at meetings and other public events.
8. Performs other related duties as assigned by management.

Education and Experience Required: Degree in Art/Graphic Design; demonstrated ability to use a MacIntosh computer hardware/software; some experience in television or public speaking; considerable knowledge of journalism principles, English grammar and usage; demonstrated ability to write newspaper, news and human interest articles, reports, brochures, and advertising copy; demonstrated ability to work and communicate effectively with others.

PART 3

DEVELOPING EFFECTIVENESS IN HUMAN RESOURCES: TRAINING, CAREER DEVELOPMENT, AND PERFORMANCE APPRAISAL

ORIENTATION/TRAINING/CAREER DEVELOPMENT

37. CASE

Career Development at Electronic Applications

Electronic Applications Corporation is a major producer of silicon chips for the computer industry. It is located southeast of San Francisco in an area of high technology firms. Since its founding in 1972, the company has grown rapidly in terms of sales and profits, thus enhancing its stock price many times over.

However, human resource policies have tended to lag behind company growth. Emphasis has been on reactive policies to meet the requirements of external organizations such as the federal government. Human resources have not been a high priority.

Recently, Harold Sweeney has been hired as Director of Human Resources for the company. Sweeney had previously served as an Assistant Personnel Director for a large "blue-chip" corporation in southern California. He took his present position not only because of an increase in pay and responsibility, but also because of what he termed "the challenge of bringing this company from a 1950s human resources mentality to one more compatible with the realities of the 1990s."

Sweeney has been on the job for four months and has been assessing the situation to determine the more significant human resource problems. One significant problem seems to be high turnover among electrical engineers who work in Research and Development. This is the core of the research function and turnover rates have averaged about 30 percent per year over the past three years.

In assessing the cause of the problem, Sweeney checked area wage surveys and found Electronic Applications paid five to eight percent *above* the market for various categories of electrical engineers. Since the company did not have a formal exit interview system, he could not check out other possible explanations through that mechanism. However, through informal conversations with a large number of individuals, including the engineers themselves, he learned that many of the engineers felt "dead-ended" in the technical aspects of engineering.

In particular, the Research and Development Department had lost some of the younger engineers who had been considered to be on the "fast track." Most had gone to competitors in the local area.

One particular Research and Development employee who impressed Sweeney was Helen Morgan. Helen was 29 years old, had a B.S. degree in Electrical Engineering from California Institute of Technology, and was studying for her M.B.A. at the University of Santa Clara at night. Helen had been employed for seven years, three in an entry-level engineering position and four as a section chief. The latter promotion was the highest position in Research and Development other than the position of Director of Research and Development.

Helen claimed that "the company doesn't really care about its good people." In her view, the present director, Harry James, doesn't want to allow his better people to move up in the organization. He is more interested in keeping them in his own department so he can meet his own goals without having to orient and train new people. Helen also claimed she was told she "has a bright future with the company" by both James and the former Personnel Director. Her performance appraisals have been uniformly excellent.

She went on to criticize the company for using an appraisal form with no section dealing with future potential or future goals, no rewards for supervisors who develop their subordinates, no human resource planning to identify future job openings, no centralized job information or job positioning system, no career paths and/or career ladders, and attitudinal barriers against women in management positions. She recommended that steps be taken to remedy each of the problems she identified.

Sweeney checked out the information Morgan had provided him and found it to be accurate. Moreover, he heard through the "grapevine" that she is in line for an excellent position with a nearby competitor. Clearly, he has an even greater challenge than he had anticipated. He realizes he has an immediate problem concerning high turnover of certain key employees. In addition, he also has a series of interconnected problems associated with career development. However, he is not quite sure what to do and in what order.

Questions

1. Describe the nature and causes of the problem faced by Mr. Sweeney.
2. What additional questions should Sweeney ask or what additional information is needed before proceeding toward a solution to this problem? Why?
3. What are the individual and organizational benefits of a formalized career development system?
4. If Sweeney decides to develop a formalized career development system at Electronic Applications, what components or types of services should be offered? Why?
5. Should the career development activities be integrated with other human resource management activities? If yes, which ones? Why?
6. What criteria should Sweeney consider to evaluate good candidates for promotion? What criteria could be used to evaluate the performance of supervisors in development of their subordinates?

38. CASE

The Safety Training Program

Houghton Refrigeration Company builds refrigerators for other large refrigerator companies such as General Electric Co. It employs about 300 people, mostly assembly line workers, and is located in a small rural town in Utah. The company typically builds, on a contract basis, chest-type freezers and small bar-type refrigerators. On occasion, however, it also builds standard size refrigerators. The president of the company is a former engineer, as are most of the other executives. These individuals are very knowledgeable about engineering, but have received little training in the basic principles of management.

During the summer months, volume at the factory increases significantly, and the company needs to hire about 40 new employees to handle the heavy workload. Most of these new employees are college students who attend a small private college located about 15 minutes from the plant. Some high school students are hired as well.

When a new employee is hired, the company asks him or her to complete an application blank and then to show up at the plant gate ready for work. Employees receive no orientation. The worker is shown to a work station and after a minimum amount of on-the-job training, the new employee is expected to start performing a job. Most of the jobs are quite simple, hence, the training is typically completed within five to ten minutes. The first-line supervisor usually shows the employee how to do a job once, then watches while the employee does the job once, leaves, and comes back in about 20 minutes to see how the employee is progressing. Typical jobs at the plant include screwing 14 screws into the sides of a freezer, placing a piece of insulation into the freezer lid, and handing out supplies from the tool room.

The company has had excellent experience with college students over the years. Much of the success can be attributed to the older workers coming to the aid of the new employees when trouble or difficulties arise. Most new employees are able to perform their jobs reasonably well after their on-the-job training is completed. However, when unexpected difficulties arise, they are not usually prepared for them and therefore need assistance from others.

The older workers have been especially helpful to students working in the "press room." However, Joe Gleason, the first-line supervisor there, finds it amusing to belittle the college students whenever they make any mistakes. He relishes showing a student once how to use a press to bend a small piece of metal, then exclaims, "You're a hot-shot college student; now let's see you do it." He then watches impatiently while the student invariably makes a mistake and then jokingly announces for all to hear, "That's wrong! How did you ever get into college anyway? Try it again, dummy."

One summer the company experienced a rash of injuries to its employees. Although most of the injuries were minor, the company felt it imperative to conduct a series of short training programs on safe material-handling techniques. The company president was at a loss as to who should conduct the training. The personnel director was a 64-year-old former engineer who was about to retire and was a poor speaker. The only other employee in the Personnel Department was a new 19-year-old secretary who knew nothing about proper handling techniques. Out of desperation the president finally decided to ask Bill Young, the first-line supervisor of the "lid-line," to conduct the training. Bill had recently attended a training program himself on safety and was active in the Red Cross. Bill reluctantly agreed to conduct the training. It was to be done on a departmental basis with small groups of 10 to 15 employees attending each session.

At the first of these training sessions, Bill Young nervously stood up in front of 14 employees, many of whom were college students, and read his presentation in a monotone voice. His entire speech lasted about one minute and consisted of the following text:

> Statistics show that an average of 30 persons injure their backs on the job each day in this state. None of us wants to become a "statistic."
>
> The first thing that should be done before lifting an object is to look it over and decide whether you can handle it alone or if help is needed. Get help if there's any doubt as to whether the load is safely within your capacity.
>
> Next, look over the area where you're going to be carrying the object. Make sure it's clear of obstacles. You may have to do a little housekeeping before moving your load. After you have checked out the load and route you're going to travel, the following steps should be taken for your safety in lifting:
>
> 1.   Get a good footing close to the load.
> 2.   Place your feet 8 to 12 inches apart.
> 3.   Bend your knees to grasp the load.
> 4.   Bend your knees outward, straddling the load.
> 5.   Get a firm grip.
> 6.   Keep the load close to your body.
> 7.   Lift gradually.
>
> Once you've lifted the load, you'll eventually have to set it down—so bend your legs again—and follow the lifting procedures in reverse. Make sure that your fingers clear the pinch points. And, finally, it's a good idea to set one corner down first.

After Bill's s speech ended, the employees immediately returned to work. By the end of the day, however, everyone in the plant had heard about the training fiasco, and all, except the president, were laughing about it.

Questions

1. Evaluate the company's on-the-job training program. Should it be changed?
2. Should the company install an employee orientation program for new factory workers, or isn't one necessary?
3. What changes should be made in the company's safety training program?
4. What other kinds of approaches might a firm take to emphasize safety and curtail accidents other than training?

39. CASE

The Mentoring Problem at Walnut Insurance

Tom Morrison, President of Walnut Insurance, was sitting at his desk reading a letter he had just received and thinking about a recent meeting with his vice presidents. He knew he had to make a decision regarding whether to implement a new mentoring program but he did not know what that decision should be.

Walnut Insurance has been selling liability insurance to firms in one particular industry for over 50 years. Its specialized niche in the insurance industry has made it highly successful. It employs about 2,400 individuals who work in 12 regional offices throughout the United States and in its midwest headquarters.

Walnut Insurance has six senior male Vice Presidents who report directly to Tom Morrison. Over the years these individuals have traveled between the various regional offices, working primarily with the insurance sales representatives. The VPs perform numerous functions when visiting the regional offices. They go out on overnight sales trips with the representatives to learn about customer problems, assist agents with policy questions, and provide training; they evaluate agents to determine who has the potential to be promoted; they pass on the firm's values and culture which places heavy emphasis on honesty and satisfying customer needs; they assist agents in interpreting company policies; and they determine what new policies need to be developed.

Over the years, these VPs have performed one other valuable service to new employees—they have informally mentored some of them. Typically, each VP would pick out five or six promising agents and take them under his wing. He would get to know the agents well, point out strengths and weaknesses, and help them develop plans for achieving management positions. Over the years, this approach has worked quite well.

However, in the last two years the firm had hired over 50 new agents and almost two thirds of them were women. These individuals were college graduates who majored in a variety of disciplines. They were hired based on their sales skills, initiative, self-confidence, assertiveness, and physical appearance. Previously, almost all of the new hires were men. Tom Morrison believed that the present informal mentoring system might result in women being excluded so he thought that a formal system should be considered.

Thus, at one of the firm's regular retreats, Tom broached the subject with his VPs. He commended them for their willingness to mentor agents voluntarily in the past, noted that many of the regional managers were a product of this mentoring, explained his concerns regarding the need for female agents to receive equal mentoring treatment, and asked them if they thought the process should be formalized by assigning specific agents to specific VPs.

Tom's suggestion went over like a lead balloon—not a single person liked the idea in the least. In fact, they strongly opposed it and told Tom so as tactfully as they could. One VP explained that he was a elder in the church and had strong religious convictions. He did not want to travel with female employees on overnight sales calls because it might tarnish his image among his evangelical friends. He had no problem working with females in regional offices and had done so for many years. But, he did not want to travel with them.

Three other VPs were opposed to the idea because they were fearful of sexual harassment suits being filed against them. They noted that a recent insurance trade publication article described numerous cases in which managers in several other insurance firms had been charged with harassment. The article explained how even if one is innocent of a charge, one's career can be ruined. The VPs demanded to know how and whether the firm would stand behind them if charged with sexual harassment.

One other VP objected to the idea because he wanted free choice in selecting employees to mentor. He argued that only the best agents are deserving of mentoring and that it would be a waste of time to mentor everyone. He asked: why should we mentor someone who does not have the potential to become a manager?

The last VP objected because he knew that his wife would not approve of any plan that would require that he work closely with young female agents, particularly at night in faraway locations.

After hearing all of these objections, Tom asked the VPs to give further thought to the issue. He restated that mentoring was critical to the firm's success and that it was important that women not be left out of the process.

In the week that followed, Tom had not heard anything more regarding the issue from any VP. However, he had received a letter from one wife (see Exhibit 3.1) and it was clear what she thought of the idea. Nonetheless, the final decision was his to make.

Questions

1. If you were Tom, would you implement a formal mentoring program? If so, how would you address the VP's concerns?
2. What alternatives to a formal mentoring program are available to Tom?

EXHIBIT 3.1   *Letter from a VP's Wife*

January 23, 19xx
1105 Edgewater Dr.
Sometown, USA

Mr. Tom Morrison
President
Walnut Insurance Company

Dear Tom,

I am writing to you regarding the new mentoring proposal that is being considered. My husband told me about it at dinner last week and I have been worried about it ever since.

As you may know, my husband and I have been married for twenty-eight years and have raised three lovely children. We are dedicated to each other and have strong family values. We try to act as good role models to our children and to others.

To be honest, I am very concerned about what effects the new mentoring program might have on our marriage. My husband is faithful to me and I trust him with other women under typical circumstances. However, the new program involves special circumstances and I do not trust the women he might need to mentor. Some of these women may be so ambitious that they will stop at nothing to get promoted. They would not hesitate to destroy a marriage or my husband's career if they thought it would help them get ahead.

I would appreciate it if you would find a different alternative. Surely, some other approach would accomplish your goals.

Sincerely yours,

Joyce Butler
Joyce Butler

40. EXERCISE

Conducting a Training Needs Assessment

I. *Objectives:*
    A. To illustrate the importance of needs assessment for organization change efforts.
    B. To show you the linkages between organization-wide, job-wide, and individual training needs.
    C. To help you learn how to identify training needs and collect supporting data.

II. *Out-of-Class Preparation Time:* 60–90 minutes.

III. *In-Class Time:* 45 minutes

IV. *Procedures:* Read the case "Strategic Human Resource Management" and the following "Update" on the College of Business Administration at Old State University. Then use Form 1 to conduct a Needs Assessment. In general, a needs assessment is used to identify any discrepancies between desired and current performance behaviors. Although the outcome of the assessment might be the identification of training needs, it could identify other organization development needs that are not necessarily met through training programs.

    Part I of Form 1 is to be used for the Organization Analysis phase of the needs assessment, which identifies "where" there is a need for improvement within the college and whether there are "system-wide" problems that exist. Factors to be analyzed include any recent or anticipated organization-wide changes and how that will affect the organization's goals, structure, culture, and/or climate. The result of this analysis is a determination of whether the "problem" (discrepancy) is an organization-wide problem as opposed to an individual training problem. Part II of Form 1 is to be used for the Job/Task Analysis, which identifies "what" tasks are in need of improvement and whether there are job-wide problems that exist. Factors to consider here include any recent or anticipated changes in the job demands and how that might affect the nature of the job requirements (tasks, skills), goals, resources, and/or performance opportunities. The result is a determination of whether the "problem" is a job-wide problem as opposed to an individual training problem. Part III of Form 1 is used for the Person/Performance Analysis and identifies "who" is in need of training and what type of training is needed. The result is a determination of whether the problem is a motivation-related training problem or an ability-related training problem.

    Complete Form 1 on your own before class. Think about the implications of your analysis for organization development programs in

Contributed by Diana Deadrick, Old Dominion University.

addition to training programs. During class, form groups of three to five, which will act as the consulting team for the college. Share your individual analyses and come to a consensus about what should be done. At the end of class, have a spokesperson from each team discuss the team's recommendations and the rationale to support them.

Update

Since your last visit to the college, the Dean has implemented those changes pertaining to the strategy of focusing on adult learners. Specifically, the college now offers (1) more evening courses for both undergraduate and graduate students, (2) a teaching schedule that accommodates students that want to earn their degree in the evening, (3) credit courses in suburban locations, and (4) M.B.A. concentrations in a variety of areas. In addition, the Dean has implemented a "TQM" philosophy for the college whereby students are treated like customers and "customer service" is the new goal for faculty to pursue. These changes had been in place for a year when the Dean decided to evaluate their effectiveness. A "customer satisfaction" questionnaire was sent out to recent graduates; the results were disappointing. Of particular concern were the findings that the graduates were dissatisfied with the quality of their education and that they would not recommend that their friends, family, or colleagues attend Old State's College of Business.

The Dean has hired a consulting team (your group) to develop a training program for faculty in order to improve the quality of teaching in the college. However, your team has decided to first conduct a needs assessment to determine whether there really is a need for faculty training.

FORM 1   *Training Needs Assessment*

PART I: ORGANIZATION ANALYSIS

"Where" is there a need for improvement within the college?

  1. What college-wide changes have occurred or are anticipated to occur? How have these changes affected faculty performance? What evidence is there to suggest that a "problem" exists?

  2. In what way are the changes described above conflicting with the college's original organizational structure, culture, and/or climate? What type of data should be collected and analyzed in order to identify these conflicts?

  3. What recommendations would you make to alleviate these conflicts?

PART II: JOB/TASK ANALYSIS

"What" tasks are in need of improvement?

  4. What job-wide changes have occurred or are anticipated to occur with respect to faculty members? How have these changes affected faculty performance?

  5. In what way are the changes described above conflicting with the faculty member's previous job expectations and responsibilities? What type of data should be collected and analyzed in order to identify these constraints?

  6. What recommendations would you make to alleviate these conflicts?

PART III: PERSON/PERFORMANCE ANALYSIS

"Who" needs to improve?

  7. Do faculty members need any training? If so, what type of training is needed, and how would you conduct it?

41. EXERCISE

Design and Evaluation of Training Programs

I. *Objectives:*
   A. To help you determine which training methods are most appropriate for achieving particular objectives.
   B. To show you the linkages between training objectives, training methods, and training evaluation.
   C. To help you learn how to identify and write training objectives.
   D. To build skill in the evaluation of training programs.
II. *Out-of-Class Preparation Time:* 1 hour
III. *In-Class Time Suggested:* 45 minutes
IV. *Procedures:* Prior to the class meeting in which this exercise will be discussed, read the entire exercise and use a pencil to complete Forms 1 and 2 in the book. Or you may use a separate sheet of paper. At the beginning of the class period, the instructor should divide the class into discussion groups of three to five students.

   Each group should begin by completing Form 1. If you are unfamiliar with any of the training methods listed, consult your text or ask your instructor.

   Look at each training objective/outcome and then determine which training methods would be *most* appropriate for achieving each of the six training objectives. Since each group member comes into the class period with his or her own ideas on which training method is most appropriate for achieving which objectives, there may be a need for some discussion and negotiation before a group consensus can emerge.

   Put an "x" beside the method that seems *most* appropriate for achieving each objective or outcome. For example, if you believe that a lecture with questions would be a good method of facilitating knowledge acquisition on the part of a training program participant, put an "x" in that space. Then put an "x" wherever the particular training method seems appropriate for achieving particular training objectives or outcomes. For each of the six objectives or outcomes, you should have at least three, but no more than eight, training methods which are identified as most appropriate.

   Now look at the data in Exhibit 3.2. These data are taken from a training needs analysis of Corporation X. The percent opposite each occupation group indicates the percentage of members in that group citing *any* training need at all. The numbers under that, opposite each of the two training needs identified for each group, indicate the percentage of that group requesting training in those subject areas.

   This company has had no previous formal training programs for its employees and the newly hired Director of Training has asked your group to answer the following questions:

1. Which two occupational groups should I provide training programs for during my first year? Why?
2. What training objectives should I set for each occupational group and training need?
3. What training methods should I use to meet these objectives?
4. What training evaluation method should I use to evaluate each training method or program?

Before completing Form 2, review the information in Form 1 and Exhibit 3.2. Select the two occupational groups which you feel should be the new Director of Training's top training priority for the coming year. Then select only one training need for each occupational group. For example, if you feel training programs for executives are a priority, choose *either* strategic planning *or* marketing. Write the two occupational groups you choose and one training need for each on Form 2.

Now develop specific objectives for each of the two training programs you are recommending be offered. If your group selected strategic planning for executives as one of the two programs, then possible objectives might be increased knowledge about the process of strategic planning or successful development of a strategic plan for the corporation or the executive's department. Likewise, an objective for a performance appraisal program for middle managers might be the design of an appropriate performance appraisal form and process for the individual middle manager's particular situation.

Once the objectives are determined, they usually fit under one of the six major objectives or outcomes listed on Form 1. Based upon your previous analysis in Form 1, select up to three training methods for achieving these objectives with the particular occupational group. For example, achieving the objective of helping executives improve their strategic planning skills might involve on-the-job coaching by consultants or other executives skilled in this process as well as business games, lectures, or cases.

The final step is to determine the most appropriate method of evaluating the particular training program or programs. The four major methods of evaluation in order of their degree of complexity and difficulty are as follows:

1. Participant reaction—usually determined by a questionnaire immediately at the conclusion of the training program.
2. Learning—assessment of knowledge about or attitudes toward a particular subject, both before and after a training experience.
3. Behavioral change—changes in on-the-job behavior or performance as measured by performance appraisals, subordinate's perceptions, supervisor's perceptions, and/or individual productivity data.
4. Organizational effectiveness—decreases in departmental or organizational costs, turnover, absenteeism, and grievances, and increases

in departmental or organizational sales, income, or productivity as compared to a control group of those not attending training.

Complete Form 3 by selecting one or two training evaluation methods for the training methods you have selected. If you selected three training methods, then fill in one or two evaluation methods for each.

Now look at the questions on Form 4 and answer them in your group. Once all the questions are answered, raise your hands and let the instructor know your group has finished the exercise. Appoint a spokesperson to discuss your group's recommendations. When all groups have finished, compare results in each of the groups and discuss possible reasons for differences between the groups.

EXHIBIT 3.2   *Results of a Training Needs Assessment*
                Survey by Occupational Group

Top Two Areas of Training Needed by Occupational Group	Percentage Citing Need
1. Executives	67
Strategic planning	38
Marketing	27
2. Middle managers	84
Performance appraisal techniques	44
Employee motivation	32
3. Professionals	27
Effective communication skills	16
Principles of supervision	14
4. Salespeople	28
How to close a sale	22
Effective communication skills	12
5. First-line supervisors	47
Employee motivation	31
Principles of supervision	21
6. Production workers	22
Discipline	16
Production scheduling	10
7. Office/clerical staff	38
Time management	25
Assertiveness training	20

FORM 1 *The Effectiveness of Alternative Training Methods for Achieving Various Training Objectives/Outcomes*

Training Method	Training Objectives					
	Knowledge Acquisition	Attitude Change	Problem-Solving Skills	Interpersonal Skills	Participant Acceptance	Knowledge Retention
Information Processing:						
Lecture (with questions)						
Conference (discussion)						
Sensitivity training						
Laboratory training						
Observation						
Closed-circuit TV						
Programmed instruction						
Correspondence courses						
Videos						
Reading lists						

FORM 1 *continued*

Training Objectives

Training Method	Knowledge Acquisition	Attitude Change	Problem-Solving Skills	Interpersonal Skills	Participant Acceptance	Knowledge Retention
Simulation:						
Cases						
Incidents						
Role playing						
Business games						
In-Basket exercises						
On-the-Job:						
Job rotation						
Committee assignments						
On-the-job coaching						
Feedback from performance appraisal						
Apprenticeships						

FORM 2   *The Relationship Between Training Objectives and Training Methods*

Occupational Group:

Training Need:

Training Objectives	Training Methods
1.	1.
2.	2.
3.	3.

Occupational Group:

Training Need:

Training Objectives	Training Methods
1.	1.
2.	2.
3.	3.

FORM 3   *Evaluation Methods*

Occupational Group:

Training Need:

	Training Methods	Training Evaluation Methods
1.		1.
		2.
2.		1.
		2.
3.		1.
		2.

FORM 4   *Questions*

1. Why did you select the particular two occupations for the highest priority in training?

2. Once you had determined the occupational group, training need, and training objectives, how did you determine which training method would be most appropriate?

3. What problems might you encounter if you attempted to implement evaluation processes based on improvements in individual participant behavior or organizational effectiveness? Why?

4. What are the most effective training or educational methods to facilitate your own learning? Why?

5. Consider the most complex job you have ever had. What would have been the most effective method of training for that job? Why? What method (if any) was actually used?

42. EXERCISE

On-the-Job Training

I. *Objectives:*
   A. To make you aware of the problems a supervisor may encounter when training employees.
   B. To provide you with practice in conducting on-the-job training.
   C. To teach you how to prepare training aids.

    D. To teach you how to evaluate on-the-job training.

    E. To familiarize you with the major on-the-job training steps.

II. *Out-of-Class Preparation Time:*   1–2 hours

III. *In-Class Time Suggested:*   45 minutes

IV. *Procedures:* An important task for most supervisors is to instruct new employees on the methods and procedures necessary to perform various operations involved in a job. Initially, the employee may be totally unfamiliar with a particular task. This places an additional burden on the manager to make his or her instructions as clear and precise as possible. In this exercise you will be asked to train one or more other members of the class on how to perform a task. After the training is complete, it will be critiqued.

Preparation for the training can be done individually or in groups of three to five members, at the instructor's option. If groups are used, the instructor will divide up the class during the class period prior to the one in which this exercise will be conducted. Each group will then meet outside of class to prepare for the training. Each individual or group should begin by selecting a task to teach one or more class members. For example, one of the following could be picked:

- How to lift heavy objects safely.
- How to fold a napkin like they do at fancy restaurants.
- How to tie a special knot used by tree surgeons, merchant marine personnel, or those in the Navy.
- How to fix a dripping faucet such as one a plumber might fix.
- How to use a volt-ohm meter such as an electrician might use.

In selecting a task, pick one which is performed in industry, one which most class members don't already know how to perform, and one sufficiently complicated that trainees can't perform it instantly. Remember, you will have to provide all of the materials necessary to perform the task.

Once a task has been selected, you (your group) should develop a training aid and make copies for each class member. It might include:

A. Training objectives.

B. Benefits of performing the task for the employee, the company, and the customers.

C. A list of tools, materials, and equipment necessary to perform the task correctly.

D. A list showing each step in sequence necessary to perform the task, including the necessary illustrations.

E. An evaluation form to evaluate the trainee.

Finally, you must choose the best approach for conducting the training (lecture, demonstrations, etc.) and the steps which will be followed when conducting the training. If you are working in groups, a spokesperson (the one who will actually conduct the training for the group) should also be selected.

At the start of class, the instructor will select four or more groups/individuals to actually conduct on-the-job training. Depending upon the task, the instructor will also select one or more students to serve as trainees. At this point, the trainer will hand out a copy of the training aid to each class member and, one at a time, conduct training. This will be followed by a critique of each training session and training aid by all class members. Toward the end of class, those groups/individuals which did not actually conduct training during class will be asked to distribute a copy of their training aid to all class members.

43. INCIDENT

The Orientation Problem

Carol Burgess is a letter carrier and a part-time trainer of letter carriers for the U.S. Postal Service in a major city on the west coast. She trains all new letter carriers in her service area which encompasses the northern half of her state. Over the past five years she has trained 318 new letter carriers. Typically, the training is offered prior to the new letter carrier's entry onto the job, although sometimes it occurs shortly thereafter.

The training program typically encompasses both the orientation of new employees to the U.S. Postal Service and the development of specific skills needed by the new letter carrier. The latter involves practice in casing mail (i.e., sorting) to appropriate locations of a case in preparation for delivery, reading maps, determining appropriate sequencing of delivery, and customer relations. The total training program takes three full days (one day of orientation and two days of skills training).

The orientation part of the training program encompasses both an orientation packet and a discussion of various Postal Service policies and procedures. The orientation packet typically includes information about employee benefits, holidays, copies of certain standard forms (i.e., I.R.S. withholding forms), outline of emergency and accident procedures, key terms used in the Postal Service, copies of the health and life insurance options, and telephone numbers and locations of the Personnel Department and other important offices. In addition, an explanation of the U.S. Postal Service operation and purpose, the training to be received, the letter carrier's duties and responsibilities, job standards and production levels, Postal Service rules and regulations, and the chain of command for reporting purposes is provided. Ms. Burgess concludes her orientation with an offer of help and encouragement for the future.

The assumption built into the orientation is that it will be supplemented at the job site by the direct supervisor who will provide all the necessary information about the particular facility, the personnel at the facility, the area covered by the route or routes to which the new employee will be assigned, and the additional written information such as the employee handbook and the union contract. According to Postal Service policy, each new letter carrier should get three days of on-the-job training of which one is paid for by the training division and two are charged to the supervisor's production.

Ms. Burgess learned from subsequent conversations with her former trainees over the past five years that the orientation provided by the direct supervisor varied from practically nothing to fairly extensive. In some stations, the supervisor greeted the new employee, introduced the person to one other employee, and explained their own expectations regarding attendance, personal conduct, and productivity. Then the employee was given an assignment and allowed to "sink or swim." Several supervisors were known in the Postal Service to be "S.O.B.s" While 83 percent of new hires have survived their probationary 90 day period over the past three years, less than 20 percent survived in certain stations.

Last night Ms. Burgess received a telephone call from Edith Jones, one of her former trainees who finished training 10 weeks ago. Ms. Jones is a single parent with two school age children who had left her job as a secretary and taken the letter carrier job in order to make more money. She was in tears as she described her experience at her station.

Her supervisor had given her no written materials, introduced her to only one other employee, and has shifted her from route to route over the ten weeks she has worked at the facility. No help or support of any kind has been offered, but the supervisor has continually berated her for the number of hours she has taken to case and deliver routes. She had tried to study maps during her days off in order to learn the various areas covered by various routes, but this only helped a little. Each route had to be delivered in a particular order and it took time to learn the sequence. The other letter carriers were all stressed-out and working overtime themselves. Consequently, they ignored her and offered no assistance. Ms. Jones told Ms. Burgess that she was on the verge of quitting. Ms. Burgess told her to "hang in there because it does get easier with time."

As a result of all the complaints she had received from former trainees (some of who survived the 90 day probationary period), Ms. Burgess decided to recommend to the area Postmaster a program to train supervisors in how to orient new letter carriers. However, she wasn't sure what specific items the supervisors should include in their new employee orientation and how to train them to do it.

Questions

1. Describe the nature and causes of the orientation problem in this case.

2. What types of orientation for new employees should direct supervisors provide at the work site?
3. What training methods should be used to train the supervisors, assuming approval of the proposal?
4. What written materials should the supervisor provide for new letter carriers in light of what Ms. Burgess already provides?
5. In addition to the written materials discussed in the previous question, what else should the supervisor do to orient new letter carriers?

44. INCIDENT

The Cultural Diversity Training Program

Dr. Jennifer Barnes is an Assistant Professor of Organization Behavior and Human Resource Management of a major state university in the Southeast. Her university is located in a large city which is 61 percent black. In recent years, the university has aggressively recruited black faculty and graduate students. Specifically, the university has funded new faculty positions and graduate fellowships for minorities.

Recently Dr. Barnes read about a new university-sponsored cultural diversity training program which was required for all academic administrators/supervisors and offered to faculty and staff. Since Dr. Barnes teaches two human resource management courses, she decided to enroll in the one-day seminar in anticipation of utilizing the material in her own courses. She expected the program would cover the full range of workforce diversity including age, race, gender, ethnicity, physicial abilities, and sexual orientation. She also thought there might be some discussion of the impact of parental status, religious beliefs, and dual-career couples. Finally, she expected to experience a high level of involvement in the process through the use of case studies, sensitivity training, incidents, and role playing.

When Dr. Barnes attended the program, she was quite disappointed. There was a series of lectures by seven different speakers including one external consultant on cultural diversity and several university administrators. While the seminar coordinator told the participants she wanted their input and involvement, the speakers were scheduled for one hour blocks and used most or all of their allotted time with their formal presentations. Throughout the day only seven comments or questions were asked by participants. In addition, the only concept of diversity discussed by the presenters was racial diversity.

Other types of workforce diversity were mentioned in passing by one presenter but otherwise ignored. The emphasis for most of the presentations was on the changing workforce demographics and the consequent necessity for the university to be more open, accommodative, and responsive to black students, employees, or potential employees. One of the speakers noted that while blacks constitute 60 percent of the city's population and 30 percent of the area's population, only 15 percent of the students and 4 percent of the faculty are black. The unspoken assumption was that the participants (most of whom were white) harbored racial animosity toward blacks. Therefore, they needed to modify their attitudes and behavior in order to better recruit, retain, and relate to black employees or students.

Dr. Barnes felt that both the content and process of the seminar left much to be desired. After the seminar, she discussed her experience with her department chair. The chair agreed to discuss it with the Dean of the School of Business. After doing so, he reported that it had been decided at the highest levels of the university that "in our environment, diversity means black."

Questions

1. What is cultural diversity?
2. Why is cultural diversity an important issue for all organizations? What are the potential disadvantages of ignoring it as an issue? What steps should a proactive organization take to respond to this challenge?
3. Evaluate the content and training method used by the university in this training program. Do you have any suggestions for improvement?

45. SKILL BUILDER

Identifying Training Needs Through Task Analysis

I. *Objectives:*
   A. To introduce you to the process and purposes of assessing training needs.
   B. To give you practice in determining training needs for a job.
II. *Time Required to Complete:* 2–3 hours
III. *Instructions:* There are generally three analyses used to determine an organization's training needs: organization analysis, task or operations analysis, and person analysis. This assignment allows you to perform a task analysis for a particular job by interviewing and observing a job holder. A task analysis involves systematic collection of data about a specific job. Its purpose is to determine what an employee should be

taught to perform the job at the desired level. It generally includes a description of the major tasks of the job, standards of performance, how the tasks are to be performed to meet the standards, and the skills, knowledge, and abilities necessary. You will conduct the task analysis by following the steps described below:

Step 1: Select a job to analyze. You may choose a job currently held by a relative, friend, fellow student, etc. (If you completed the Job Description Exercise in Part II, you may use that job.) Ask the job holder if you may interview him or her about the position and/or also observe him or her performing the job.

Step 2: Obtain a job description for the job you selected or prepare one by interviewing the job holder. The job description should describe in general terms the worker's major duties and responsibilities. For example, a job description for an accounts receivable clerk might include the following duties and responsibilities:

a. Invoice shipments to customers on a monthly basis.
b. Prepare journal vouchers at the end of the month to record cash receipts and sales by product lines.

When preparing the job description, be sure to include those things that are critical to performing the job satisfactorily, no matter how infrequently or briefly they occur, and the knowledge, skills, and abilities needed.

Step 3: This step involves identifying the tasks associated with performing each of the major duties of the job. You are to identify the overt, observable behaviors that are involved in performing the job. Arrange (if possible) to observe the worker performing his or her job and develop a list of the tasks involved. A task listing includes behavioral statements of how the job is to be performed. Using the example presented earlier for the accounts receivable clerk, the tasks associated with invoicing customers might include:

a. Pull and review invoice master.
b. Extend and update invoice master.
c. Add correct discount and freight charges.
d. Make necessary amount of copies on copy machine.

When you complete this step, you should have a report which includes the title of the job, the major duties (responsibilities) of the job, the tasks associated with each duty/responsibility, and the knowledge and skills required of job incumbents.

Step 4: Once you have completed steps 1–3, answer the following questions and include them in your report:

a. What training would benefit a person performing the job? If you had to design a training program for the job, what content areas would be needed based on your analysis?
b. What training method would be best? Why? (On-the-job training, seminars, apprenticeships, vestibule, etc.).

PERFORMANCE APPRAISAL

46. EXERCISE

EvalSim—A Performance Evaluation In-Basket

I. *Objectives:*
   A. To familiarize you with some of the problems related to the use of performance appraisals and to provide alternative approaches for solving these problems.
   B. To give you practice in making decisions and writing memos to employees regarding performance appraisal issues.
   C. To familiarize you with the major duties or tasks which personnel specialists must perform with regard to a firm's performance evaluation system.

II. *Out-of-Class Preparation Time:* 20 minutes to read exercise plus one hour to complete In-Basket Items either individually or with group members and write memos

III. *In-Class Time Suggested:* 45 minutes to discuss all In-Basket Items

IV. *Procedures:* This exercise can be done individually or in groups of three to five members, at the instructor's option. You are to begin by reading all of the material presented in this exercise. You are to assume that you are responsible for developing and maintaining the O'Leary Organization's performance appraisal system. You are to assume further that the items that follow were waiting in your in-basket when you arrived at work after a three-week vacation. You (or your team) are (is) to respond in writing to each employee who wrote a memo. Secondly, explain on a separate sheet of paper what additional actions you would take with reference to each item. For example, if you believe that you should gather additional information before making a final decision on an item, explain what information you would want. Or, if you believe that additional memos or discussions with someone in the company are needed, explain this. You (or your team) should bring both the memos and the "Additional Action" sheets to class. Be prepared to present and defend these materials during the class discussion.

Situation

The O'Leary Organization is a medium-sized organization whose headquarters is located in the midwestern United States. You may assume that the organization is a manufacturing company, a hospital, an insurance company, a university, or virtually any other medium-sized organization with which you are familiar.

The O'Leary Organization's Personnel Department is organized in the manner shown below:

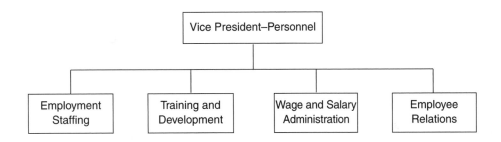

The Training and Development section consists of you or your team. In addition to conducting training, one of your other major duties is that of having full responsibility for the organization's performance evaluation system. Included among your duties are:

1. Determining which employees will be evaluated.
2. Determining how frequently employees will be evaluated.
3. Determining which appraisal format should be used.
4. Determining which job categories will be used to evaluate the employee's job performance.
5. Determining who should evaluate each employee.
6. Insuring that all evaluators know how to complete the organization's performance appraisal form and to conduct evaluation interviews.
7. Establishing the performance appraisal system and insuring that all employees adhere to it.
8. Maintaining all performance appraisal records.

The O'Leary Organization's present performance appraisal system, which you are to assume you or your team designed, requires that all employees be evaluated by their supervisor on a periodic basis. All employees are evaluated at the end of a 90-day period (the probationary period) and on a yearly basis thereafter. The performance appraisal form used by the organization is shown in Exhibit 3.3. Supervisors are required to complete this form covering each of their employees at the appropriate time, discuss the evaluation with him or her, ask the employee to sign the form at the end of the evaluation interview, and return the completed form to the Personnel Department.

EXHIBIT 3.3   *The O'Leary Organization Performance Appraisal Form*

NAME	SOCIAL SECURITY NO.	
TITLE	DEPARTMENT	
TODAY'S DATE	APPRAISAL PERIOD FROM_____ TO_____	Annual 90 day Special

PART I Performance Rating
(All Employees)

	1	2	3	4	5
Ability					
Attendance					
Attitude					
Appearance					
Conduct					
Initiative					
Work with Group					
Promotability					
Quantity of Work					
Quality of Work					
Overall Level of Performance					

REMARKS

Prepared by_____   Title_____
COMMENTS BY REVIEWED EMPLOYEE:

Employee's Signature_____   Date_____
(Employee signature does not indicate agreement, merely acknowledgment of this report.)

1 — Unsatisfactory   2 — Below Average   3 — Satisfactory   4 — Good   5 — Excellent

In-Basket Items

Item 1

MEMORANDUM

TO: Personnel Department
FROM: Tom Morrison, Accounting Department
SUBJECT: 90-Day Employee Evaluation

I just received my 90-day employee evaluation and received mostly "3's" on it. My boss explained his evaluation to me by saying that I was making good progress on the job. He added that, if I continue to show improvement, I will receive "4's" and "5's" like the more experienced employees do. Why am I being evaluated against older, more experienced workers? That doesn't seem right. I believe that considering my limited experience I deserve "excellent" evaluations.

Item 2

MEMORANDUM

TO: Personnel Department
FROM: Paul Lands, Computer Center
SUBJECT: Performance Evaluation

Joe Meena and I both started together at the O'Leary Organization two years ago. We are both in the Computer Center doing the same job, only he works one shift, and I work another. Two weeks ago when we compared our performance evaluations, I discovered that he received all "5's" whereas I received mostly "4's." The thing that irks me is that he and I both know we are doing an equally good job. His boss is just more lenient in his evaluation than is my boss. I don't think this whole system is fair, particularly since he may get promoted (based on his performance evaluation) before I do. Can't something be done about this?

Item 3

MEMORANDUM

TO: Personnel Department
FROM: Jill Best, Manager
SUBJECT: Lost Performance Appraisal Form

Six weeks ago when our offices were being remodeled, one of the janitors accidentally threw away a small stack of papers. Included in the stack was a performance appraisal form which I had just completed on one of my subordinates, Karen Whitmore. I know you need this form, but it is gone. What should I do?

Item 4

MEMORANDUM

TO: Personnel Department
FROM: Sue Peters, Supervisor
SUBJECT: Administering Employee Evaluations

I have recently received from your office a request to conduct evaluations this month on three of my employees. As you probably know, I was promoted to this supervisory position just one week ago as a result of the former supervisor's termination. I don't feel that I can presently conduct a fair evaluation of these employees. Do you want me to do them anyway?

Item 5

MEMORANDUM

TO: Personnel Department
FROM: Sandra Kelly, Supervisor
SUBJECT: Evaluation of Karen Bicknell

Yesterday afternoon I conducted an evaluation interview with Karen Bicknell and when I told her I gave her a "3" on "Work with Group" she got quite upset and defensive. She said the evaluation should have been at least a "4" and probably a "5." I attempted to explain my evaluation to her, but she wouldn't listen. Instead, she continued to argue with me. Karen received a "4" evaluation last year on "Work with Group" and a 3.5 overall evaluation this year. What should I do if this happens again?

Item 6

MEMORANDUM

TO: Personnel Department
FROM: Howard Adams, Supervisor
SUBJECT: Necessity of Signing Evaluation Forms

Recently I conducted a performance evaluation interview with Harold Wallace. At the end of the interview, when I asked him to sign the appraisal form at the bottom, he refused. I asked him if the evaluation was accurate, and he said yes. I also explained to him that signing the form only represented an acknowledgment that he had been evaluated. He replied that he had nothing to gain from signing the form, and, therefore, why sign it? I don't know what I should do. Harold is somewhat of a problem and is often quite stubborn.

Item 7

MEMORANDUM

TO: Personnel Department
FROM: Margaret Windell, Purchasing
SUBJECT: Annual Performance Review

I have a rather troublesome question to ask you. I would ask it of my boss but she is currently in the hospital. For the last 23 years I have received an overall performance review, and my evaluations have all shown that I am an excellent employee. I am six years from retirement and, frankly, I have reached the point where performance evaluations aren't of any consequence to me. I know I am doing a good job. I know I won't get promoted or transferred, and I am at the top of my pay grade. So why should I continue to be evaluated formally?

Item 8

MEMORANDUM

TO: Personnel Department
FROM: Sarah Wade, Maintenance Engineer
SUBJECT: Employee Appraisal Form

When I was over in the Personnel Department yesterday looking at my personnel file, I saw the appraisal form which was completed on me one month ago. I was shocked to see the following statement written on it under "Remarks": "Sarah has a very poor work attitude and doesn't appear willing to change it." My boss, Marilyn Turner, had also changed my evaluation on "attitude" from "4" to a "2." I am positive the negative statement was not on the evaluation form when I signed it. Needless to say, I want you to do something about this!

Item 9

MEMORANDUM

TO: Personnel Department
FROM: Chris Green, Supervisor
SUBJECT: Performance Evaluation of Bill Young

Next week I must conduct a performance evaluation interview with Bill Young who works by himself in the evenings. While I was completing the evaluation form on him, I realized that it was impossible for me to evaluate him on one of the evaluation categories, "Work with Group." What should I do? I am afraid if I leave it blank it will affect his "Overall Level of Performance" score and hence his chances of promotion.

Item 10

MEMORANDUM

TO: Personnel Department
FROM: Jeff Skala, Finance Department
SUBJECT: Confidentiality of Performance Evaluation

As you know, I have been experiencing a series of personal problems during the past year all of which have adversely affected my job performance. These problems reflected themselves on my recent performance evaluation as my "marks" slipped from mostly "4's" to mostly "2's." I can't disagree with my evaluation, but I don't think it was right for my boss, Helen Jackson, to tell two of my co-workers that she had given me a "1" on "Quality of Work." It seems to me that this type of information should be none of their business.

47. EXERCISE

Performance Appraisal Interview Role Play

    I. *Objectives:*
      A. To allow you practice in conducting a performance appraisal interview.
      B. To compare and contrast different approaches to the performance appraisal interview.
      C. To help you develop sensitivity toward communication problems in performance appraisal interviews.
    II. *Out-of-Class Preparation Time:*   20–30 minutes
   III. *In-Class Time Suggested:*   45 minutes
   IV. *Procedures:*
      A. Read the exercise before coming to class.
      B. Four students should be selected to participate in two different performance appraisal interviews (A and B). Two of you will play the role of the employee and two will play the role of the supervisor. Role assignments should be made in the prior class period or before class begins. The instructor will provide role sheets.
      C. The persons playing the role of the employee should read "Employee's Role."
      D. The person playing the role of supervisor A should read the "Supervisor Role A," and the person playing the role of supervisor B should read the "Supervisor Role B."
      E. During the class period in which the role plays will occur, all role play participants should be taken outside of the classroom and given time to prepare their respective roles. All other members of the class are to observe the two different sets of interviews and record their observations on separate sheets of paper.
      F. Supervisor A conducts a 10–15 minute appraisal interview with one of the employees in the front of the class. The other role play pair remains in the hall outside the classroom until their turn.
      G. After the first role play is completed, the second role play pair enters the classroom and conducts its appraisal interview. The first role play team joins the rest of the class to observe the interview.
      H. The entire class discusses both interviews.

Situation

Tri-City Health Services is a large non-profit center providing basic outpatient health services and health education programs to low-income families in the Southwest. The center employs over 40 physicians and nurses and over 200 other workers in various staff positions. Pat Smith has been working as a junior assistant in the Fund Raising and Grants Department for the past two years and has worked on the children's healthcare program. Pat has done well in performing the job—all performance objectives have been met or surpassed for the year. However, this year Pat has been consistently late for work on many occasions. Each year on the anniversary date of the employee's hire, his or her supervisor must conduct a performance appraisal interview. Chris Jackson, the supervisor, has completed the performance evaluation form shown in Exhibit 3.4 and is ready to discuss the evaluation with Pat.

Instructions for Observers

Your task is to evaluate two different sets of performance interviews. As you observe the interviews, consider the following:

1. How did the supervisor begin the interview? Was the purpose of the interview clearly stated?
2. What type of interview approach did the supervisor use? Who did most of the talking?
3. Did the supervisor learn how the employee feels about the job? About his or her performance?
4. Did both parties gain a clear understanding of the problem and its solution?
5. Were any specific action plans made to resolve the problem(s)?
6. Are there any ways in which the supervisor could improve the interview? How?
7. Which interview was most effective? Why?

EXHIBIT 3.4   *Performance Evaluation Form*

I. RATING CATEGORIES

Performance Dimensions	Performance Level	Points (Maximum = 5)
Quality of Work (The degree to which the employee's work is free of flaws)	*Excellent*	5
Quantity of Work (The total amount of acceptable work completed within time and resources available)	*Excellent*	5

(continued)

EXHIBIT 3.4   *continued*

Attendance (Includes absences and tardiness)	*Poor*	1
Cooperation (The degree to which the employee cooperates with and is respected by co-workers)	*Average*	3
Initiative and Self-Reliance (The degree to which the employee is independent and self-directed)	*Excellent*	5
Work Timeliness (The degree to which the employee exhibits skill in planning and scheduling activities)	*Average*	3
Responsibility (The degree to which the employee is willing to accept responsibility for details in work)	*Above Average*	4
Total Points		26

II. OBJECTIVES AND GOALS

A. Did the employee set any specific work-related goals this performance period?
Yes (X)   No ( )

B. If yes, what were they?
To complete and implement a fund-raising program by April 1.
To obtain a 15 percent increase in federal grants by April 1.

C. To what extent were they met?
Employee met or exceeded both objectives. The fund-raising effort was very successful (over $25,000 was raised) and federal grants have been increased by 18 percent this year.

Overall evaluation of goal achievement?   *Excellent*

III. OVERALL EVALUATION OF EMPLOYEE PERFORMANCE
(Support evaluation with comments.)

The employee has done a fine job on performance objectives but continues to have a problem with tardiness. Based on this, the overall rating for the year is average (26 out of 35 points). I do not recommend the employee for a promotion at this time.

Supervisor Signature	Date	Employee Signature	Date

48. EXERCISE

Which Performance Appraisal Format Is Most Effective?

I. *Objectives:*
  A. To examine the strengths and weaknesses of four different methods for appraising employees
  B. To enhance your oral communication skills.
II. *Out-of-Class Preparation Time:* 30 minutes to prepare for the debate
III. *In-Class Time Suggested:* 50–75 minutes
IV. *Procedures:* Your instructor will divide the class into five groups at the end of class prior to conducting this exercise. There will be four debating groups consisting of three to five members each and one or more groups of "judges" that consist of the remaining class members. Debaters will be assigned one of four positions and told to prepare to argue in favor of that position. Judges will be told to read the textbook chapter pages that cover those positions. The issue to be debated is: Which approach to appraising employees is the most effective? The positions are: (1) the graphic rating scale; (2) the behaviorally anchored rating scale; (3) a ranking or forced distribution system; and (4) management by objectives.

  At the start of the next class, your instructor will announce that a four-way debate will be held. The judges' role in the debate is to "search for the truth." They are to listen to all four different sides presented and then, after the debate is over, to tell the class what they believe is the "correct" answer to the debate question, not who "won" the debate.

  The debate consists of two rounds. The purpose of Round One (15–20 minutes) is for each team to learn the position of the other debating teams. Hence, each team has up to five minutes to explain their position as comprehensively as possible. At the completion of Round One, the debating teams are given up to ten minutes to prepare criticisms of each of the other three teams for Round Two. During this intermission, judges are to discuss what they have heard and begin to formulate their own position.

  In Round Two (15–20 minutes), each debating team is given up to five minutes to criticize the position of each of the other teams. Unlike a traditional debate, teams are not allowed to rebut the criticisms made by others. They must simply listen to them. Round Two ends when Team Four has finished criticizing the position of the other three teams.

  After the debate has ended, the judges have five minutes to discuss the case among themselves and to arrive at a consensus, if possible. The judging team(s) then explains its decision to the debaters.

PART 4

*IMPLEMENTING COMPENSATION
AND SECURITY: COMPENSATION,
INCENTIVES, BENEFITS, AND SAFETY
AND HEALTH*

49. CASE

The Overpaid Bank Tellers

The State Bank is located in a southwestern town of about 50,000 people. It is one of four banks in the area and has the reputation of being the most progressive. Russell Duncan has been the President of the bank for 15 years. Before coming to State Bank, Duncan had worked for a large Detroit bank for ten years. Duncan has implemented a number of changes that have earned him a great deal of respect and admiration from both bank employees and townspeople alike. For example, in response to a growing number of Spanish-speaking people in the area, he hired Latinos and placed them in critical bank positions. He organized and staffed the city's only agricultural loan center to meet the needs of the area's farmers. In addition, he established the state's first "uniline" system for handling customers waiting in line for a teller.

Perhaps far more than anything else, Duncan is known for establishing progressive personnel practices. He strongly believes that the bank's employees are its most important asset and continually searches for ways to increase both employee satisfaction and productivity. He feels that all employees should continually strive to improve their skills and abilities and hence cross-trains employees and sends many of them to courses and conferences sponsored by banking groups such as the American Institute of Banking.

With regard to employee compensation, Duncan firmly believes that employees should be paid according to their contribution to organizational success. Hence, ten years ago he implemented a results-based pay system under which employees could earn raises each year from 0 to 12 percent, depending on their job performance. Raises are typically determined by the bank's Personnel Committee during February and are granted to employees on March 1 of each year. In addition to granting employees merit raises, six years ago the bank also began giving cost-of-living raises. Duncan had been opposed to this idea originally but saw no alternative to it.

One February another bank in town conducted a wage survey to determine the average compensation of bank employees in the city. The management of the State Bank received a copy of the wage survey and was surprised to learn that its 23 tellers, as a group, were being paid an average of $22 per week more than were tellers at other banks. The survey also showed that employees holding other positions in the bank (e.g., branch managers, loan officers, and file clerks) were being paid wages similar to those paid by other banks. (See Exhibit 4.1.)

After receiving the report, the Personnel Committee of the bank met to determine what should be done regarding the tellers' raises. They knew that none of the tellers had been told how much their raises would be but that they were all expecting both merit and cost-of-living raises. They also realized that, if other employees learned that the tellers were being overpaid, friction could develop and morale might suffer. They knew that it was costing the bank over $26,000 extra to pay the tellers. Finally, they knew that as a group the bank's tellers were highly competent, and they did not want to lose any of them.

Questions

1. If you were on the bank's Personnel Committee, what would you do regarding raises for the tellers?
2. How much faith should the Personnel Committee place in the accuracy of the wage survey?
3. Critique the bank's policy of giving merit raises which range from 0 to 12 percent, depending on job performance.
4. Critique the bank's policy of giving cost-of-living raises. Should they be eliminated?

EXHIBIT 4.1 *Wage Survey Results: Comparative Salaries of Local Bank Officers*

Position	Bank 1	Bank 2	Bank 3	State Bank
Commercial Loan Officer	$38,600	$39,500	$37,900	$38,400
Consumer Loan Officer	39,200	28,700	29,300	39,300
Mortgage Loan Officer	37,100	35,900	39,500	37,200
Branch Manager	33,700	35,400	34,800	34,400
Assistant Branch Manager	24,800	24,400	26,600	23,300
New Accounts Officer	20,900	20,800	20,700	20,800
Officer Trainee	20,200	20,000	20,400	20,300
Average Weekly Earnings of Local Bank Employees				
Accounting Clerks	$ 323	$ 316	$ 328	$ 326
File Clerks	286	292	279	283
Safe Deposit Clerks	378	380	370	380
Tellers	312	309	315	334

50. CASE

Rewarding Volunteers

Background

Northern University is a large university in a small college town in the Northwest. After several years of political pressure, internal conflicts, and negotiations, the university applied for, and was granted, an FCC license for a new public radio affiliate. The general goals of the station were to provide quality noncommercial alternative broadcasting with an emphasis on local and national news, jazz, and classical music. The station would have no paid commercials, but would broadcast public service announcements and cultural events.

A short-term objective was to assemble and train a volunteer staff (mostly students and faculty) until funds could be provided for an all-professional administrative staff. A longer-term objective was to develop all-professional announcers.

Exhibit 4.2 shows the organization structure of the radio station. The General Manager, Chief Engineer, News Director, Administrative Assistant, and Program Director were all full-time paid positions. All of the other positions were either part-time employees, part-time work-study students, or unpaid part-time volunteers.

The largest segment of the staff were the volunteers comprised of college students, faculty, or faculty spouses. The students volunteered to get training and experience which they hoped would propel them into careers in the media. Faculty volunteered either for the new experience or because they liked playing particular types of music. The others volunteered to help the station and to meet new people. Volunteers were trained and used as both announcers and in "behind the scenes" positions such as board operators. Many of the board operators were told they could become announcers in the future.

The Program Director's responsibilities included developing the on-air program schedule, developing a volunteer training program (including both equipment operation and on-air announcing), and scheduling/supervising the volunteers and work-study students. The Program Director also did some on-air announcing and worked as the internal liaison coordinating the various departments. He reported directly to the Station General Manager, who was responsible for all aspects of internal station management as well as developing and sustaining relationships with external constituencies.

Problems

The person hired initially as Program Director had a leadership style that did not fit well in a volunteer-oriented organization. Specifically, he was task-oriented and had few skills in managing others. This leadership style contributed to conflicts within the organization, and the Program Director left the organization by mutual consent after nine months on the job. The position of Program Director remained unfilled for nine months.

During that time period the General Manager and the Administrative Assistant split the work ordinarily done by the Program Director, including recruitment, selection, training, and scheduling of the volunteers. However, none of these activities were ever institutionalized in terms of written policies and procedures. For example, there were no written job descriptions for volunteers explaining duties and responsibilities for particular positions. Nor was there any formal feedback system for evaluating volunteer performance and receiving volunteer input. Opportunities for volunteer training were also reduced during this period.

After nine months a new Program Director was hired. He had previous experience as a Program Director at another public ratio station and came highly recommended. His initial statement was one of amazement at the high quality of announcing among the volunteers. In fact, he sent out a memorandum to that effect during his second week on the job. However, as time passed more and more of the volunteer announcers were told by the Program Director that their services were no longer required as announcers. They were offered the opportunity to work behind the scenes as board operators with no on-air announcing. Most chose to simply quit.

When challenged by the volunteers, the Program Director stated that there was too much voice variation among the volunteers and an all-professional sounding station needs more uniformity. Since there was no money to hire full-time professional announcers, the Program Director (as well as several other paid staff) began to do more and more of the on-air announcing. The Program Director himself was working more than 60 hours per week. No new volunteers were being trained. Most of the old volunteers had either quit or been demoted. The five still doing on-air announcing then requested a meeting with the General Manager.

At the meeting these volunteer announcers indicated their displeasure concerning the decisions of the Program Director. They indicated that they had contributed not only their time but also had made monetary contributions to the station and had encouraged others to do so. The General Manager thanked the announcers for their contributions of time and money, but indicated he had given the Program Director control of the programming including personnel matters. They were still welcome to do volunteer work at the station and could continue announcing "for the time being." The volunteers were not happy with this response and promptly submitted their resignations.

The General Manager now had an even more severe problem. The paid staff were already spread too thin and stretched to the limit even before the latest volunteer resignations. The station was committed to 20 hours of programming each day and prerecorded tapes could not fill the entire programming gap since they also required staff time to produce. The station clearly was in a crisis situation.

Questions

1. Describe the fundamental problem in this case together with its causes.
2. What specific mistakes were made by (a) the General Manager and (b) the Program Director?
3. What types of rewards are most appropriate for volunteers? To what degree were these provided to volunteers at the radio station?

EXHIBIT 4.2 *Organizational Structure of the Station*

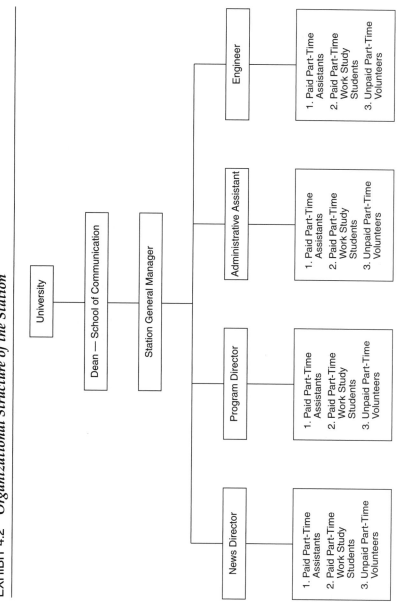

51. CASE

Managing Nonmonetary Compensation

Andrew J. (Drew) Nelson supervised the respiratory therapy department at Dunesbury Medical Center in Owatonna and Waseca, Minnesota, towns of 16,000 and 2,000, respectively. Though he worked mainly at the local hospitals, he was employed by Breathing Care Associates (BCA), which was affiliated with St. Luke's Hospital in Rochester, Minnesota.

Nelson had graduated from the Mayo Clinic Respiratory Therapy Program and had earned a Bachelor's degree in Biology from a Minnesota state college. Before accepting this supervisory position three years ago, he had been a staff therapist at Mount Olympus Medical Center in Milwaukee, Wisconsin.

A highly respected professional, Nelson tried to keep up with current developments in his field. He was well liked by staff and patients, and had a good sense of humor. If there was one thing Nelson lacked, it was formal management training. He now wished he had taken some business courses during college.

Nelson did not belong to a labor union. His parents had owned a trucking business and had dealt with Teamsters. Stories about their shenanigans had soured Nelson on union membership. However, therapists at St. Luke's who were employed by BCA were represented by a bargaining unit.

Nelson's supervisor, Matt Barnes, used to call or visit the Owatonna hospital regularly to see how things were going or to bring supplies. Lately, Barnes' visits were less frequent. Months could go by before Nelson saw him.

Since 1963, Dunesbury Medical Center had operated another facility in Waseca, about 12 miles west of Owatonna. In 1985, Dunesbury's Board of Directors decided to close the Waseca hospital on June 30th for economic reasons.

Below in Exhibit 4.3 is an organizational chart for the respiratory therapy department at Dunesbury Medical Center in January, 1985.

EXHIBIT 4.3   *Dunesbury Medical Center Organizational Chart*

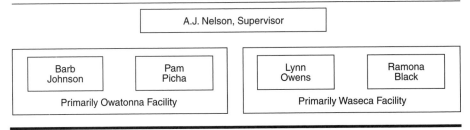

Contributed by Margaret Foegen Karsten, The University of Wisconsin, Platteville.

Beginning January 3, 1985, Barb Johnson took a six-week paid maternity leave permitted under BCA's temporary disability program. At the end of January, Ramona Black had surgery and took a six-week medical leave. That left only Nelson, Pam Picha, and Lynn Owens to staff the two facilities.

Nelson was under pressure from BCA to cut labor costs. For about a month, he worked six days per week. The length of his workday varied from 8 to 12 hours or more. On the days Nelson worked, he also was "on call." If a patient had breathing difficulties, Nelson was called to the hospital after normal working hours. Sometimes he would not get "called in" for several days. On other nights, he might get called in two or three times. If a doctor wanted a patient to be on an artificial breathing machine, called a respirator, Nelson had to provide staff at the hospital 24 hours a day.

Since he supposedly was an "exempt" employee, Nelson received no overtime pay. Originally he was not paid for on-call hours either. Then he successfully negotiated with BCA to get $1.00 per hour call pay. In January and February 1985 combined, Nelson worked more than 140 hours beyond his normal scheduled workweek. His salary was about $24,000.

In March, Pam Picha resigned to move to Texas. Lynn Owens gave two weeks' notice on April 2nd. She had accepted a position in a Minneapolis hospital. While Nelson attended a Minnesota Association of Respiratory Therapists' Convention in mid-April, Ramona Black quit without giving notice. Nelson left the conference early to fill in at the Owatonna facility.

Nelson began to feel he needed some time off work. He was getting "burned out." His "earned time" account, which could be used for sick leave, vacation, holidays, etc., had almost reached the 400-hour maximum.

On April 21st, Nelson asked Barnes if he could take a vacation from May 20–26. His wife had to attend a business meeting in New Orleans, and this would be a good chance for the family to spend a few extra days sightseeing.

Hearing no reply from Barnes, Nelson sent him a note with the weekly payroll report of May 5th asking what decision had been made on his vacation request. In the meantime, Barb Johnson found out that Nelson was planning to take time off. She refused to work seven days in a row, which would have been necessary to provide adequate staffing in Nelson's absence. The previous summer Nelson had worked seven days in a row so that she could take a vacation.

Finally, on May 12th, Barnes called Nelson. "Good morning, Drew. Say about this vacation request . . . I really can't let you take off right now. I can't force Barb to work seven days in a row. Besides, if she did, I'd have to pay her overtime." Nelson swallowed hard. Before he could reply, Matt ended the conversation.

BCA's policy on earned time accrual and use are presented in Exhibit 4.4.

Questions

1. What are Nelson's alternatives?
2. What do you think Nelson should do? Justify your answer.
3. Does the hospital administration have any obligation to help alleviate Nelson's situation?

EXHIBIT 4.4   *BCA's Policy on Earned Time Accrual and Use*

EARNED TIME

Personal time off from the workplace is important in maintaining good health. Breathing Care Associates is introducing an innovative program for earned paid time off. The program is called EARNED TIME, and has been nicknamed "ET."

EARNED TIME combines traditional programs of paid vacation time, paid legal and personal holiday time, and paid sick time into one "bank" of paid benefit time off. For each hour you work—up to 80 per pay period—an amount of Earned Time is deposited into your personal "Earned Time Account." Then, as you decide you want to schedule time off, the hours accumulated in your personal ET Account are yours to use.

You begin to earn time with your first hour of work at Breathing Care Associates. And for each hour you work—up to 80 per pay period—Earned Time continues to accrue. The amount of Earned Time you accrue depends on your length of continuous service at Breathing Care Associates, your exemption status (Nonexempt or Exempt), and the number of hours you work.

These are also the usual components for determining accrual rates for paid holiday, sick, and vacation time. With this new program, however, you have the flexibility to schedule time off for whatever purpose you choose.

MAXIMUM ACCUMULATION AMOUNTS

The emphasis of Earned Time is to offer you scheduled time away from work for whatever purpose you choose. Full-time employees are strongly encouraged to take 15 days off each year. Because unused Earned Time can be forwarded from year to year, it is possible to reach your Account Maximum if you do not use enough Earned Time each year.

Your personal ET Account has a *Maximum Accumulation Amount of Two Times Your Annual Accrual Rate.* When you near your Account Maximum, it is your responsibility to schedule Earned Time off. If the Account Maximum is reached, no ET will accrue beyond it.

| | Example of Maximum Accumulation Amounts | |
Years of Service	Annual Accrual	Maximum ET Accumulation
2–4	200 hours (25 days)	400 hours (50 days)
10	248 hours (31 days)	496 hours (62 days)

SCHEDULING ET

ET is available as you accrue it. However, requests for paid time off must be approved by your supervisor, who will consider staffing arrangements and departmental operations before granting your request. Schedule ET with your supervisor as far in advance as possible. Often, at least a two-week notice is required for a scheduled absence.

52. CASE

Controlling Employee Benefit Costs

John DeCarlo is President and CEO of Quality Auto Parts, an automotive parts equipment manufacturer and supplier in the Southwest. The company was started by DeCarlo and his father in 1968 and now employs 812 people at four different sites. Revenues and profits increased steadily from 1968 until 1992. Both were down in 1992 and 1993. During the remainder of the 1990s both were erratic as a result of the increased foreign competition in both the auto parts industry and the auto industry itself.

The Problem

DeCarlo recently met with his Vice President for Finance (David Schramm) and his Vice President for Human Resources (Harriet Poster) to determine how costs could be cut so the company could price its products more competitively relative to foreign competitors. At this meeting, he learned that employee benefit costs had increased at approximately twice the rate of increase for wages alone (12 percent versus 6 percent yearly) from 1988 to 1998. In particular, the employee health insurance costs increased from $2,184 per employee per year in 1988 to $5,316 in 1998. DeCarlo expressed frustration at these increases and asked what could be done.

Foster and Schramm invited DeCarlo to a meeting of health-care providers, insurers, and employers scheduled for the following week. At this meeting, they learned that their problem was quite common and being experienced by most other corporations in the area. One consultant surveyed the chief human resources executives at *Fortune 500* and *Fortune Service 500* corporations and found "controlling employee benefit program costs" to be the most critical issue facing these executives. Another national survey found that health benefit costs amounted to a whopping 26 percent of corporate earnings. Moreover, health care costs have grown faster than overall inflation and faster than any other segment of the economy since 1990.

They also learned more about the nature and causes of this problem. Many of the speakers at the conference cited large catastrophic-illness claims, increased use of mental health and substance abuse services, increased use of medical services, high-technology medicine, cost-shifting from government programs (Medicare and Medicaid) to private insurance, high physician fees, the AIDS crisis, the demographics of employees in the auto industry (i.e., a higher percentage of older employees), and recent premium increases by both traditional and managed care plans attempting to recoup recent losses. One speaker noted: "If businesses in the private sector don't make a profit, they are not going to exist. The continuing escalation of healthcare costs are threatening the very survival of some companies, particularly small companies. Smaller businesses increasingly bear the brunt of the spiraling costs because they have no one else to whom they can shift their costs."

Several possible solutions were discussed although there was no consensus regarding their effectiveness or applicability to particular situations. Among the cost containment suggestions were self-insurance, utilization review, managed care (i.e., health maintenance organizations and preferred provider organizations), wellness programs, flexible benefits, cost-sharing (i.e., higher deductibles and co-insurance), and insuring ambulatory alternatives to hospitalization.

Many speakers emphasized that employers should not wait passively for the government to solve the problem because that was unlikely to happen any time soon. In addition, health-care reform raises fundamental questions regarding societal priorities, and there is currently no consensus regarding these questions. Health-care reform is not currently a top priority of the public, and there is a strong anti-tax sentiment among the public. Consequently, there is little political will to take on such reform, particularly since the failure of the Clinton health reform proposals in 1994. When Congress has intervened, it has usually made the problem worse by mandates which raise costs for insurance companies and employers.

The Challenge

DeCarlo came away from the conference with a greater appreciation of the complexity of the problem and a greater determination to do something about it. However, he wasn't sure what to do. He viewed his company as a "preferred employer" because it had always paid above the market wage rates and its benefits were always more liberal than those of other U.S. companies and particularly those of foreign competitors. DeCarlo did not want to do anything to jeopardize his company's advantage in attracting and retaining high-quality personnel. At the same time, he realized that if no changes were made, his health insurance premiums would be greater than his total projected earnings by the year 2005.

Quality Auto Parts' present health insurance plan (Blue Cross–Blue Shield) is a traditional indemnity insurance plan. All employees have one plan which makes no effort to control the health-care services provided. Employees select their own physicians and the insurance company pays reimbursement for whatever services are provided at whatever price the particular provider charges. Neither physicians nor employees have a financial incentive to economize in the use of services or to seek out low-cost providers.

DeCarlo decided to establish an Employee Health Benefits Committee that would report to him in one month with recommendations for containing health benefit costs while minimizing adverse employee reaction. Membership on the committee consisted of Foster, Schramm, and two other employees. You have been asked to serve as an employee member of this committee.

The committee has recommended that DeCarlo consider three general options for the future: (1) stay with the current traditional indemnity policy with an average cost of $5,316 per year; (2) offer an HMO option in addition to the current plan; and (3) establish a special self-insurance fund and negotiate preferred provider arrangements (PPOs) with local providers. (i.e., discounted prices in exchange for the directing of these employees to these providers).

The committee members are split on the three options. The other employee wishes to continue with the current plan. Mr. Schramm wants to adopt the self-insurance option and Ms. Foster wants to offer the HMO option. All three are looking to you to make a recommendation and help them reach a consensus.

Questions

1. Describe the nature and causes of the cost problem in this case.
2. What information should the committee gather before making any recommendations? Why?
3. Given the desire of most employees to protect themselves from high health-care costs, is there any way for the company to continue to attract the best employees while containing health benefit costs? Why or why not?
4. On the basis of what you know about this company, which of the three specific proposals would you be likely to recommend? Can the company adopt some combination of the three options? What do you recommend and why?

53. CASE

Evaluating Nontraditional Incentive Systems: Howe 2 Ski Stores

The Howe 2 Ski Stores are a chain of three ski and windsurfing shops located in the suburbs of a large eastern city. Maria Howe, a ski enthusiast and business school major, opened a store ten years ago after her college graduation with some financial backing from her family and several friends. From its inception, the Howe 2 store was intended to provide state-of-the-art equipment and clothing for skiers at all skill levels from beginners to champion. It was to be staffed by employees who were themselves advanced skiers and could provide expert advice on the choice of clothing and equipment, and it was intended to have a quick response time that would permit the last-minute purchase of equipment and clothing prior to a ski trip.

Howe originally drew from a pool of skiing friends and fellow students to staff the stores and still prefers to hire part-time employees with skiing expertise who might leave in a year over more stable, full-time employees with less expertise and interest in the sport. Whether administrative staff, cashiers, clerks, or molders (employees who fit bindings to skis), employees were encouraged to keep up on the latest skiing equipment and trends, attend ski vendor shows, try out demo equipment, and give feedback on the store's inventory in order to help provide the highest quality state-of-the-art equipment and advice for the customer. Suggestion boxes were placed in the store and Howe herself regularly collected, read, and acted upon the suggestions made by the clerks and customers. She developed special advertising campaigns to build an image for the nearby slopes in order to increase the market. As the business grew, Howe even added a line of rental equipment in order to lower the costs and encourage people to try the sport.

Although profits grew irregularly due to weather effects and the faddish nature of the sport, Howe's efforts paid off in the long term, and within four years business had grown sufficiently to permit the opening of a second Howe 2 Ski Store in another suburb about ten miles from the first. In order to even out sales across the year, about six years ago Howe took a chance on the growing windsurfing market and the East Coast location and added a line of equipment for this sport. The move turned out to be a very good one. The windsurfing market increased by more than 300 percent in the next four years and continues to experience a slower but stable pattern of growth as families and older adults attempt the sport. This market has enabled her to smooth out the number of sales occurring throughout the year.

Three years ago, Howe was able to open a third store, located within a 15-mile radius from the other two. Although managers have been hired to

Contributed by M. Susan Taylor, University of Maryland, and J. Kline Harrison, Wake Forest University.

run each of the stores and the total number of employees has grown to 65, Howe's basic strategy has remained the same—high quality, state-of-the-art products, a knowledgeable staff, and quick response time. Profits from the stores have continued to grow, although at a slower rate. Competition from other ski stores has also increased noticeably within the last two years.

The threat of increased competition has been exacerbated by signs that employee productivity has begun to slide. Last year there were eight occasions where expensive ski orders were not delivered in time for the customer's ski vacation. Although Howe used a variety of maneuvers to retain the customers' patronage (e.g., paying for the customers to rent equipment of equivalent quality, expressing the equipment to the customer as soon as it was delivered, and lowering the price of the equipment), the costs of these late orders were high. She realizes that word of these kinds of incidents could significantly damage the store's reputation. Furthermore, at least 15 percent of all ski orders were more than two days late, even though customers did not miss a trip or vacation because of it.

In an attempt to respond to these difficulties, Howe instituted a merit performance system for the molders (employees who fit the binding to skis). Although productivity seemed to increase for awhile, waves of discontent popped out all over the stores. The molders felt that their merit ratings were inaccurate because the store managers could not observe them much of the time. Further, they argued that their performance would have been much higher had not other employees interrupted them with questions about appropriate bindings or failed to clearly identify the appropriate equipment on the sales tickets. Other employees also complained because they were not given the opportunity for merit pay. The buyers, who visit ski shows, examine catalogs, and talk with sales representatives in order to decide on the inventory, argued that their work was essential for high sales figures and quality equipment. Sales clerks claimed that their in-depth familiarity with an extensive inventory and their sales skills were essential to increasing sales. They also noted their important role in negotiating a delivery date that the molders could meet. Similar arguments were made by the people in the credit office who arranged for short-term financing if necessary and the cashiers who verified costs and checked credit card approvals. Even the stockers noted that the store would be in a bad way if they did not locate the correct equipment in a warehouse full of inventory and deliver it in a timely manner to the molders.

Howe had to concede that the employees were correct on many of these points, so she suspended the merit plan at the end of the ski season and promised to reevaluate its fairness. Even more convincing were several indications that productivity problems were not limited to molder employees. Complaints about customer service increased 20 percent during the year. Several customers noted that they were allowed to stand, merchandise in hand, waiting for a clerk to help them, while clerks engaged in deep conversations among themselves. Although Howe mentioned this to employees in the stores when she visited and asked the store managers to discuss it in staff meetings, the complaints continued. A record number of "as is" skis were sold at the end of the season sale because they were damaged in the warehouse, the store, or by the molders. The closing inventory revealed that 20 percent of the rental equipment had been lost or seriously damaged without resulting charges to the renters because records were poorly maintained. Regular checks of the suggestion boxes in the store revealed fewer and fewer comments. Although less extreme, similar problems occurred in windsurfing season. Employees just didn't seem to notice these problems, or worse, didn't seem to care.

Howe was very bothered by all these factors and felt they could not be attributed to the growth of the business alone. She knew it would be impossible to maintain her competitive position with these events occurring. At a recent Small Business Forum meeting, Howe heard the guest speaker, a university professor, suggest that employers consider a group of nontraditional incentive plans in order to increase employee motivation and involvement and reduce the costs of operating. She decided to investigate the topic further to see whether these plans might be appropriate for her stores.

Questions

1. Given the background information about Howe 2 Ski Stores, discuss the feasibility of implementing lump sum bonuses, pay for knowledge, profit sharing, and gainsharing plans in this situation. What plan or plans would you recommend that Howe look at most closely and why?
2. Assuming that she decides that a gainsharing plan is feasible, what could be done to increase the likelihood of success?
3. What negative effects are likely to result from even the successful implementation of a gainsharing plan?

54. EXERCISE

Job Evaluation at Smithfield County Health Services

I. *Objectives:*
   A. To help you develop an understanding of the point system of job evaluation.
   B. To provide you with experience in evaluating jobs using a point system.
   C. To give you practice in evaluating the consistency of job descriptions.
II. *Out-of-Class Preparation Time:* 30 minutes
III. *In-Class Time Suggested:* 45 minutes

Developed by Gary F. Kohut and Gerald E. Calvasina, The University of North Carolina, Charlotte.

IV. *Procedures:*
   A. Review the Job Evaluation Manual (Exhibit 4.5) and the job descriptions (Exhibit 4.6) before class.
   B. The class should be divided into groups of three to five students to complete the exercise.
   C. Read the scenario below and follow the instructions given.

Smithfield County Health Services

Smithfield County is part of one of the largest SMSAs (Standard Metropolitan Statistical Areas) in the southeastern United States. Census figures indicate that the current population of Smithfield County is 1.4 million people and growing. The major city in the county, Newberry (population, 475,000 people), is a banking, health-care, and transportation center for the region.

Smithfield County Health Services (SCHS) is the primary provider of health-care services for the region. Services include vaccinations, screening and treatment of communicable diseases, and programs on nutrition and mental health. SCHS employs 2,500 people in various professional, technical, and administrative support positions. Due to steady economic growth in the county and increasing demands for health care, competition for qualified personnel is keen across all areas.

The Director of SCHS is concerned about the turnover rate at the facility. Turnover at similar facilities averages 20 percent; SCHS experienced a 30 percent turnover rate this past year.

You have been asked by the Director to evaluate six key job descriptions (See Exhibit 4.6) according to the SCHS Job Evaluation Manual (See Exhibit 4.5). Review the SCHS Job Evaluation Manual and record your point ratings in the form provided (See Exhibit 4.7). When the group has finished, your instructor will give current mid-point salaries for each job. Construct a wage curve using this information and points assigned (See Exhibit 4.8). Evaluate the consistency of information with respect to the point evaluations.

EXHIBIT 4.5   *Smithfield County Health Service Job Evaluation Manual*

Smithfield County Health Service (SCHS) utilizes the point factor method to evaluate jobs.

FACTOR ONE—JOB COMPLEXITY (JC). This factor measures the judgment, creativeness, and resourcefulness required to perform the work assigned to a position and the amount of discretion to carry out the assigned tasks. The factor is measured in terms of two subfactors:

> **Subfactor A: Problem Solving.** The degree to which a position is required to use judgment, decision making, research, and creativity to carry out work assignments.

(continued)

EXHIBIT 4.5 *continued*

Degree One: Position applies physical dexterity in carrying out its work assignments. There is little or no discretion or judgment. The work assignments are repetitive and routine.

Degree Two: Position applies judgment to follow work methods and procedures and/or to interpret work policies and/or analyses in carrying out its work assignments. Work assignments are more complex but repetitive and interrelated.

Degree Three: Position applies judgment and/or research analysis to determine work approaches and to recommend courses of action where no precedent exists. Work assignments are varied and usually encompass a single discipline.

Degree Four: Position applies judgment to create, formulate, and evaluate operating policies, objectives, and systems in analyzing and carrying out broad organizational activities.

Subfactor B: Latitude. The degree of supervision or guidance received by a position or the amount of freedom given the position to perform its work assignments.

Degree One: Position receives regular supervision and work directions. No latitude given to alter work methods.

Degree Two: Position receives regular supervision and work directions. Position has considerable latitude to select work methods.

Degree Three: Position receives broad work supervision and direction. Position has complete latitude to accomplish work goals and objectives.

Degree Four: Position receives presidential work supervision and direction. Position has complete latitude to accomplish and/or develop strategic goals and objectives for a major segment of SCHS.

FACTOR TWO—ORGANIZATIONAL IMPACT (OI). This factor measures the position's influence and contribution to SCHS. It is measured in terms of two subfactors:

Subfactor A: Internal Impact. Measures the scope and breadth of work responsibility and accountability assigned to a position.

Degree One: Position is accountable for carrying out assigned work tasks that have limited impact on SCHS.

Degree Two: Position is accountable for carrying out assigned job duties that have an indirect impact on SCHS. The work assigned to the position supports other positions that have an impact on the accomplishment of organizational goals and objectives.

Degree Three: Position is accountable for an assigned work department or operations headquarters of SCHS. Position's work results have a significant impact on the accomplishment of broad organizational goals and objectives of SCHS.

(continued)

EXHIBIT 4.5   *continued*

Degree Four: Position is accountable for the accomplishment of corporate goals and objectives across a number of work departments and operations headquarters within SCHS.

Subfactor B: External Impact. Measures the scope and breadth of work responsibility and accountability assigned to a position for programs, policies, services, and operating systems that directly impact SCHS activities outside of the local environment.

Degree One: Position has no direct impact on the accomplishment of SCHS activities outside of the local environment.

Degree Two: Position has limited direct impact on the accomplishment of SCHS activities outside of the local environment. The external impact is limited to giving support to other positions that directly serve SCHS affiliates outside of the local sector.

Degree Three: Position has a contributory impact on the accomplishment of SCHS activities outside of the local environment.

Degree Four: Position has direct impact on the accomplishment of SCHS activities outside of the local environment. The position works directly with SCHS affiliates to design, develop, and execute various programs, services, and operating systems within their organization.

FACTOR THREE—SUPERVISORY RESPONSIBILITY (SR). Factor measures the human resource responsibilities delegated to a position over other positions. Factor is measured in terms of two subfactors:

Subfactor A: Type of Supervision. There are two basic types of supervision: Functional supervision is delegated to a position if it has responsibility determining work assignments, priorities, and methods used by other positions. It does not have responsibilities for determining work performance reviews. Administrative supervision is delegated to a position if it has responsibilities for recommending and/or approving all personnel actions that affect other positions.

Degree One: Position exercises no supervisory responsibilities over other positions.

Degree Two: Position exercises work guidance or lead direction over other positions but no functional supervision.

Degree Three: Position exercises functional supervision.

Degree Four: Position exercises functional supervision and is delegated responsibilities for most personnel actions except for work performance reviews.

Degree Five: Position exercises administrative supervision over other positions.

Subfactor B: Employees Supervised. Measures the total number of full-time employees supervised by a position.

Degree One: Position is responsible for no employees.

(continued)

EXHIBIT 4.5   *continued*
___

Degree Two: Position is responsible for between one and three employees.

Degree Three: Position is responsible for between four and ten employees.

Degree Four: Position is responsible for between 11 and 20 employees.

Degree Five: Position is responsible for more than 21 employees.

FACTOR FOUR—WORK REQUIREMENTS (WR).   Factor measures the minimum work qualifications required to satisfactorily perform the duties and responsibilities delegated to a position, whether gained through formal education or on-the-job experience. Two subfactors:

Subfactor A: Knowledge. Measures the minimum level of knowledge gained through formal education or equivalent work experience.

Degree One: Position requires a basic knowledge of reading and writing to perform the assigned work.

Degree Two: Position requires technical or special knowledge to perform the assigned work.

Degree Three: Position requires advanced knowledge of a technical skill or discipline to perform the assigned work.

Degree Four: Position requires expert knowledge of a technical skill or discipline to perform the assigned work.

Subfactor B: Experience. Measures the minimum amount of work experience, beyond the level of knowledge, required to perform the duties and responsibilities assigned to a position.

Degree One: Position requires a minimum of fewer than six months of prior related work experience.

Degree Two: Position requires a minimum of six months to one year of prior related work experience.

Degree Three: Position requires a minimum of one to two years of prior related work experience.

Degree Four: Position requires a minimum of two to four years of prior related work experience.

FACTOR ONE—JOB COMPLEXITY

A. Problem Solving	B.	Latitude		
Degree	1	2	3	4
1	20	35	50	70
2	61	75	95	115
3	102	117	135	156
4	143	160	180	201

(continued)

EXHIBIT 4.5   *continued*

FACTOR TWO—ORGANIZATIONAL IMPACT

A. Internal Impact	B.	External Impact		
Degree	1	2	3	4
1	10	25	40	55
2	25	40	55	70
3	42	57	72	87
4	59	74	89	104

FACTOR THREE—SUPERVISORY RESPONSIBILITY

A. Kind of Supervision	B.	Employees Supervised			
Degree	1	2	3	4	5
1	0	22	44	66	88
2	25	47	69	91	113
3	50	72	94	116	138
4	75	97	119	141	163
5	100	122	144	166	188

FACTOR FOUR—WORK REQUIREMENTS

A. Knowledge	B.	Experience		
Degree	1	2	3	4
1	10	25	40	55
2	25	40	55	70
3	42	57	72	87
4	59	74	89	104

EXHIBIT 4.6   *Job Descriptions*

Position Title: Assistant Director, Public Relations
Department: Public Relations
Title of Immediate Supervisor: Director, Public Relations

POSITION SUMMARY:

Implement communications projects and programs to gain and maintain public understanding and support for Smithfield County Health Services (SCHS).

JOB FUNCTIONS:

I. **External Communications**
    A. Write, edit, and produce printed materials directed to Smithfield County Health Services as identified by organizational marketing objectives making full use of desktop publishing.

(continued)

EXHIBIT 4.6   *continued*

 B. Produce audiovisual presentations/programs for SCHS.
II. **Internal Communications**
 A. Provide consultation and the appropriate communication vehicles to keep volunteers and paid staff informed about and involved in organizational objectives.
 B. Publish newsletter and other internal communications.
III. **Media Relations**
 A. Work with the media through news articles, radio and TV news, public service announcements, and editorials to reach SCHS external publics with strong and positive messages about programs and services. Activities involve telephone calls, personal visits, contact through professional organizations, dissemination of news releases, answering media inquiries, news conferences, interviews with staff and/or volunteers as appropriate.

JOB REQUIREMENTS:

Broad background in public relations, including strong oral and written communication skills, and publication design experience, including desktop publishing. Plan and implement projects and programs using organizational skills, creativity, and resourcefulness. Requires media or media relations experience. Three to five years experience required.

SUPERVISION OF OTHERS:

Supervises five staff members and approximately 20 volunteers.

Position Title: Administrative Assistant
Department: Purchasing
Title of Immediate Supervisor: Purchasing Agent

POSITION SUMMARY:

The purpose of this position is to provide clerical support within the purchasing department.

JOB FUNCTIONS:

 I. **Purchasing Duties**
 A. Verify receipts as proof that the product(s) were received against the original invoice insuring prompt and accurate payment.
 B. Complete disbursement voucher and/or purchase order for payment of services rendered to the appropriate vendor.
 C. Update and maintain files (maintenance, technical supplies, equipment, etc.) as needed.
 D. Type letters, memorandums, and reports as needed.
 E. Assist with in-house duplicating as needed.

(continued)

EXHIBIT 4.6   *continued*

F.   Responsible for telephone coverage in the department.
G.   Responsible for typing approved major/minor equipment packets during the budget process.
H.   Assist stock room personnel with quarterly inventories.

JOB REQUIREMENTS:

This position requires a high school diploma and typing speed of 60-80 words per minute. Good math background and related work experience is helpful.

SUPERVISION OF OTHERS:

None

Position Title: Systems Analyst
Department: Management Information Systems (MIS)
Title of Immediate Supervisor: Senior Systems Analyst

POSITION SUMMARY:

The purpose of this position is to assist in the design and development of various systems programs.

JOB FUNCTIONS:

I.   **Program Design**
   A.   Defines functional capabilities required to meet the determined needs.
   B.   Designs computer applications working with system specifications.
II.   **Program Testing and Documentation**
   A.   Generates test data, as necessary.
   B.   Runs program tests to ensure correctness.
   C.   Meets standards for documentation.
   D.   Assists with the user documentation of programs/systems.
III.   **Program Resolution**
   A.   Assists other MIS staff with problems.
   B.   Assists other departments with daily MIS operational problems.
   C.   Must be able to work independently with little or no supervision.
IV.   **Security**
   A.   Access to system hardware as an authorized MIS staff.
   B.   Access to data is restricted to "test" data only.
   C.   Access to "live" data is kept to a minimum as an authorized MIS staff.
   D.   Authorized to assist with maintenance of system/user security.

JOB REQUIREMENTS:

Degree in computer science plus 5 years experience programming; or minimum of 8 years programming.

(continued)

EXHIBIT 4.6   *continued*

SUPERVISION OF OTHERS:

Does not directly supervise others but is authorized to support the supervision function as necessary.

Position Title: Production Technician I
Department: Screening Services
Title of Immediate Supervisor: Operations Supervisor

POSITION SUMMARY:

The purpose of this position is to prepare and maintain specimens and records of analysis.

JOB FUNCTIONS:

I. Specimen Analysis
   A. Prepare all specimens for analysis.
   B. Maintain thorough and accurate records (manual and computerized).
   C. Participate in the maintenance and quality control procedures for department equipment.
   D. Label products.
   E. Prepare frozen specimens for storage and shipment.

II. Other Laboratory Functions
   A. Participate in special products and studies.
   B. Attend continuing education seminars.

JOB REQUIREMENTS:

This position has a minimum requirement of a high school diploma. Must be able to stand for long periods of time; must be able to lift and carry up to 30-pound loads. Must be able to learn skills required for computer data entry. Must be able to work on weekends on a rotating basis. Must apply professional ethics and maintain confidentiality about information gained from access to test results.

SUPERVISION OF OTHERS:

Not required

Position Title: Staff Nurse
Department: Specimen Services
Title of Immediate Supervisor: Head Nurse, Specimen Services

(continued)

EXHIBIT 4.6   *continued*

POSITION SUMMARY:

The purpose of this position is to assist with all aspects of specimen collection operations.

JOB FUNCTIONS:

I.   Specimen Collection Duties
  A.   Collect specimens according to standard operating procedures.
  B.   Delegate and assure proper orientation of volunteers.
  C.   Consult appropriate supervisor when deemed necessary.
II.   Administrative Duties
  A.   Perform administrative functions to assure Specimen Collection Operation is in accordance with written policies.
  B.   Complete assignments and fulfill responsibilities in a timely manner.
  C.   Prepare daily operation reports and quality control records.
  D.   Accept and adapt willingly to changes in procedures.
  E.   Exhibit courteous, tactful, and sensitive communication skills.
III.   Other Duties
  A.   Share in driving staff car and refueling as needed.
  B.   Attend CPR class annually.
  C.   Attend First Aid class every three years.
  D.   Attend all staff meetings.
  E.   Demonstrate knowledge of and compliance with nursing regulations, i.e., dress code, punctuality, etc.

JOB REQUIREMENTS:

Graduate of an accredited School of Nursing. Bachelor of Science in Nursing preferred. Current license to practice nursing in state. Continuous telephone service and a valid driver's license required. Must support and promote philosophies and policies of SCHS. Full knowledge of pertinent skills and demonstrated technical proficiency. Must be flexible and accept irregular hours, including last minute changes in work schedule.

SUPERVISION OF OTHERS:

None

Position Title: Coordinator, Emergency Services
Department: Emergency Services
Title of Immediate Supervisor: Director of Emergency Services

POSITION SUMMARY:

The purpose of this position is to provide administrative leadership to Emergency Services.

(continued)

EXHIBIT 4.6   *continued*

JOB FUNCTIONS:

I. **Administrative Duties**
   A. Identify and provide supervisory training and developmental needs to paid and volunteer staff.
   B. Maintain up-to-date job descriptions for staff and volunteer positions.
   C. Provide work performance reviews for paid and key volunteer staff.
   D. Provide technical and logistical support to Director of Emergency Services.
   E. Prepare disaster reports according to correct procedure.
   F. Prepare annual reports according to guidelines.

II. **Public Relations Duties**
   A. Participate in community emergency planning.
   B. Develop public information materials.
   C. Maintain relationships with other health service agencies.

III. **Staff Development Duties**
   A. Train staff and volunteers for disaster assignments.
   B. Maintain roster and skills file for paid and volunteer staff.
   C. Maintain adequate coverage by staff and volunteers.

JOB REQUIREMENTS:

Graduation from an accredited college with three to five years experience in an administrative or supervisory capacity. Social welfare background is preferred. Ability to interpret programs to personnel and to the public through effective speaking and writing. Decision-making skills. Knowledge of SCHS policies, procedures, and services. Ability to work with and promote volunteer strengths.

SUPERVISION OF OTHERS:

Supervision of two staff members and approximately 25 volunteers

EXHIBIT 4.7 *Job Evaluation Scoring Sheet*

Job Title	JC	OI	SR	WR	TOTAL

JC = Job Complexity, OI = Organization Impact; SR = Supervisory Responsibility; WR = Work Requirements

EXHIBIT 4.8   *Plotting a Wage Curve*

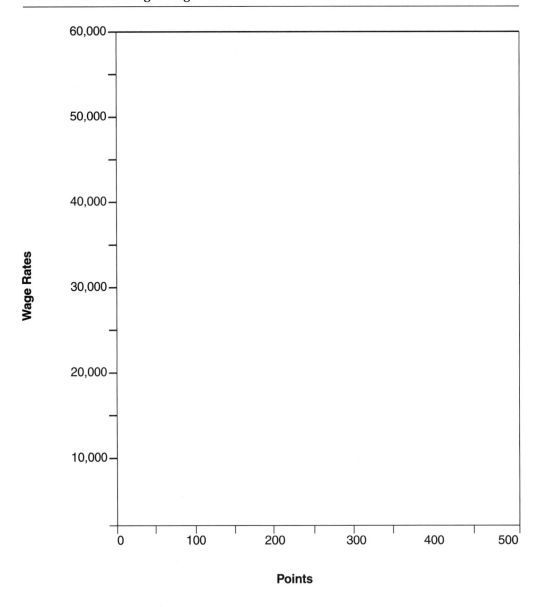

55. EXERCISE

WageSim—A Compensation Administration In-Basket

I. *Objectives:*
   A. To familiarize you with some of the problems involved in building and maintaining a compensation system.
   B. To provide you with alternative approaches for solving some typical compensation-related problems.
   C. To give you practice in writing memos to employees regarding compensation issues.
   D. To familiarize you with job evaluation procedures.

II. *Out-of-Class Preparation Time:* 20 minutes to read exercise plus one hour to complete In-Basket Items either individually or in a group and write memos

III. *In-Class Time Suggested:* 45 minutes to discuss all In-Basket Items

IV. *Procedures:* This exercise can be done individually or in groups of three to five members, at the instructor's option. You are to begin by reading all of the material presented in this exercise. You are to assume that you are responsible for developing and maintaining the Mack Organization's wage and salary system. Assume further that the person who previously had these responsibilities has just quit and left you all of the items which follow in your in-basket. You (or your team) are (is) to respond in writing to each employee who wrote a memo. Secondly, explain on a separate sheet of paper what additional actions you would take with reference to each item. For example, if you believe that you should gather additional information before making a final decision on an item, explain what information you would want. Or, if you believe that additional memos or discussions with someone in the company are needed, explain this. You (or your team) should bring both the memos and the "Additional Action" sheets to class. Be prepared to present and defend these materials during the class discussion.

Situation

The Mack Organization is a large organization whose headquarters is located in the midwestern United States. It has offices located throughout the country and employs over 700 individuals. You may assume the organization is a chemical company, a manufacturing company, a hospital, a university, or virtually any large organization with which you are familiar.

The Mack Organization's Human Resource Department includes a Compensation Administration section that consists of two individuals, one of whom is you (or your team). The company has several different wage structures, including one for executives and one for clerical personnel. For compensation purposes, all clerical employees are divided into five job classifications. The organization's current wage structure for clerical personnel is shown in Exhibit 4.9.

MACK ORGANIZATION
Compensation Policies
(Excerpts from policy manual)

How Salaries Are Determined

Employee salaries directly relate to the work they do and how well they do it. Two major factors work together to establish the salaries payable for various jobs—position evaluation and salary ranges.

Job Evaluation

Job evaluation is a method of measuring the relative worth of each job in the organization compared to all the other jobs, based on an objective analysis of the duties and responsibilities of the position. The concept is not unique to us; determining the relative value of jobs within an organization is an integral part of any salary administration program, regardless of the company.

At the Mack Organization, job evaluation works like this:

First, a description is written for each job. The information for it comes from a questionnaire completed by the person performing the job. The description defines the function of the job and lists the major duties performed. Each description is then evaluated by a standing committee of people from various areas of the organization who have a broad knowledge of the jobs that exist throughout the organization. Their evaluation is based on "yardsticks," including knowledge required, freedom of action, accountability, contacts with employees and customers, physical effort required, unusual working conditions, research responsibilities, and supervision or management responsibilities. Based on these yardsticks, the job is assigned a point value. By listing all positions according to their point value, the relative worth of each position is established.

When a new job is developed, or duties change on an existing one, the job description is submitted to the position evaluation committee. The committee analyzes it, determines the overall point value, and assigns it to its proper place within the ranking structure. The result is an up-to-date listing of all the jobs in the organization from entry level to management. This is the first phase in determining salaries. The second phase is the assignment of jobs to grades and the establishment of salary ranges.

Grade Levels and Salary Ranges

Based on the total points received in job evaluation, jobs are assigned to a grade level. Each grade has an entry or minimum rate and a maximum salary payable for the jobs in that grade: the amounts between the entry rate and maximum comprise the salary range for the grade.

To ensure that the organization's salaries remain at a fair, competitive level, ranges and rates are checked continuously against those paid for similar positions in other organizations. Adjustments to the ranges are made periodically as area market rates change.

Usually employees begin at the bottom of each salary grade. Employees are considered for a merit increase after six months of satisfactory service. After this, they may receive an annual merit increase upon completion of satisfactory service. There are a total of six possible merit increases. Cost-of-living increases are granted periodically by the organization to all employees.

Payday

The Mack Organization's staff is paid on a biweekly basis, every other Friday. There are 26 pay periods each year. For pay purposes a normal week is Friday through Thursday.

Normally a full-time employee is quoted a weekly salary when hired. To compute the annual salary, multiply the weekly salary by 52, or the biweekly salary by 26. Their monthly salary equals their annual salary divided by 12.

All employees are paid by check. Attached to the check is a statement indicating gross pay, deductions required by law, any voluntary deductions, and net pay.

Full-time employees are paid up-to-date on payday—the amount they receive includes what they have earned through that payday. Any overtime or premium earnings are paid on a two-week delayed basis. Part-time employees are paid through the previous Thursday so that their hours may be properly credited.

Employees who have lost their checks or have had them stolen are requested to contact the Personnel Department, which issues a stop payment and prepares a new check.

Pay Advances

In extreme emergencies, it is possible for employees to be paid for those hours already worked during the current pay period. It is also possible for employees to receive a vacation advance before they go on vacation. All advances need the approval of an employee's supervisor. Six hours are needed to prepare checks.

EXHIBIT 4.9   *Mack Organization's Wage Structure for Clerical Personnel*

Job Title	Salary	Number of Employees
Office Services Aide	$14,259 min $22,262 max	40
Office Services Assistant	$15,588 min $24,337 max	30
Secretary	$17,041 min $26,604 max	20
Senior Secretary	$18,628 min $29,083 max	40
Executive Secretary	$20,364 min $31,794 max	20

In-Basket Items

Item 1

MEMORANDUM

TO: Wage & Salary Division
FROM: Mary Wallace—Vice President
SUBJECT: Request for promotion

This is to formally request your endorsement of my intent to promote Susan Anthony, an Office Services Aide in my office, to the position of Office Services Assistant. Ms. Anthony has taken the clerk typist test administered by your office and scored 55 wpm. Though I realize the requirement for Office Services Assistant is 70 wpm, Ms. Anthony possesses the necessary skills to perform all tasks in this office. Ms. Anthony has been with this office for five years and is a loyal and dedicated employee. I wholeheartedly encourage your endorsement of this recommendation. A vacant Office Services Assistant position is available in this office. Please advise as soon as possible.

Item 2

MEMORANDUM

TO: Wage and Salary Section
FROM: Kelly Actor
SUBJECT: Request for pay increase

I have been with this company for ten years. My present position with this company is Senior Secretary, at the maximum pay level.

The Wispette Company has offered me a position which would give me a 9% increase in salary for similar duties.

Since I do enjoy my work, I hate to leave. However, my financial obligations to my family leave me no choice. My husband recently has been disabled, with no hope of employment for three years. As I mentioned, I have enjoyed my ten years with this company. My supervisor and I get along well. I have not missed any work during the ten years except for the two-week vacation during the summer.

If you will match the Wispette Company's offer, I would prefer to stay with your company. I understand there is no opening for an Executive Secretary which would be a comparable position. I need an answer soon.

Item 3

MEMORANDUM

TO: Wage and Salary Section
FROM: Jane Swenk, Supervisor
RE: Long-term employee wage dispute

M. O. Scott, a secretary, expressed concern that her daughter, also a secretary, was making an equal amount of money. M. O. has been employed for twenty-eight years, her daughter for five. Merit raises are given yearly only for the first five years, and M. O. has not gotten one in twenty-three years. I don't think this policy is fair. M. O. should get something for her longer service. Please respond so I can explain the situation to M. O.

Item 4

MEMORANDUM

TO: Compensation Administration
FROM: Personnel Director
RE: Payroll budget for next month

Please prepare a payroll budget for next month for clerical employees. Make whatever assumptions you feel are necessary in doing your calculation. Just let me know what the assumptions are. Many thanks.

Item 5

MEMORANDUM

TO: Wage and Salary Section
FROM: Bob Franklin, Office Services Assistant
RE: Lost paycheck

Please issue me a new paycheck for the last pay period. I can't seem to find mine. I asked my wife if she had it or cashed it, and she doesn't remember. I don't think she did because I think she would have remembered it if she did cash it. My pay is $15,588 per year. Please do it as soon as possible.

Item 6

MEMORANDUM

TO: Compensation Section
FROM: Betty Dyer, Supervisor
SUBJECT: Promotion for Tammy Tuff

Tammy Tuff is an excellent secretary in my office. She does an outstanding job with all assignments and performs beyond standards for a secretary in everything she does. She completes her assignments in half the time of other secretaries and voluntarily assumes extra duties after finishing her assignments.

In addition to her outstanding performance, Ms. Tuff has improved morale in the office since she entered on duty nine months ago. She always has a smile on her face and brightens the day for co-workers with her pleasant disposition. Best of all, she makes others feel important, and this has carried over to their work. Everyone seems to take pride in their work; consequently, performance and productivity are up.

Due to Tammy's influence, the turnover rate is zero, leaving her with no promotion potential in this office. Based on Tammy's excellent performance, skills that exceed the requirements of the job, and attitude that has improved morale, I feel that Tammy deserves a promotion within the office even though there is no Senior Secretary vacancy.

Item 7

MEMORANDUM

TO: Wage & Salary
FROM: Hal Markley, Supervisor
SUBJECT: Early issuance of pay

I am leaving town in two hours and will be gone for four days on emergency business. Since I will be out of town on payday three days hence, it is essential that I receive my check before I leave.

Item 8

MEMORANDUM

TO: W & S
FROM: McNamara, Department Manager

Mary White, an Office Services Aide, left two hours early yesterday, without permission, to attend a civil rights rally. Should she be paid for this time or not?

Item 9

MEMORANDUM

TO: Wage and Salary Section
FROM: Sue L. Ross, Supervisor
SUBJECT: Promotion for Julie Tate

Julie Tate, Senior Secretary, has been temporarily assigned some of the duties of an Executive Secretary position. The position is temporarily vacant due to the Executive Secretary being on vacation.

Julie has been told by me that she may be assigned higher-level duties on occasion, but she is not satisfied. She has threatened to take her complaint to the Human Resources Office, insisting that she deserves financial compensation for absorbing some duties of an Executive Secretary. None of the additional duties is too difficult for Julie to handle, and she actually does an excellent job on all assignments when she stops complaining about her unfair treatment.

I am recommending that Julie be promoted to an Executive Secretary position so that I can assign her higher-level duties whenever my Executive Secretary is on vacation or sick leave. This way Julie would not complain about the grade level of her work, and the flow of work in the office would proceed smoothly without disruption.

Please respond to this recommendation.

Item 10

MEMORANDUM

TO: Wage and Salary Section
FROM: Doris Pope
SUBJECT: Merit pay increase for Frances Brown, Secretary

I would like you to approve an extra eight percent pay increase for my personal secretary, Ms. Frances Brown, to be effective immediately. Ms. Brown has served in this position throughout my eight-year tenure and that of my predecessor, for a total of 25 years. Ms. Brown will be presented with a letter of commendation at a departmental meeting this P.M. It would be helpful if you could complete the paperwork for this salary adjustment by 5:00 P.M. so that I can present it with the commendation.

Thanks,

Doris Pope

Doris Pope
Department Head

---

56. EXERCISE

Safety and Health Programs

  I. *Objectives:*
    A. To familiarize you with contemporary health and safety policies and procedures.
    B. To give you an understanding of the possible gaps that may develop between health and safety policies and procedures and actual practices on-the-job.
 II. *Out-of-Class Preparation Time:*   3 hours
III. *In-Class Time Suggested:*   45 minutes
 IV. *Procedures:*
    A. You or your group of two or three students (at the option of your instructor) select one organization and obtain its policies concerning

health and safety. Examples might include workplace injuries, AIDS, employee assistance programs, and smoking. The information is often contained in the *Employee Handbook.*

B. You or your group then interviews one person in the organization who is knowledgeable about these policies.

C. You or your group then writes up a short report which answers the following questions:

1. What safety and health policies/procedures currently exist? Are any changes in these policies contemplated for the near future? If so, why?
2. What safety and health problems were the policies above designed to eliminate or minimize?
3. To what extent do employees abide by these policies? How do employees feel about these policies? Why?
4. Are these policies enforced and who is responsible for enforcement? If the policies are not enforced, why not?
5. What impact does OSHA (both the act and the agency) have on the organization?
6. What future changes does the organization anticipate in the areas of health and safety?

D. At the option of the instructor, you or your group reports the results of your study either (1) to the class as a whole or (2) to a small group.

E. The reports are then turned in to the instructor.

57. EXERCISE

Ethical Compensation Dilemmas

I. *Objectives:*

A. To make you aware that many compensation decisions involve ethical issues.

B. To familiarize you with four to ten different ethical compensation dilemmas and issues.

C. To enhance your ability to identify ethical issues in case situations.

D. To familiarize you with various criteria that can be used to distinguish between ethical and unethical behavior.

E. To examine the interrelatedness between ethical choices, individual values, and ethical organizational climates.

F. To examine the causes of ethical dilemmas.

II. *Out-of-Class Preparation Time:* 5 minutes to read all or some of the Ethical Compensation Dilemmas below, as assigned by your instructor

III. *In-Class Time Suggested:* 20–75 minutes, depending on how many of the dilemmas below are assigned by your instructor

IV. *Procedures:* At the start of class, you will be divided into groups of three to five and assigned one or more of the following ten dilemmas to analyze. Your group should answer the following three questions and be prepared to present your decisions:

A. Are there any ethical issues presented in the dilemma? If so, what are they?

B. How can the dilemma be resolved most effectively and ethically?

C. How important are the issues presented in the dilemma?

For the purpose of this exercise, use the following definition of compensation ethics:

Compensation ethics are the rules, standards, or principles that provide guidelines for morally correct behavior, and for truthfulness in the remuneration and reward of employees.

In answering the three questions, your group may want to address the questions below. They are designed to help you determine if an issue involves ethical considerations.

A. Does the action involve intentional deception?

B. Does the action purposely benefit one party at the expense of another?

C. Is the action fair and just to all concerned? The Golden Rule not only dictates that we "do unto others as we would have them do unto us" but also commands that we treat others as we might wish to be treated.

D. Would the manager feel comfortable if the action were made public or must it remain a secret?

E. Are managers justifying the action by telling themselves that they can get away with it or that they won't need to live with the decision's consequences?

F. Would the decision maker recommend the action to other managers or firms?

G. Will the action build goodwill and better relationships?

In answering the questions, you also may want to consider three different schools of thought regarding ethical decision making. The *Utilitarian Approach* argues that decision outcomes should result in the greatest good for the greatest number of people. The *Moral Rights Approach* holds that decisions should be consistent with fundamental rights and privileges as set forth in the Bill of Rights or some other document such as the United Nations' Declaration of Human Rights. The

Justice Approach stresses that decisions should be equitable and follow the distributive justice and fairness principle. Some argue that the ideal decision occurs when it is supported by the ethical standards of all three ethical approaches.

After your group has finished its analysis (ten minutes or less), each group will make a short, two- to three-minute, presentation to the class. This will be followed by a discussion (six to ten minutes long) that focuses on each group's answers.

Ethical Compensation Dilemmas

1. Based on an evaluation of the knowledge, skills, and abilities needed to do each job, a company has determined that two jobs (Job A and Job B) are equal. However, when the firm studies the labor market, it finds that applicants for Job A are plentiful whereas those for Job B are very scarce. Should the firm offer less to those who apply for Job A or should the pay be equal?

2. Assume that the supply of electrical technicians is low so a firm hires a group of them at $18 per hour. Two years later, due to a recession, the supply of technicians is high so the market rate for them is now $15 per hour. Should the firm pay new hires $18 or $15? Given that the firm bases pay on supply and demand, should it lower the pay of existing technicians to $15?

3. Jim is given an extremely large raise because of his superb work record one year. As a result he is currently earning $55,000 whereas others at the firm holding the same job are earning $45,000. Everyone expects Jim to continue to excel and enhance the entire unit's productivity. Unfortunately, Jim's performance drops off after the first year and his performance is now just average. What should be done about his pay? Should it be reduced to reflect his current performance or should he continue to earn more than all of the others?

4. One year, Ethan's performance is truly spectacular, just as good as Jim's had been in the previous case. However, the company has no raise money available that year so no one, including Ethan, receives a merit raise. Given that Jim received a large raise for past performance, is this fair to Ethan?

5. Mary and Sue both work in the same department. Mary believes that Sue is being paid considerably more than she is. In fact, both employees are being paid about the same amount. Mary complains to her boss and the compensation manager and wants a pay raise. What should the compensation manager say, assuming the firm follows the policy of not revealing the pay of individual employees? Should Mary be told the amount of Sue's pay? Or, should Mary only be told that there is a "misunderstanding" and that her belief is incorrect? Or, should some other approach be taken?

6. When Mary was hired she was told verbally that she would receive a raise when she finished her college degree and yet another raise when she was given added responsibility. She accepted the job offer based on this understanding. However, during the next two years, the firm experienced slow sales and had to ask all factory employees to accept a 12% pay decrease. But Mary, who does not work in the factory, has finished college, and has accepted more responsibility. Should she receive a raise?

7. Two firms in the chemical solvent industry decide to merge. Employees in the testing department of Firm A have enjoyed high pay for many years. However, Firm A is purchased by Firm B which has a history of paying low wages. As a result, employees in Firm A's testing department earn on average $1.00 more per hour than those at Firm B. Upon completion of the merger, what wage levels should prevail? Should wages be cut for those who worked for Firm A? Or, should wages be increased for those in Firm B?

8. Sue is a 55 year old employee of Company A. Her children are out of college and her parents have both died. Company A offers a child care program to all employees along with an elder care program. However, Sue, like many other employees, has no need for these services, neither now or in the future. Should the firm retain these programs? Should alternative benefits for employees who have no use for such services be offered?

9. Helen works as an accountant for a firm in the textile industry. During non-working hours she does extensive volunteer work for the American Red Cross, Meals on Wheels, and the American Heart Association. Helen's employer wants to maintain a favorable image in the community so it wants every employee to donate money to the United Way. Should the firm pressure Helen to donate money? Keep in mind that if Helen doesn't donate money, other employees may not either which could result in the firm having an unfavorable image in the community. On the other hand, Helen already donates time which has a monetary value and she may feel that it is unfair to be asked to donate even more.

10. Frank works 25 hours per week for a mail order firm in the packaging department. He receives no benefits other than those required by law. Frank does the same work as three other employees all of whom work full time. These employees qualify for pensions, medical care, long-term disability, child care, etc. Is this ethical? Assume that Frank would like to work full-time, really wants to receive benefits, and feels harmed because of his shortfall. On the other hand, the firm is not legally required to pay Frank benefits, Frank only works part time, and it would be expensive to pay benefits to all part-time employees, including Frank.

58. INCIDENT

Merit Increases

Dr. Carl Jones is chairperson of the Department of Management in the College of Business Administration at a large state university in the East. He has been a member of the department for 14 years and a full professor for five years. Last summer he was asked to assume the chair after a screening committee conducted interviews and reviewed resumes for him and three other candidates.

Carl was very excited about the new challenges and has begun several innovative projects to enhance faculty research and consulting. The teaching function in the department has always been first-rate while research has been somewhat weaker. Carl has continued to be very productive as a scholar, publishing three articles, two book chapters, and one proceedings article over the past year. He also made considerable progress on a management text which he was co-authoring. Finally, he remained active in his professional association, the Academy of Management, where he served as chair of one of the professional divisions.

The university's policy is that all salary increases are based only on merit. Carl had developed a very sophisticated performance appraisal system for his faculty to help him quantify salary recommendations. His point system considers and weighs different items in the areas of teaching, research, and service. Teaching and research are given weights of 40 percent each with service at 20 percent. For the coming academic year, his recommended salary increases averaged seven percent and ranged from three to 14 percent. Carl felt he had good documentation for all his recommendations.

Carl submitted his recommendations to Dean Edmund Smith and was pleased when all these recommendations were accepted. He then proceeded to schedule appointments to meet with each faculty member to discuss his recommendation, the reasons for the recommendation, and goals for the coming year. While a few of the faculty receiving lower increases indicated dissatisfaction with his weighting system, particularly the emphasis on research, these meetings generally went well.

Carl then submitted his own annual report detailing his accomplishments as chair as well as his more personal accomplishments. From his perspective, he felt he deserved at least a 10 percent increase since his department had made major strides in a number of areas while the other departments had been standing still. Moreover, none of the other chairs were professionally active on the national level and none had published in the past year. His teaching evaluations were also in the top 15 percent of faculty in the college.

Dean Smith sent out letters to all the department chairs in August. Carl was shocked to learn that his salary increase was just seven percent. Information he received through the "grapevine" was that all the chairs had received the seven percent increase. He also learned from one of the other chairs that the Dean always gave the chairs equal percentage increases each year. Contrary to the official university policy, there were no distinctions based on merit.

Carl was visibly upset about what he considered to be a major inequity. He then called the Dean's secretary to schedule an appointment to discuss the situation with Dean Smith.

Questions

1. Describe the nature and causes of the compensation problem described in this incident.
2. Are "merit" salary increases always based on "merit"? Why or why not?
3. Why has Dean Smith had a policy of equal percentage salary increases for all department chairs despite the stated university policy? Are all the chairs equally meritorious?
4. How do you think Dean Smith's "merit" increases will affect Carl and his performance as department chair and faculty member? Why? What can Dean Smith do to motivate Carl if a large differential pay increase based on performance is out of the question?
5. What are the long-range benefits of a true "merit" program? What are the problems associated with the lack of such a "merit" system for department chairs?

59. INCIDENT

The Medical Leave Problem

Maura Currier has been working for ComputerTech for four years as a Lead Supervisor. During the past two years, Maura's mother has needed frequent medical attention for her diabetes. Being the only child, Maura has helped her mother, Jane, as often as her work schedule would allow. Unfortunately, during the past two years, Jane's condition has worsened.

With the passage of the Family and Medical Leave Act, Maura asked the firm for, and was granted, an unpaid leave to care for her mother in accordance with company policy (see policy in Exhibit 4.10). The agreement stated that Maura could miss work every Friday for 60 weeks rather than take off 12 straight weeks. At the end of 60 weeks, Maura returned to work full-time and immediately began missing work to care for her mother until all of her allotted vacation and sick leave days were exhausted. She then asked that her Friday leave be extended indefinitely, because her mother's condition remained serious and she required on-going assistance.

The firm's Human Resource Director was uncertain what her response should be. The firm needed Maura to be at work regularly because of the increasingly heavy work load, the fact that her job duties were critical, and because other supervisors and employees preferred not to have to cover for her. On the other hand, Maura was an excellent supervisor and had worked four years for ComputerTech. In addition, everyone was concerned about Maura's, and her mother's, welfare and wanted to be supportive of them.

Questions

1. What are the advantages and disadvantages of extending Maura's leave?
2. If you were the Human Resource Director, would you grant Maura's request? Explain your answer.

EXHIBIT 4.10   *Family Medical Leave Policy*

Employees who have worked for at least one year and worked 1,250 hours during the 12-month period preceding the commencement of the leave year are eligible to take up to 12 weeks of unpaid job-protected leave for one or more of the following reasons:

1. Because of the birth of a son or daughter of the the employee and to care for such son or daughter;
2. Because of the placement of a son or daughter with the employee for adoption or foster care;
3. To care for the spouse, son, daughter, or parent of the employee, if such spouse, son, daughter, or parent has a serious health condition; or
4. Because of a serious health condition that makes the employee unable to perform the functions of the position of such employee.

Employees who wish to take advantage of this policy must fill out a Leave Request Form at least 30 days prior to the date they wish the leave to commence or as soon as possible in cases where the reason for the leave (such as sudden illness) was unforeseeable. You will be entitled to return to your same job or an equivalent position as the one you held before, and all normal benefits will be restored. Eligible employees will also be entitled to maintain group health care coverage during the period of leave to the same extent as if they had continued to work during the leave period.

60. INCIDENT

The Educational Leave Problem

Rollermakers Corporation is a midwestern manufacturer of rollers used by most industrial firms to move products and packages from one location to another. For example, the U.S. Postal Service uses rollers to slide packages from one area of the post office to another, thereby minimizing the lifting of heavy parcels. Coal companies use rollers underneath conveyor belts to move coal from the mine to empty coal train cars. Rollers are usually made to customer specifications rather than mass produced. Typically, customers determine the type of rollers needed with the help of design engineers or one of Rollermaker's sales staff.

Rollermaker's staff consists of a production crew, inside sales force, outside sales force, and administrative offices. The administrative offices and the inside sales force work closely together to process quotes, orders, and invoices in the most efficient manner possible. The inside sales force is hired using a placement firm and are trained internally. Administrative staff are usually hired from the same recruiting agency with some exceptions. Purchasing managers and accounting positions are salaried and are filled through advertising and recruiters. The company in the recent past has faced threats of racial discrimination lawsuits from former inside sales employees, and lawyers have contacted the firm on behalf of those who are issuing these threats. No lawsuits have been filed but management has become more careful in all human resource matters.

The present purchasing manager was hired from another competitor a little over a year ago. At that time the manager was also attending an evening M.B.A. program at a local university and, as part of his compensation package, would be allowed tuition reimbursement and time off to attend classes with the understanding that the classes would not cause a major disruption to the daily work schedule. For the past year, this has worked well because classes do not start until 5:45 p.m.

With the new fall semester starting, two inside sales employees informed the inside sales manager of their intentions of returning to college on a part-time basis. Jan, an African-American female, wanted to return to college to finish a degree in accounting. She is a junior now and hopes to finish within the next two years. She is scheduled to take two accounting classes, one on Tuesday and Thursday from 11:00 until 12:20, and the other on Monday, Wednesday, and Friday from 2:00 until 2:50. These are the only times the required classes are offered. The college is located about five minutes from work. Jan has made it known that she will be leaving the company upon graduation. She has been with the company for 18 months and is well liked and competent. She is one of the more efficient and accurate of the inside sales staff.

The second employee, Josephine, is a white female, starting community college after achieving a G.E.D. She would like to take classes that meet from 2:00 until 2:50 and from 3:00 until 3:50 on Monday, Wednesday, and Friday. The community college is located within 20 minutes of work. She also plans to earn a degree or certificate in accounting and has stated that she wishes to stay with the company "for as long as they will have me." She wants to earn more money and was told if she obtained her degree she would be eligible to be promoted to an appropriate position. The current bookkeeper is planning on retiring in three years and Josephine has her eye on this job. Josephine is likewise well liked by most, but not all, of the inside sales force. Her error rate on specifications and pricing of specialty work is higher than most others.

Josephine submitted her classes to the inside sales manager as a request and had not registered or paid for classes. Jan had registered and paid for her classes. The schedules chosen by the employees drastically conflicted with the regular business day. Nonetheless, both employees demanded that their schedules be worked around and accommodated. They contended that the precedent set by the purchasing manager should apply to them. Rollermakers does not currently have any formal policy regarding educational leaves. However, both employees were told when they were first hired that they were expected to be at work during business hours.

Questions

1. Should the firm allow the two inside sales people to miss work in order to attend classes? Should it pay for the tuition? Why?
2. Should the firm continue to allow the purchasing manager to attend the evening M.B.A. program and to pay his tuition?
3. Should there be a formal policy regarding educational leave or should it remain informal? If the firm decides to formalize its policy, what provisions should it contain?

61. INCIDENT

The Lost Vacation Days

Ships, Inc. is a large shipbuilding company located in one of the eastern states. One September afternoon the firm made the decision to shut down operations due to an approaching hurricane. This was based on the forecasted arrival of tropical storm force winds to the local area as early as noon on Wednesday. They made that decision at approximately 2:00 p.m. on a

Tuesday afternoon and some employees were told Tuesday by supervisors that the shutdown would occur beginning with the next morning's shift and that they were not to report to work. They were also told that the time they lost would be excused with pay.

By Tuesday evening it was very clear that the hurricane would not hit the area until Thursday at the earliest. Nonetheless, the shipyard decided to maintain the decision to shut down on Wednesday. The emergency hotline message confirmed this information but also said that missed time for salaried personnel would be charged against each employee's vacation bank.

By Wednesday evening the emergency hotline message was updated to state that the shutdown would be continued through the first shift on Thursday with normal operations commencing on the second shift. The hurricane subsequently hit the area Thursday night (during the second shift), leaving many roads littered with branches and debris.

On Friday morning when all personnel reported for work again (many of them without electricity), they were hit with the fact that they had just lost two days of vacation—two days gone with the wind. Hourly personnel had the option of charging the two days off to their vacation bank or taking time off without pay, but salaried personnel did not have a choice—they were required to charge the leave to their accrued vacation bank. This action was in line with the company's policy for complete shutdowns despite what some personnel were told prior to the shutdown.

Within a few days, many people became very upset with the way the company handled the situation and the fact that they just lost two vacation days for no good reason. Why did the firm close down operations so soon instead of waiting for the storm to hit? Why didn't it close down operations on Thursday, the day the storm actually did arrive? Some had already scheduled vacation for over Thanksgiving and the Christmas holidays and now realized that they had insufficient vacation days left. Those who had already paid for their airline and cruise tickets were particularly upset. Others were offended by the fact that they would now need to work uncompensated overtime to make up for the work missed, an action expected of all salaried employees.

The company's vacation policy states that salaried employees accrue vacation time based on length of service. Employees with less than five years seniority receive one day per month, those with five to ten years experience earn one and one half days per month, and those with more than ten years earn two days per month. Employees have the right to carry over unused vacation time to the next year. The policy also states that if the shipyard is shut down for any reason the time lost by salaried employees will be charged to each person's vacation bank. Furthermore, the policy states that in the event of a partial shutdown, salaried employees who report to work and are then sent home will be paid for any time missed and will not be required to charge lost time to their vacation banks.

Questions

1. What, if anything, should the company do with regard to salaried personnel who have vacations planned later this year and now don't have enough vacation time?
2. What, if anything, should the firm do regarding the lost vacation time for all of the other employees, both salaried and hourly?
3. Should the firm change its current policy that requires salaried employees to charge their vacation bank whenever a shutdown occurs?

62. INCIDENT

The Safety Problem

Belcher Manufacturing Company employs 300 workers in its main plant in the upper-Midwest. One of its major product lines is compressors for air conditioners. All compressors are tested when they come off the assembly line. Two years ago Mr. William Carlson was 28 years old, a high school graduate, and had been employed in the compressor division for five years. His job was to test each compressor using a standard procedure.

Each inspector goes through an extensive training program where proper procedures for testing compressors are explained and demonstrated. In addition, inspectors are required to follow the detailed procedures for testing each unit specified in the company manual. No deviations from those procedures are permitted by company policy.

Two years ago Mr. Carlson was testing a compressor when it exploded. He was killed on the spot. The company expressed sympathy to the family but also indicated that the company had provided proper training, proper clothing, proper warnings, and proper procedures. It reiterated its commitment to employee safety and implied that the cause of the explosion was probably due to improper employee testing procedures which were neither known or approved by the company.

The family hired an attorney on a contingency basis to pursue a lawsuit against the company. Recently, the case was heard in federal district court. During court testimony it was revealed that most of the inspectors, including Mr. Carlson, had developed various "shortcuts" to reduce the time required to test each compressor. Some continued to use the shortcuts even after the accident. The plaintiff's lawyer argued that it was not clear that Mr. Carlson had violated procedures, but if he did, the company had an obligation to know about the deviations and take steps to bring inspectors back to the proper testing procedures. In addition, he argued the company was responsible for providing training, periodically reinforcing proper procedures, and monitoring practices to assure conformity to proper procedures. The jury then retired to consider a verdict and, if the company is found guilty of safety violations, to assess appropriate penalties.

Questions

1. In this particular case, was the company guilty or innocent of safety violations which resulted in the death of Mr. Carlson?
2. Irrespective of the jury's decision in this case, what should the company do now to avoid a similar incident in the future?

63. SKILL BUILDER

Applying the FLSA—Is This Job Exempt?

I. *Objectives:*
  A. To familiarize you with the requirements of the Fair Labor Standards Act.
  B. To show you how to apply the law in determining whether jobs are exempt or nonexempt.
II. *Time Required to Complete:* 30–45 minutes
III. *Instructions:*
  A. Assume that you are working as a job analyst for your state. One part of your job involves determining whether administrative jobs are exempt from the wage and hour provisions of the Fair Labor Standards Act (FLSA).
  B. Read the excerpt from the FLSA provisions pertaining to exempt status for administrative positions (Exhibit 4.11). Your instructor may also require you to review pertinent state laws.
  C. Review the Federal Wage and Hour Exemption Determination Form completed for two different jobs in a state agency (Exhibits 4.12 and 4.13) and determine the exempt status of each job. Prepare a half-page summary of your findings and justification thereof.

EXHIBIT 4.11   *FLSA Wage and Hour Exemptions*
for Administrative Personnel

EXEMPTIONS

Executive, administrative, professional, or outside sales personnel: An exemption from both the minimum wage and overtime pay requirements is provided in section 13(a)(1) of FLSA for any employee employed in a *bona fide* executive, administrative, professional, or outside sales capacity, as these terms are defined and delimited in regulations of the Secretary of Labor. An employee will qualify for exemption if he or she meets *all* of the pertinent tests relating to duties, responsibilities, and salary as stipulated in the applicable section of Regulations, 29 C.R.F. Part 541.

Administrative: In order to be exempt as a bona fide administrative employee, all of the following tests must be met:
   (a) The employee's primary duty must be either:
      (1) Responsible office or nonmanual work directly related to the management policies or general business operations of the employer or the employer's customers; or
      (2) Responsible work that is directly related to academic instruction or training carried on in the administration of a school system or educational establishment; and
   (b) The employee must customarily and regularly exercise discretion and independent judgment, as distinguished from using skills and following procedures, and must have the authority to make important decisions; and
   (c) The employee must:
      (1) Regularly assist a proprietor or *bona fide* executive or administrative employee; or
      (2) Perform work under only general supervision along specialized or technical lines requiring special training, experience or knowledge; or
      (3) Execute under only general supervision special assignments; and
   (d) The employee must not spend more than 20 percent of the time worked in the work week (no more than 40 percent if employed by a retail or service establishment) on work that is not directly and closely related to the administrative duties discussed above; and
   (e) The employee must be paid on a salary or fee basis at a rate of not less than $155 a week (or $130 a week in Puerto Rico, Virgin Islands, or American Samoa), exclusive of board, lodging, or other facilities, or in the case of academic administrative personnel in public or private schools, the salary requirement for exemption must be at least $155 a week or one which is at least equal to the entrance salary for teachers in the employing school system or educational establishment or institution.

Special proviso for administrative employees paid on a salary or fee basis of at least $250 per week: An administrative employee who is paid on a salary or fee basis of at least $250 a week ($200 per week in Puerto Rico, Virgin Islands, or American Samoa), exclusive of board, lodging, or other facilities will be exempt if:
   (a) The employee's primary duty consists of either:
      (1) Responsible office or nonmanual work directly related to the management policies or general business operations of the employer or the employer's customers; or

(continued)

EXHIBIT 4.11   *continued*

---

    (2) Responsible work that is directly related to academic instruction or training carried on in the administration of a school system or educational establishment; and

  (b) Such primary duty includes work requiring the exercise of discretion and independent judgment.

Source: U.S. Department of Labor, Employment Standards Administration, Wage & Hour Division, WH Publication 1281.

EXHIBIT 4.12   *Federal Wage and Hour Exemption Determination Form A*

Inventory Control Officer	*2054*	*9/5/9x*
Position Title (Classification)	Position Number	Date

Purchasing	*Mary Lincoln, Director*
Department or Office	Department or Office Head

Harry Phipps	*(60) $45,070*	*Todd Jenkins, Asst. Director*
Incumbent	Grade/Salary	Immediate Supervisor

JOB SUMMARY

State in general terms the overall purpose and/or function of the position: The responsibilities of the inventory control officer can be divided into three categories:

(1) Taking the Annual Physical Inventory, (2) Tagging new equipment as it arrives, and (3) Direct responsibility for surplus property.

MAJOR DUTIES AND RESPONSIBILITIES

Summarize the major duties and responsibilities of the position and indicate the approximate percentage of time required for each:

1. Schedule inventories in advance.
2. Supervise the actual inventory-in-progress to insure that every precaution is taken to produce accurate inventory records.
3. Locate any items not accounted for.
4. Maintain accurate records for fixed assets.
5. Train inventory staff in the proper procedures for conducting the inventory.
6. Tag all new fixed assets.
7. Arrange for the disposal of surplus property.

(Percentage of time for responsibilities: physical inventory 70%; tagging new equipment 20%; and surplus property 10%.)

(continued)

EXHIBIT 4.12   *continued*

Answer the following questions regarding the position:

1. *Number of people directly supervised:*

    Full-Time Supervision
    _____ Administrative
    _____ Clerical
    _____ Service

    Part-Time Supervision
    _____ Administrative
    __6__ Clerical
    _____ Service

2. *Describe the responsibility for hiring, firing, promoting, etc. of subordinates:*
    None; handled by Director of Purchasing.

3. *Describe supervision and guidance received:*
    Most of the instructions for the job come from guidelines established by the State Fixed Assets System and the State Auditors.

4. *What special training, experience, or knowledge is necessary to perform the duties of the job?*
    No special training required or education. Must be knowledgeable of Fixed Assets System.

5. *Describe the use of discretion and independent judgment:*
    Some. Most procedures are routine, however.

6. *Describe any original and creative work you may do requiring invention, imagination, or special creative talents (if applicable). What percentage of time is spent on creative work and what percentage is spent on routine (non-creative, non-discretionary, or non-analytical) work?*
    Not applicable. Procedures are routine.

The above statements constitute an accurate and complete description of the duties of the position.

_____
Incumbent Signature

_____
Supervisor Signature

EXHIBIT 4.13   *Federal Wage and Hour Exemption Determination Form B*

Director of Administrative Computing	*3159*	*9/5/9x*
Position Title (Classification)	Position Number	Date

Computing Services	*William Bern, Director*
Department or Office	Department or Office Head

Earl Atwood	*(75) $69,150/year*	*Vincent Pollard, Assoc. Director*
Incumbent	Grade/Salary	Immediate Supervisor

JOB SUMMARY

State in general terms the overall purpose and/or function of the position: Direct systems and programming staff support for computer systems for Business Affairs. Includes accounts payable, purchasing, cash receipts, accounts receivable, general ledger, chart of accounts, security and traffic payroll, personnel, statewide reporting system, physical plant, fixed assets, internal auditing, and auxiliary services.

MAJOR DUTIES AND RESPONSIBILITIES

Summarize the major duties and responsibilities of the position and indicate the approximate percentage of time required for each:

1. Recruit and staff available positions at budgeted level.
2. Direct, supervise, and train programmers and analysts.
3. Evaluate staff performance and recommend promotions and other actions.
4. Maintain existing computing systems.
5. Develop new systems and direct development of user training and documentation.
6. Assist in establishing and implementing departmental objectives.
   (50 percent of time is spent on management and supervision of staff and the other 50 percent is spent on developing new systems, maintaining present systems, and departmental planning.)

1. *Number of people directly supervised:*

Full-Time Supervision	Part-Time Supervision
__8__ Administrative	_____ Administrative
__1__ Clerical	_____ Clerical
_____ Service	_____ Service

2. *Describe the responsibility for hiring, firing, promoting, etc. of subordinates:*
   Full responsibility for the 9 employees who report to me.

3. *Describe supervision and guidance received:*
   Overall direction and priorities are provided by the Associate Director and Director of Computing Services.

4. *What special training, experience, or knowledge is necessary to perform the duties of the job?*

(continued)

EXHIBIT 4.13   *continued*

Four-year college degree in Business Administration or Management Information Systems, with courses of study in Business, Computer Science, and Accounting; minimum of four years experience in systems design, programming and project management and/or advanced studies; and five years of experience in computer systems design, programming, and management including supervision of technical and professional employees; proficient in programming languages, especially COBOL.

5. *Describe the use of discretion and independent judgment:*
   The position involves a great deal of discretion and judgment in designing new systems, responding to user needs, and managing personnel in the department.

6. *Describe any original and creative work you may do requiring invention, imagination, or special creative talents (if applicable). What percentage of time is spent on creative work and what percentage is spent on routine (non-creative, non-discretionary, or non-analytical) work?*
   The majority of my work is analytical involving the design of new computer systems to handle various administrative needs at the agency. About 60 percent of my job is non-routine requiring intense mental concentration and problem-solving skills.

The above statements constitute an accurate and complete description of the duties of the position.

Incumbent Signature   Supervisor Signature

64. SKILL BUILDER

Developing a Wage Structure

I. *Objectives:*
   A. To familiarize you with how data obtained when using the point system approach to job evaluation can be used to develop a wage structure.
   B. To give you practice in developing a wage structure.
II. *Time Required to Complete:* 1 hour or less

Contributed by Steve Maurer, Old Dominion University.

III. *Instructions:* Examine all of the pay data below.

Pay Grade	Job Evaluation Points	Top of Grade	Position
1	100–200	$18,000	Office Services Aide
2	201–300	$19,500	Secretary
3	301–400	$23,750	Senior Secretary
4	401–500	$26,900	Executive Secretary

Exhibit 4.14 shows a partially completed pay structure for office staff positions. Your task is to complete the chart for pay grades 2, 3, and 4. Construct pay steps for each of the remaining pay grades based on the following guidelines for "time in service" in each pay grade (*round total to nearest $10*).

Pay Step Data

Entry wage = 65.5% of top for each pay grade
Step 1: After 1 year within the pay grade = 70% of top
Step 2: After 3 years within the pay grade = 75% of top
Step 3: After 5 years within the pay grade = 82% of top
Step 4: After 8 years within the pay grade = 90% of top
Top of grade: After 10 years within the pay grade.

In addition, listed below are the names of employees in each pay grade and their current salaries. Plot each one on Exhibit 4.14. Which of the current salaries fall outside the appropriate pay step? What action should the firm take with regard to the pay of these individuals?

Office Services Aides:
Charles Hamilton—6 years services—paid $15,109
Mary Richardson—10 years service—paid $16,125

Secretaries:
Jerry Smith—2 years service—paid $14,625
Theresa Jones—5 years service—paid $15,800

Senior Secretaries:
Alicia Wadsworth—5 years service—paid $19,475
Connie Johnston—7 years service—paid $20,190
Velda Prescott—1 year service—paid $16,625

Executive Secretaries:
Gloria Lopez—3 years service—paid $20,175
Rosemary Jensen—5 years service—paid $22,060

EXHIBIT 4.14   *Pay Structure for Office Staff Positions B*

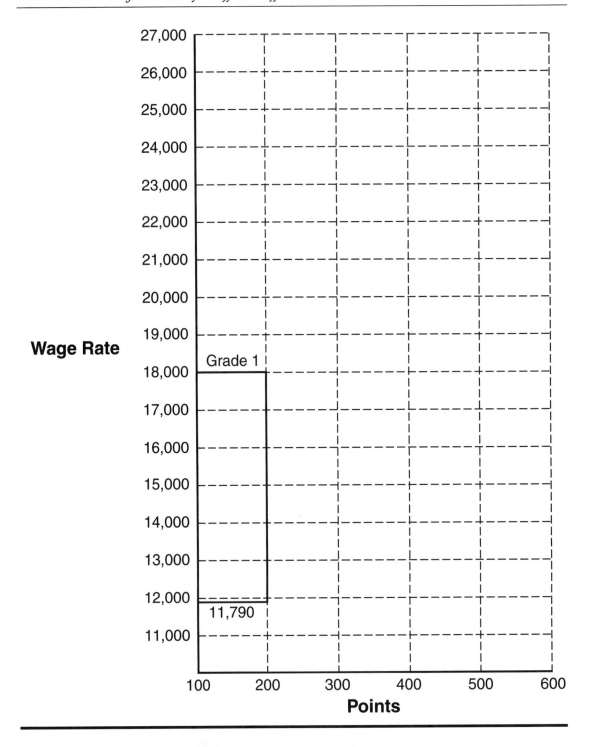

PART 5

ENHANCING EMPLOYEE RELATIONS:
MOTIVATION, EMPLOYEE RIGHTS AND
DISCIPLINE, LABOR RELATIONS, AND
COLLECTIVE BARGAINING

MOTIVATION AND DISCIPLINE

65. CASE

The Broken Employment Contract?

Arthur Wayne walked out of Sara Bell's office shocked. It was hard for him to understand what had just transpired. Bell, Treasurer of EcoCare, a large health insurance company located in Michigan, had just told Wayne of the decision to terminate his employment and had requested his immediate resignation in return for a severance pay arrangement whereby he would continue to receive his salary for six months or until he found other employment. As he looked at the date on his watch calendar, May 7, Wayne realized that he had been hired exactly five years ago by Bell. Bell had told Wayne that EcoCare was not satisfied with his administration of the company car program and that given the number of complaints about the program from other employees, it was in the best interest of the company to ask for his immediate resignation. Wayne, Assistant to the Treasurer, had been in charge of the program for the past year. During a meeting the day before with both Bell and the Vice President of Operations, George Findlay, he had been unable to explain why there were so many complaints about the program. One such complaint had involved the claim that someone had "set back" the odometers on several company cars while the vehicles were under Wayne's control.

After his termination, Wayne requested that the decision to ask for his resignation be reviewed by the company President and the Chairperson of the Board of Trustees of EcoCare. Wayne felt that he had been wrongfully discharged and that he had been under the impression that he had a contract for continued employment as long as his performance was satisfactory. He further maintained that his supervisor had not properly followed the termination policies and procedures of EcoCare.

In preparation for the review, the President asked the Director of Human Resources, Chris Miller, to investigate the facts of the situation and the events leading up to Wayne's termination.

Human Resource Department's Investigation

In order to prepare its report for the President, the Human Resource Department decided not only to review Wayne's personnel file but also to interview Wayne, Bell, and others involved in the case. Two weeks later, Miller prepared the following summary of what had been learned.

After seven years with a local bank in Michigan, Arthur Wayne sought the assistance of an employment agency to obtain a job that would give him more opportunities for advancement. Wayne had graduated with a degree in business administration and had completed 15 hours toward his M.B.A. degree in Finance. The employment agency referred him to our company. After several preemployment interviews and a psychological test, Wayne was hired as an assistant to the company Treasurer, Sara Bell. His duties primarily consisted of analyzing and preparing certain financial reports under the direction of Bell. Wayne came to us with excellent work experience and admirable references from his previous employers.

According to Wayne, he felt at the time of his employment that he had a "contract" with EcoCare that was partly oral (Bell's statements during the job interview) and partly written. Wayne told us that during his preemployment interview with Bell, he had specifically asked about job security and was told that "as long as he did his job" he could remain with the company until he reached retirement age. He further indicated that he had been told by Bell that if he came to EcoCare he wouldn't have to look for another job because she knew of no one ever being discharged. Wayne also told us that a copy of the "Supervisory Manual" was handed to him during his interview with Bell. He said he specifically recalled reading through the sections of the manual that pertained to discipline and termination procedures at that time (see Appendix for relevant sections). At the end of that interview Bell made Wayne a job offer, which he accepted. The manual is given to all management employees as an aid in supervising persons in their charge and not as a declarative of the contract terms of an employee's hire. Our personnel policy has always been to discharge for "just cause only" pursuant to the procedures described in the manual. These procedures apply to all EcoCare employees who have completed their probationary period.

During his five years as Assistant to the Treasurer, Wayne received above average performance ratings. Last year he was given the responsibility of administering the company car program. In April of this year, other employees began complaining to Bell and Findlay about Wayne's handling of the program. Wayne indicated that he had only a brief conversation with Bell about these complaints before the meeting of May 6.

We also spoke with Bell and Findlay about Wayne's employment and subsequent termination. According to Bell, she did tell Wayne during the interview that he would have a job as long as his performance was satisfactory. Bell told us that she made that statement based on her understanding of our company's policies and did not intend her statement as a promise of a permanent job.

Bell and Findlay report that Wayne was fired because of continued personality conflicts with other employees. They report that he was unable to work with other employees and that this was an important job requirement for anyone managing the company car program. After receiving numerous complaints about Wayne's handling of the program, they finally requested from him various reports and documents concerning the odometer discrepancies. Ultimately, they called a meeting with Wayne in an attempt to resolve the problems. During the May 6 meeting, Wayne was reported to have been defensive and insubordinate and unable to provide any satisfactory answers to their questions. At the conclusion of the meeting, they both felt that it would be in the best interest of the company if Wayne were asked to resign. Bell called Wayne into her office the next day and asked for his resignation.

APPENDIX
EXCERPTS FROM SUPERVISORY MANUAL

Section IV. Disciplinary Procedures

(Note: If the unacceptable behavior is repeated between six months and one year, the last disciplinary action will be applied. If the behavior is repeated after one year, it will be treated as a new occurrence for disciplinary purposes.)

A. All discipline shall be administered in a fair, consistent, and reasonable manner within EcoCare.

B. Whenever the work performance or personal behavior of an employee is below department standards, a series of progressive, corrective steps will be taken. Before any of these steps are undertaken, however, the employee shall be counseled about his or her performance discrepancy, what he or she must do to improve the performance, and the action the supervisor will take if the performance is not corrected.

C. Within our discipline system, discipline will be given only for cause. Furthermore, the disciplinary action should fit the problem it is intended to correct.

D. All disciplinary action should be duly documented and reported by the supervisor on Form 29B. The form also requires the employee's signature.

E. The following series of steps shall be followed in administering discipline within EcoCare:

1. *Oral Warning:* Supervisor should discuss the unacceptable behavior with the employee and document such by completing Section A of Form 29B and obtaining the employee's signature.
2. *Written Warning:* A written warning should be issued if the unacceptable behavior continues. The supervisor completes Section B of Form 29B and gives the employee the blue copy. The Human Resource Department receives the canary copy.
3. *Suspension:* If the employee's behavior continues uncorrected, the employee shall be suspended for a given time without pay. Normally, suspension should not exceed five working days. Supervisors should consult with their immediate supervisor and the Human Resource Department before implementing this action. The supervisor shall

complete Section C of Form 29B and also include the date the employee should return to work.

4. *Discharge:* If the employee's behavior is not corrected, the employee shall be terminated. Due to the serious nature of termination, it is recommended that the supervisor review the case with both his or her immediate supervisor and the Human Resource Department before discharging the employee. Examples of reasons for termination without prior corrective discipline are covered in Section V. Note, however, that in such cases the employee should first be suspended according to the following procedures:

Suspension Pending Discharge: (This paragraph applies to all proposed discharges except those which are a result of application of the normal disciplinary procedures.)

   a. When an employee's misconduct warrants immediate discharge under Section V, the employee should be first suspended without pay.

   b. At the time of suspension, the employee should be informed by the supervisor to leave the premises and that he or she will be notified if and when he or she is to return to work.

   c. The supervisor should document the suspension by completing an Employee Discipline Report. The supervisor should consult with the Human Resource Department to determine the appropriate course of action.

Section V. Termination
(Reasons for Immediate Termination):

1. Misconduct, such as fighting, gambling, or use of profane or abusive language toward others.
2. Furnishing proprietary company information to unauthorized agents or persons.
3. Refusal to obey direct orders from the immediate supervisor (insubordination).
4. Willful damage of company property.
5. Failure to notify supervisor or manager during three successive working days of absence.
6. Engaging in a business likely to conflict with the business of the company without prior permission.
7. Dishonesty, falsification of employee's own or other employee's time cards, company records, employment application, etc.
8. Illegal use or possession of alcohol, drugs, etc.
9. Reporting to work or engaging in company business under the influence of alcohol or drugs.

Questions

1. Did Wayne have an employment contract, either oral or written, with EcoCare? Why or why not?
2. What problems, if any, do you see with EcoCare's preemployment process?
3. Can an employer's written human resource policies ever be construed as a contract between an employer and an employee?
4. Was Wayne terminated for "just cause"? Why or why not?
5. How can companies protect themselves against a claim of "wrongful discharge"?

66. CASE

The Crack in the Wall

Standard Chemical Company's Camden Division processes volatile, toxic chemicals that are sold for commercial use. The division consists of 500 employees. Approximately half are in the bargaining unit of the Machinists and Aerospace Workers Union at the Division. Safety is a critical issue at the plant because of the potential for environmental hazards resulting from accidents.

Vicky Jacobson, Human Resource Manager, had attended a seminar on drug abuse in the work force and was concerned that some of the job-related accidents in the Camden Division might be drug related. As a result of Ms. Jacobson's concerns and the concerns of management at the other plants, the company decided to implement a Drug and Alcohol Program.

Notification was sent to the president of the local union. When Ms. Jacobson met with union representatives at the plant she found little opposition to the policy. However, there was concern about how the policy would be enforced. Bob James, union representative, was concerned that the policy would be used by supervisors as a witch hunt to get rid of people they do not like. Ms. Jacobson assured him that there would be checks and balances so that the program would be administered even-handedly. She further assured the union that the emphasis would be on rehabilitation, not termination.

Notification of the Program

The program was presented to employees during a series of group meetings. Ms. Jacobson read a prepared statement at each meeting to be certain that the policy was presented uniformly to all employees:

> Standard Chemical is implementing a company-wide Alcohol and Drug Abuse Program effective January 1, 1989. We do not believe we have a serious problem with drug or alcohol abuse at Standard. However, we are committed to maintaining high standards of job performance and to protecting the safety of our employees, our community, and our environment. Therefore, we have implemented a policy that will reduce significantly the possibility that our employees or our environment might be harmed through alcohol or drug use of any individual employed at Standard Chemical. Please familiarize yourself with the policy as described to you in the brochure.

Brochures were distributed to each employee at the group meetings (see Exhibit 5.1 for a description of the brochure's contents).

Contributed by Susan Corriher, The University of North Carolina, Charlotte.

Suspension Under the Program

During the time in which the policy has been in effect, Ms. Jacobson has, in practice, enforced the policy by suspending employees when there was reasonable suspicion of drug use. Suspended employees were then given three options regarding drug testing:

1. Refusing to undergo drug testing which resulted in immediate termination.
2. Taking the drug test. If the drug test was negative, back pay was awarded for the time on suspension. If the drug test was positive, the employee was given the opportunity to participate in the Employee Assistance Program (EAP).
3. Enrolling directly in the EAP's drug and alcohol program in lieu of submitting to a drug test.

On March 7, Ms. Jacobson was in her office when John Martin, the company's security guard, asked to speak to her. "Ms. Jacobson, I thought I better report this to you. The forklift driver on the last shift must have been out of it when he parked that machine. The blade was driven through the crack between the concrete floor and the outer steel wall. The next shift driver is out there and he's having a heck of a time getting it out." The guard also told Ms. Jacobson that other employees had commented, "It was probably that 'pothead' Peter Carpenter."

When Ms. Jacobson and the guard walked over to the forklift she noticed that the lower portion of the steel wall had buckled. During that day she talked to several employees who had information about the accident. She discovered that Peter Carpenter was the driver of the forklift and that he had been seen driving the lift too fast around the corner at the end of his shift. Mr. Carpenter had worked for Standard Chemical for five and a half years.

Ms. Jacobson met with Mr. Carpenter, his supervisors, and union representatives and questioned him about the forklift accident. According to Ms. Jacobson, the following conversations took place.

"Look, Ms. Jacobson, I admit that I parked that forklift there, but I had no idea I had parked so close to the wall."

Ms. Jacobson responded, "Mr. Carpenter, I have worked in this plant for 23 years and have seen my share of accidents. The blade of the forklift was wedged in the crack between the wall and the floor with enough force to buckle the steel wall. In my opinion this accident is evidence enough for reasonable suspicion of drug or alcohol abuse."

After talking to Mr. Carpenter's supervisors and conferring with the plant manager, Ms. Jacobson met again with Mr. Carpenter and told him, "Mr. Carpenter, you are suspended effective immediately, based on reasonable suspicion of drug or alcohol use on the job. Company policy requires that you submit to a drug test or be terminated, effective immediately. If your drug test is negative, you will be paid for the time of your suspension. If it is positive, then you must enroll in the Employee Assistance Program and demonstrate a sincere commitment to the treatment program. You do have the option of enrolling directly into the EAP's alcohol and drug program. If you choose that option, you can forego the drug test at this time."

"Ms. Jacobson, I'd like to go ahead and get some help. I'll go on and get started with the EAP," replied Carpenter.

In Ms. Jacobson's presence, he then signed the company's EAP consent form which included the following statement:

> If I fail to meet my obligation to the EAP program, I will be subject to disciplinary action, including termination of employment.

After he signed the form, Ms. Jacobson telephoned the EAP (conducted by the local Alcoholism Council). Mr. Carpenter was given an appointment the next evening, March 8.

Mr. Carpenter kept his scheduled appointment. During that first meeting with the counselor he signed a Release of Information form authorizing the EAP to release information about his participation in the program including keeping appointments, following EAP suggestions, and reporting to the designated lab for drug testing. He refused to give the EAP counselor permission to release the results of his drug tests to Standard Chemical.

Report from the Counselor

Mr. Johnson, the EAP counselor, telephoned Ms. Jacobson to confirm that Mr. Carpenter had kept his appointment and explained that he had not given permission for the EAP to disclose results of the drug testing. Mr. Johnson also recommended that Mr. Carpenter be allowed to return to work while attending counseling sessions on an outpatient basis.

On March 13, Ms. Jacobson sent Mr. Carpenter a letter stating that his discharge was "held in abeyance" while he received counseling sessions. The letter further stated that Mr. Carpenter must attend counseling sessions and follow the guidelines of the program and submit to urine testing if instructed to do so by his EAP counselor. The letter also included the following statement:

> Any incident in the future which would indicate failure to comply with the EAP program would result in disciplinary action up to and including termination of employment.

Mr. Carpenter attended EAP sessions regularly for the next eight weeks. Reports to Ms. Jacobson from his supervisors during that time period were extremely positive. His job performance was excellent and he had no safety violations.

On May 9, Mr. Johnson, the EAP counselor, called Ms. Green, the plant nurse, to discuss several EAP-related matters. They specifically discussed Mr. Carpenter's case because of his concerns about Carpenter. He noted that, while Mr. Carpenter had attended every session and his supervisors reported that he had been an exemplary employee, his lab tests showed ascending levels of cannabinoids (marijuana metabolites). Johnson intimated that he was not sure that the EAP counseling sessions would be successful.

Ms. Green called Ms. Jacobson and reported that Mr. Carpenter's lab reports were positive. Ms. Jacobson telephoned Johnson and confirmed what had been said to the plant nurse. She also telephoned the company's medical department and was told that cannabinoids normally stay in a person's system for 35-45 days.

Later that same day, Ms. Jacobson met with Mr. Carpenter and the Union representatives and confronted him with the information she had received about his drug tests. Carpenter argued with Ms. Jacobson and said that he did not understand why she was questioning him. He told her that he had attended every counseling session and felt like the sessions were helping him. Carpenter told her that his performance and his safety record had been great since he started the program. Carpenter further told her that he knew that his supervisors had reported his excellent work record to her. He also told her that he had stopped smoking marijuana. Ms. Jacobson then asked him to submit to a urine sample test. She told him that if he refused he would be terminated in compliance with company policy. Carpenter agreed to take the drug tests.*

On May 17, the lab reported that the results of both drug tests were positive. Later that same day Ms. Jacobson met with Mr. Carpenter and informed him that he was fired. Mr. Carpenter immediately filed a grievance.

On May 26, the union recommended that Mr. Carpenter take another drug test. Standard Chemical agreed to take into consideration the results. Later that same day Mr. Carpenter took the drug test.

On May 30, Standard Chemical received the lab report that was negative for cannabinoids.

On June 21 and July 12 Mr. Carpenter's drug tests were again negative for cannabinoids. Ten months later Mr. Carpenter took another drug test that was also negative.

Questions

1. Was Carpenter's suspension justified?
2. Was Carpenter's termination justified?
3. Evaluate the adequacy of the company's drug and alcohol abuse policy. Are there any components that need improvement?
4. Were Carpenter's privacy rights protected?

*The company uses two tests: the enzyme multiplied immunoassay technique (EMIT) and gas chromatography/mass spectrometry.

EXHIBIT 5.1   *Excerpt from the Brochure Given to Employees During the Group Meetings*

STANDARD CHEMICAL ALCOHOL AND DRUG ABUSE POLICY

1. Use or abuse of any substance that may have an adverse effect on job performance or safety is a violation of Company policy.
2. Reporting to work or working while under the influence of alcohol or unauthorized drugs is a violation of Company policy.
3. Unauthorized drugs are any drugs that cannot be obtained legally or have been illegally obtained. Prescription drugs obtained without a prescription, or over-the-counter drugs used other than as instructed, are considered to be unauthorized drugs.
4. Drug testing is required as a condition of employment when there is reasonable suspicion of drug or alcohol use.
5. Reasonable suspicion is a basis for drug testing when, in the opinion of management, a job-related accident may have been caused by human error that may be drug or alcohol related.
6. Employees who test positive may, if circumstances warrant, be permitted to continue employment provided they agree to undergo periodic drug/alcohol screening and participate in the Company approved Employee Assistance Program (EAP).

67. CASE

Violence at Work: Westside Health Systems

Maryanne Walker arrived at work relaxed and refreshed from her two-week vacation in Florida. Maryanne was Director of Pharmacy Services at Westside Health Systems, and the first item on her calendar was a regularly scheduled total quality management meeting with the four supervisors who directly report to her. During the meeting, routine business matters and normal progress reports on projects were covered. However, Maryanne was very disturbed by what occurred at the close of the meeting. Rhonda Carter reported that one pharmacy technician, Susan Miller, had allegedly assaulted another, Brenda Lawson, in the receiving area of the main hospital pharmacy. Neither of the technicians reported the incident, there were no witnesses, and Rhonda learned of the altercation from another employee. Maryanne stressed her desire to be kept informed on all matters and her complete confidence in an open communication system on which total quality management was based. Maryanne asked Rhonda why she did not view the event as important enough to contact her during her vacation. Rhonda reported that the episode did not occur during her vacation but six weeks earlier. Maryanne was perplexed to find that something happened six weeks ago, and it was just being brought to her attention.

Maryanne had dealt with problems of job performance but had never faced personnel problems unrelated to performance. It never occurred to her that physical fighting would be a problem in a pharmacy whose workforce was predominately women. Upon returning to the office, Maryanne received the following memo from her supervisor, Nancy Smith:

"While you were away, I was made aware that Susan Miller grabbed Brenda Lawson by the shoulders, shoved her against a partition, and perhaps drew her fist back as if to hit her. I suggest that you do further research into this matter. Dependent upon the outcome of the investigation, the appropriate responses could range from ignoring the incident as hearsay or as gossip to termination. This is not the way I would wish for your week to start but I really need to talk to you as soon as possible."

As Maryanne's boss had already learned of the incident, some action must be taken.

Background

Westside Health Systems was a private, nonprofit health care system located in Chicago. The system consisted of a 150 bed hospital, an 80 bed nursing

Contributed by I. E. Jernigan and Joyce M. Beggs, University of North Carolina, Charlotte.

home, and five "minor emergency" clinics. Although Westside was non-union, many of the hospital's personnel practices and policies were similar to those found in unionized settings.

Maryanne directed pharmacy services that included the main pharmacy located in the hospital, a pharmacy at the nursing home, and four satellite pharmacies. There were 35 employees in pharmacy services [14 pharmacists (10 full-time and 4 part-time), 18 technicians, 2 secretaries, and 1 records clerk]. In addition to Maryanne, there were four other supervisors in pharmacy services: an operations supervisor, an inventory supervisor, an administrative supervisor, and a supervisor of sterile products and chemotherapy. All of the supervisors, except the operations supervisor, were female.

Both of the employees (Susan and Brenda) involved in the altercation were pharmacy technicians. Eleven of the eighteen pharmacy technicians (60 percent) were women. While licensed pharmacists were required by law to fill prescriptions, pharmacy technicians did most of the routine work. At first, Susan worked as a technician in the main pharmacy where technicians accepted orders from the nursing floors. Pharmacists checked the orders for harmful drug interactions and passed the prescriptions to the technicians to fill. The technicians printed out a label, filled the prescription, and returned the orders to the pharmacist to check for accuracy such as the right drug or the correct dosage. The technicians delivered the medication to the floor nurse or placed the drugs on a cart for delivery. The work was continuous and very fast paced. However, pharmacy technician jobs were seen as very desirable since the starting pay was over $9.00 per hour and did not require extensive education. Due to the unrelenting work pace and stress and perhaps due to the unfulfilling nature of the job, the turnover rate among technicians was 50 percent.

Brenda worked in receiving, and Susan was later transferred to receiving. Rhonda was the inventory supervisor to whom Brenda and Susan directly reported. In receiving, deliveries were accepted, orders were processed after receipt from the manufacturers, shipping documents were checked for accuracy, and drugs were tracked in inventory for expiration dates and placed in storage for inventory. Drugs were delivered in bulk from manufacturers, and technicians repacked them into unit doses. The work pace in receiving was much less hectic than in the main pharmacy.

Maryanne had been the Director of Pharmacy Services for two years, and this was her first management position. She was trained as a clinical pharmacist, and her educational background included an A.A. in Liberal Arts, a B.A. in Sociology, a Bachelor of Pharmacy, and a Pharmacy Doctorate. In addition, Maryanne had been a clinical pharmacist and Associate Director of Pharmacy Services for two years at another hospital and a staff pharmacist for six years. Maryanne earned the reputation throughout Westside as "a good boss." However, none of her pharmacy education or training prepared her to face this dilemma.

The Incident

Following the total quality management meeting, Maryanne initiated an investigation of the incident between Susan and Brenda. Maryanne interviewed the supervisor, Rhonda, and both Susan and Brenda. Maryanne also gathered all the pertinent policies from human resources management such as the policies for Standards of Behavior and for Corrective Action (see Exhibits 5.2 and 5.3). Maryanne kept copious notes and recorded the following interviews.

Interview with Rhonda, Inventory Supervisor

"On October 20, the day of the altercation, Susan and Brenda were working alone in the receiving department of the pharmacy. Brenda was training Susan to operate the packing equipment that repacked bulk drugs into unit doses."

"Susan was 28 years old, had been at Westside for one year, and was somewhat of a 'misfit.' Although her job performance was fine, her attitude caused problems. Susan worked hard to complete her assignments on time and was extremely organized. Although Susan was articulate and her written communication skills were excellent, she seemed to have difficulty dealing with ambiguity. For example, two technicians showed Susan two different ways to do a task. Susan did not seem to understand how the same job could be done two different ways. She voiced her aggravation by calling both the job and the people doing it, 'stupid.' She huffed, puffed, and shoved things around, and she always seemed to be mad. As a result, she was not as careful as she should have been and injured herself twice."

"Susan seemed obsessed with organization. If things were not organized just the way she thought they should be, she became frustrated. There were a few times when she returned to work a few hours after her scheduled shift to work on organizing things such as our filing system, emergency boxes, or narcotic forms. Sometimes she came in on her days off to reorganize the work area. I finally stopped her from coming at unauthorized times. As she caused problems for the other employees, I formally warned her about working unauthorized overtime. One Sunday afternoon, Susan made some changes to the inventory control computer program. She thought that she was making it better, but it took the Management Information Systems Department three days to fix the program."

"Susan was moved to receiving from the main pharmacy. The sterile products and chemotherapy supervisor requested the move because Susan had difficulty handling the fast paced work and the pressure to make no mistakes. Last year, there was an incident when Susan lost her temper, yelled at another employee, threw a pencil across the room, and then ran out of the pharmacy. Later, her supervisor found her curled up in ball, on the couch in the hallway leading to the main entrance of the pharmacy. Susan blamed her actions on the stress of the job and had been diagnosed as suffering from clinical depression. She took both Prozac and Klonopin, and she was in counseling for her depression. Those antidepressant drugs have side effects such as erratic behavior. In fact, some of the other employees were really afraid of Susan because of her severe mood swings."

"Actually, Susan was overqualified for this job. The mental challenges of pharmacy technician underutilized her abilities. No wonder she was frustrated. I recall that Susan was hired during a period of high turnover and turmoil in the pharmacy. Her boyfriend worked here as a computer programmer in Management Information Systems. He talked to me incessantly about Susan and her qualifications. Everyday he asked me if there were any openings. He told me that Susan was a displaced worker who had been reengineered out of her job as an assistant curator at a museum. Susan had a B.A. in Archeology from the University of New Mexico and had done some graduate work. She had also completed the three-month pharmacy technician certification program at the community college. Perhaps we did not do as thorough a background check on Susan as we normally do. Quite frankly, we had not had many college graduates apply for these positions. Because of Susan's education and background, we thought she would have no problems handling the job. Later, there were rumors that reengineering was not the real cause of Susan's job loss at the museum. Some speculated that Susan was asked to leave the museum after a series of threatening confrontations with other employees on a dinosaur dig in Utah."

"Brenda was a pharmacy technician employed at Westside for 18 months and trained on the job. She was a 25-year-old high school graduate. Her previous work experience consisted of clerical jobs such as store sales clerk and cashier, and she was married to an assembly line worker at a manufacturing plant."

"Brenda was a good employee. I would call her a steady and consistent performer and not a problem employee at all. However, Brenda had a habit of frequently checking to ask if her performance was satisfactory. Although I found this habit a little annoying, I shrugged it off as a need for approval. Brenda had a baby who died suddenly a few months ago. The baby had not been sick and died while Brenda held her in her arms. Brenda accepted the death as a sign that she was not destined to be a mother. This seemed to be a fatalistic attitude, and perhaps Brenda did not report the argument with Susan for similar reasons. I heard about the incident through the grapevine from another pharmacy technician who was unsure about exactly what happened. Only after making several inquiries did Brenda tell the story."

Interview with Brenda

"On October 20, I started work at 11:30 a.m. Susan mentioned that she was going to be off the week of Halloween (October 26 to November 2). She taunted me that she switched her work schedule easily with little notice. She knew that I had asked for the Friday after Halloween off six weeks in advance and I was refused. I was upset and said, 'You can do anything, you punch in when you want, you leave when you want, and you make personal phone calls when you want.' I suppose Susan losing that good job at the museum and not being able to find a similar job was difficult. In fact, I know she was seeing a psychiatrist. Susan then said, 'I'm sick and tired of everyone treating me like an alcoholic, like I'm incompetent.' I said, 'Susan, watch your mouth.' Susan pushed me against a partition wall, held my left shoulder against the wall, and drew back her right fist in a posture to strike me. Then I said 'Susan, if it's going to make you feel better, go ahead and hit me.' Susan ran out the back door of the pharmacy and came back about 20 minutes later. Susan said, 'Don't worry, I'd never hit you.'"

"Three weeks later, a pharmacist reprimanded Susan about some pills that she had packed incorrectly and also questioned the higher than average inventory count of crushed and unusable pills (Prozac). Susan grew angry and glared at me and said, 'Why didn't you tell me about the problem with the pills? Are you afraid of me?' I said, 'No Susan, I'm not afraid of you, but I am afraid to say anything to you because you take everything too personally and are too easily upset.' I also knew that Prozac was the same drug that Susan kept popping in her mouth at work."

"Susan told me she had spoken with Rhonda, our supervisor, about our argument over work schedules. I said, 'Did you tell her that you shoved me and were going to hit me?' Susan said 'No, I told her you were upset about scheduling time off.' I asked her, 'Why not tell Rhonda about the shove?' and Susan said, 'Because I really need this job.' I looked at her and said, 'I guess if I shoved someone and was going to hit them, I wouldn't tell either.'"

"About a week later, Rhonda, my supervisor, and I were leaving work. I could sense that Rhonda had heard of my trouble with Susan. Rhonda asked me if I was tired. I said 'No, I'm just disgusted with Susan,' and then told her about the assault. Rhonda asked me why I didn't say anything earlier, and I said 'I was willing to accept the situation and give Susan the benefit of the doubt. I was taught to handle my own problems and never to tell on others. However, Susan tried to intimidate me by asking if I was afraid of her!' After that, I figured the situation was going to degenerate. So, I decided to report the incident. Rhonda thanked me and said she would take care of the situation."

Interview with Susan

"Because of personal reasons, I had requested four days off between October 23 and November 2. When my request was approved, I told Brenda about it. It was not out of the ordinary for us to discuss scheduling changes since our working schedules could almost be described as a time sharing situation. As part-time employees, we split a 40-hour workweek. Upon hearing of my scheduling change, Brenda became very agitated over the possibility that my schedule change might interfere with her plans to be off on one of the days I would be gone. I told her that I had talked to our supervisor, Rhonda Carter, and had been assured that both of our absences on that day would not pose any problems for the receiving department. My assurances did not satisfy Brenda. She became very agitated, and suggested that special favors were granted to me. Brenda contended that I was a 'favored employee' while she was being singled out for unfair treatment."

"After several attempts to calm her and defend myself against charges of favoritism, I grasped Brenda by the shoulders, looked her in the eyes, and asked her to calm down and be reasonable. Brenda was unresponsive to this gesture and her agitation was not abated. I certainly do not think my gesture was threatening. My intent was to calm Brenda and to reassure her. As friends, I did not view this act as inappropriate. I decided that the best thing for me to do was to leave the pharmacy and go on to lunch. So that's what I did."

"On the days we worked together following this incident, our relationship returned to normal, and I was unaware of any problem between the two of us. In fact, Brenda told Rhonda that she did not report the incident because 'It didn't seem like a big deal.' I really don't know what all the fuss is about; Brenda and I are friends!"

Conclusions

Following the interviews and the collection of relevant policies, Maryanne must decide on a course of action (see Exhibits 5.2 and 5.3). She scheduled a meeting with her supervisor, Nancy, for the next morning. Maryanne continued to be perplexed that the total quality management and open communication had not prevented this altercation. In addition, Maryanne was burdened with knowledge, which had not been publicly released, that Westside planned a massive reengineering project. Maryanne thought about the workers who would be displaced by the reengineering. She wondered whether the employees would be able to find suitable employment or would they become 'misfits.'

Questions

1. If you were Maryanne, what actions would you take and why?
2. In light of this incident, should Westside change any of its "Standards of Behavior Policies" or "Corrective Action Policies?" Explain.
3. How can Westside prevent future incidents of workplace violence?

EXHIBIT 5.2 *Standards of Behavior Policies*

The following are types of behavior which could result in disciplinary action up to and including dismissal. This list is not all inclusive.

1. Falsification or omission of facts on application for employment or any Westside Health System records.
2. Giving out information of a confidential nature to unauthorized persons.
3. Altering work records or time cards.
4. Falsifying work records or time cards of another employee.
5. Insubordination or refusal to perform a work shift or job assigned.
6. Failure to perform work or assigned jobs.
7. Reporting to work unfit to assume assigned duties.
8. The sale, purchase, transfer, use or possession of illegal drugs, or the misuse of prescription, over-the-counter drugs or alcohol, and/or working under the influence of such is forbidden.
9. Possession or use of firearms, weapons, or explosives on the premises without authorization.
10. Unauthorized removal of Health System property, property of other employees, patients, or visitors from the premises.
11. Theft of services (i.e., telephone, parking)
12. Abuse, mistreatment, improper care of patients.
13. Fighting or attempting to injure another person on the premises.
14. Conducting or participating in unlawful games of chance on the premises.
15. Making statements of a defamatory nature about other employees, patients, or the company.
16. Violation of the solicitation policy.
17. Sleeping on the job.
18. Excessive absenteeism.
19. Altering the work shift without authorization.
20. Failure to report absences in accordance with established procedure.
21. Unsatisfactory job performance.
22. Use of threatening or abusive language towards patients, visitors, or other employees.
23. Violation of policies and procedures.

EXHIBIT 5.3 *Corrective Action Policies*

In order to provide continuous and efficient operation and to maintain acceptable employee behavior, the Health System has developed a system of corrective action to promote these goals. The system provides the employee with the opportunity to correct behavior when minor violations have occurred. Minor violations may result in verbal or written reprimand. Serious or repeated violations may result in written reprimand or suspension. Repeated violations which were not corrected previously, or more serious violations, may result in termination.

The system of corrective action is not necessarily a progressive one. The corrective action may vary depending on the nature, frequency, and gravity of the offense and on the employee's past record. The Health System reserves the right

(continued)

to discharge an employee without prior warning when such action is considered to be in the best interest of the System.

The corrective actions consist of: verbal counseling, written counseling, written reprimand, special review, suspension, and dismissal.

Verbal Counseling

Verbal counseling is an initial discussion between the employee and department management to address a performance deficiency or disciplinary problem of a minor degree of seriousness.

Written Counseling

Written counseling is a written record of a discussion between an employee and department management to address minor performance or disciplinary offenses that have persisted despite verbal counseling or as an initial corrective measure for more serious offenses. The written counseling is also used to raise an employee's awareness of performance deficiencies.

Written Reprimand

A written reprimand is a strong, written expression of management's disapproval concerning an employee's conduct or performance. It is intended to address serious disciplinary problems or repeated minor offenses.

Special Review

A special review is a period of time, usually 60 days, for close monitoring of an employee's conduct and performance, with opportunities for interaction with management to discuss problems, and assist the employee to overcome deficiencies. Repeated substandard performance, violations of rules and regulations, or a return to work following a disciplinary suspension are situations that warrant special review. During this period, the employee is ineligible to bid on open positions or receive a wage or salary increase. At the end of the special review period, an employee may be returned to regular status if the problem is corrected, have the special review extended, or be dismissed if the deficiencies have not been corrected.

Suspension

Suspension is a management imposed absence from work without pay following a serious or repeated violation. Suspended employees are ineligible to bid on open positions or to receive wage or salary increases.

Dismissal

Dismissal is a management imposed and authorized separation from employment at the System.

All forms of written corrective action are placed in the employee's personnel file. The signing of the approved record of employee conference form indicates only that the document has been read. An employee has the right to comment on the form. An eligible employee who disagrees with a written corrective action may access the formal grievance procedure.

68. INCIDENT

Spiked Milk

A reputable northeastern construction company employs six experienced construction supervisors for its various construction jobs. These supervisors have the overall responsibility of hiring and firing and seeing that the construction proceeds as close to time and cost schedules as possible. They also have the responsibility of overall quality control of the construction.

Larry Werst, age 55, has been a supervisor for this company for many years. He is never absent and has established a reputation for getting the job done close to schedule and doing it right. He has supervised the construction of several prominent buildings and is now supervising the construction of a college fraternity house. Larry's approach to handling his employees is firm and sometimes harsh. He doesn't take any back talk, and everyone who works for him usually earns his or her pay or isn't on the job for very long.

The owner and manager of the company had become concerned about Larry because rumors implied that he was an alcoholic and that he drank on the job. The owner knew that Larry drank a lot and had a stormy, cavalier home life, but he didn't know whether he was drinking on the job.

One day, the manager was talking with Larry and noticed a definite bad breath odor smelling quite alcoholic. This happened on several occasions, and office and storeroom employees noticed the odor when they talked to him. Also, the storeroom clerk noticed that almost every day he would come in and buy two cokes at a time and then take off in his company truck, presumably back to his job site.

The manager decided to talk to Larry about this subject. When he confronted Larry with the rumors, the bad breath, and two cokes at a time, Larry denied that he was drinking. He said that the rumors were just that and that the two cokes were for himself and his carpenter supervisor. The manager told him that he would have to let him go if he were ever caught drinking on the job. He reminded Larry that the firm's progressive discipline system included a rule that states, "No employee is permitted to go on duty or remain on duty if he or she possesses, is under the influence of, or is consuming an alcoholic beverage. Violation of this policy will result in dismissal."

About a year later, when the construction season was again in full swing, stories began floating around about Larry's drinking. The employees on his job talked about the quart of milk he drank every day. They wondered why he had started drinking so much of it lately and wondered if he "spiked" it and used it to combat his odorous breath. Sometimes his speech seemed definitely slurred, but Larry was gravel-voiced and had sloppy speech habits anyway. The workers also were amused by the stories he'd tell about things

Contributed by Arno F. Knapper, School of Business, The University of Kansas.

that had happened to him. They were just stories, of course, but lately they were getting pathetically far-fetched and made no sense at all.

The manager couldn't help finding out about some of the things that were said about Larry, and he wondered what he should do. Larry had never actually been caught drinking. His construction job was going up satisfactorily, but it was a little behind schedule due to the inability to get good carpenters and laborers at the beginning of the construction season. Worker turnover was perhaps a little higher on this job than the average.

Questions

1. What course of action should the manager follow? Why?
2. To what extent should the manager go to try to catch Larry drinking on the job?
3. What action, if any, should the manager take if Larry confesses to being an alcoholic?
4. Does the manager presently have sufficient proof that Larry is working under the influence of alcohol?
5. Critique the firm's alcoholism rule.

69. INCIDENT

Motivating Employees During Downsizing

The Rutledge Company is an organization involved in the retail industry, operating 100+ retail stores. The company's headquarters is going through what is termed "modernization." A new information system is being implemented which will completely alter the way the firm does business. In addition, it will affect the staffing required by the company. The new software began to be rolled out last year, and it is projected that at least another year is required before the rollout will be complete. All personnel within the corporate office, including the large clerical staff, attended a four day, comprehensive, hands-on computer training program and were told to incorporate the new software into daily use.

The completion of the rollout will primarily affect the clerical staff. It is the company's objective to eliminate the majority of these individuals. The idea behind this is that the technology of the new software will enable all management-level personnel to perform their jobs efficiently without the need for clerical support. The Rutledge Company has informed its large clerical staff that most, but not all, of their jobs will disappear once the rollout is complete. The prospect of future unemployment along with the uncertainty regarding when their jobs will be terminated has greatly affected the staff morale. Complacency, lack of initiative, and complaining have accompanied the loss of morale.

The firm has one additional problem, which is that some of the clerical staff are long-term employees who are accustomed to how the company operated ten years ago. These employees have not adapted to the new software or the other new programs that have been implemented. Thus, these employees do not provide the full clerical support needed by management. Rather, they perform only those aspects of their jobs that existed prior to the introduction of the new software plus other menial jobs sufficient to keep them busy.

Individual managers must determine how to motivate all of the clerical support staff for the remaining time that they will be employed and must also determine how to motivate some employees to use the new software. Someone must also determine which clerical help should be retained once "modernization" is complete. The firm wants to keep all of its clerical staff until then.

Questions

1. What actions should be taken in order to increase the morale and motivation level of the clerical staff?
2. What actions can be taken to motivate those employees who are not using the new technology required of their job?
3. What criteria should be used to determine which clerical employees should be retained?
4. Should the firm attempt to solve its motivational problems by conducting further training?

70. INCIDENT

The Awards Dinner

Radio, Inc. is a holding company for over 20 radio stations located throughout the West Coast. At its headquarters it employs approximately 65 media professionals. The firm has been in the news frequently with speculations of a buyout. Wall Street analysts and broadcasts indicate that "the company is for sale." These statements have been circulating for a month now, and insiders know that they are not unfounded. Radio, Inc. is viewed as a cash cow and has been coveted by many outsiders for years because of its high listening audiences.

Earlier this week, Radio, Inc. was visited by the president of a large firm. As he toured the facility, everyone recognized him and rumors reached a feverish pace. Accountants were asked to prepare current financial statements; that added fuel to the rumors. Officially, this has all been "hush-hush," but headquarters' staff members had worked many overtime hours to provide the needed information. Employee morale is at an all-time low and most employees are fearful about their jobs and their future.

Meanwhile, the *Performance Improvement and Awards Committee* is finalizing plans for the second quarter meeting. This committee was created several years ago to promote continuous improvement, reward individuals for performance excellence, and plan an off-site meeting each quarter. The first quarter meeting was a huge success! Awards were presented with great fanfare and specific accomplishments of every recipient were cited. Slides of employees at work and play gathered over the previous six months were shown. The meeting boosted employee morale and provided incentives to improve performance with hopes of gaining recognition at the next quarterly meeting. The Committee has created numerous awards that employees cherish. These include:

People's Choice Award—given to the employee who has an infectiously positive influence on the company and on co-workers. This person is nominated by peers, voted on by management, and ultimately selected by the Performance Improvement and Awards Committee.

Fiscal Responsibility Award—given to an employee who implemented a program that saved the company the most money. The recipient is nominated by department heads or middle senior management and is ultimately selected by the Performance Improvement and Awards Committee.

Winning Attitude Award—given to the employee who performs both routine and special job tasks with a cheerful, "can do" attitude.

Extra Effort Award—given to an employee who gives extra effort, goes the extra mile, and contributes more than 100 percent to accomplish his or her job.

Technical Achievement Award—given to the employee who invents and implements a new program or process that uses technology and results in improvements for internal/external customers.

Out of the Box Award—given to the employee who thought of innovative, new ways of accomplishing his/her job, or contributed fresh ideas that focused on continuous improvement, or coordinated department efforts that enhanced the change process.

Since March, the committee has prepared for the second quarter event. They scheduled the "Shark Room" at a local Marine Science Aquarium for the afternoon, put together a great slide show, ordered sandwiches from a well-known catering firm, solicited senior and middle management for award nominations, and purchased gifts for the award recipients.

The quarterly awards meeting was scheduled to be held on a Friday. However, on the preceding Wednesday, the President of Radio, Inc. received an attractive buyout offer that she knew the firm's Board of Directors would accept. The details of the sale were expected to be finalized and announced on the same day as the awards banquet. The announcement could not be postponed due to the risk of having confidential information leak out to the public. The President is now faced with the issue of whether the awards meeting should be held.

Questions

1. Should the awards banquet be held as scheduled or should it be canceled or postponed?
2. Assuming that the firm is bought out, what can the firm do to retain desirable employees and to enhance employee motivation and morale?

71. INCIDENT

"She's Just a Temp"

A large consumer products manufacturing company with 800 employees had more than 200 pending job requisitions, and the facility's Human Resources Department was overrun with applications. In order to process the new applications, the department hired three temporary employees (JoAnn, Jack, and Jill). All three were hired on the same day, and all had adequate job experience to help the HR staff get through a very intensive ten-week project.

JoAnn was performing her job duties like a real professional. Several members of the permanent staff were impressed by her performance. It was recommended that she be considered for a potential opening created by the promotion of a member of the HR permanent staff.

Jack also was doing well in his job assignment. However, two weeks into the project, he accepted an offer for a permanent position at another firm. The supervisor called the temporary agency and was sent a qualified replacement the next day.

Jill's performance, in the view of the supervisor, was another story. Halfway through the project, the supervisor felt that Jill's deliberate style was slowing down the process and that a change needed to be made. The supervisor had two options. First, he could counsel Jill on improving her performance. Jill seemed to be well liked by her co-workers and to fit well in the department. However, this counseling option would take time, and the

Contributed by Gerald E. Calvasina and Joyce M. Beggs, University of North Carolina, Charlotte.

department had only five weeks to finish processing and sorting the applications. The supervisor's second option was much simpler. So he decided to get a replacement from the temporary agency. On Friday, the agency called Jill after work and informed her that her assignment ended immediately. On Monday, the agency had a qualified replacement to finish the project. Other members of the HR staff were surprised at Jill's termination since they personally liked her. Staff members questioned Jill's abrupt termination and wanted to know why they were not informed of it. Some said they would have at least appreciated the chance to say goodbye. The supervisor responded, "She was just a temp."

Questions

1. Were any employee's rights violated in this case? Why or why not?
2. What employee relations fallout might the supervisor have to deal with as a result of Jill's termination?
3. If you were the supervisor, what would you do? How and why?

72. INCIDENT

Alan Garfield

You are the director of the METRO Division of a large manufacturing organization. You have just received the following memo:

MEMORANDUM

TO: Director, METRO Division
FROM: Sales Manager
SUBJECT: Customer Complaints

I am sure that you are well aware that, when you appointed me as sales manager, you also emphasized that this was a sales-oriented, customer-oriented business, and you advised me to come straight to you whenever I felt that other departments were not giving sufficient support to our sales staff. We now have such a situation. It seems to be centered on one individual, Alan Garfield, supervisor of our shipping department.

What it amounts to is that our customers cannot get their inquiries about shipments answered satisfactorily. We have followed the practice of establishing a direct link between customers and the shipping department so that customers can get the fastest and most accurate information possible on the status of their shipments. Now, when anybody calls with a question or a complaint about a shipment, the people on Garfield's staff always switch the call to him, after which there is an annoyingly long wait. Then Garfield finally gets on the line and gives a complex, detailed explanation of shipping department problems, ending with a lecture on customer patience.

As you know, Garfield is an older employee with many years of service in the company, but only three-months experience in the shipping department job. His previous experience was in the credit department, purchasing, and mail room.

When we promoted him to the job last fall, I tried to impress on him the importance of being tactful with complaining customers, but it doesn't seem to have done any good. I would appreciate it if you would remedy this situation as soon as possible, to ensure that our customers get satisfactory service from the shipping department.

Questions

1. How difficult do you anticipate it will be to change Garfield's behavior? Why?
2. What action would you recommend in this situation?
3. What are the advantages and disadvantages of assigning someone else to handle the calls?

73. INCIDENT

Caught in the Act

It was about 1:30 in the morning when Mike Morrison, Night Supervisor at HITEC Corporation, a west coast manufacturer of computer software, finally returned to his office to finish up a report. As he begin writing, he heard a strange noise coming from the Quality Control Lab down the hall. He knew that no one was assigned to work in the lab at that time so he walked down to see what was up. After knocking, he opened the door and was stunned to see two of his Lead employees. Jim, a Lead Supervisor in Maintenance, had his back turned and was pulling up his underpants and pants. Mary, a Lead Supervisor on one of the production lines, was next to an inspection bench and was likewise pulling up her pants. Mike quickly shut the door and returned to his office, aghast at what had happened. Given the embarrassing nature of the situation, he decided to take no action.

Two weeks later, Teya Simpson, the Human Resource Director, was talking to another Lead Supervisor when she finally heard about the incident. Apparently, everyone in the plant knew the story, except top management, because both Jim and Mary had spread the word that they were "caught in the act."

Teya immediately called Wayne Purdy, Plant Manager, to see what action, if any, should be taken. Both recognized that the firm had no work rule that specifically covered sexual relationships on the job and that the offense had occurred two weeks ago. On the other hand, both believed that the employees' behavior was highly unprofessional and noted that both managers had left their work areas unattended. Furthermore, they were concerned about the effect that this incident might have on future employee behaviors if no disciplinary action was forthcoming.

Questions

1. What action should the firm take, if any, with regard to Jim and Mary? Justify your answer.
2. What action should the firm take, if any, with respect to Mike? Why?

74. SKILL BUILDER

Writing/Developing Employee Discipline Policies

I. *Objectives:*
   A. To familiarize you with how organizations resolve employee discipline problems.
   B. To allow you practice in writing a model discipline policy statement.
II. *Time Required to Complete:*   2–3 hours
III. *Instructions:*   Go to the library and read four articles which deal directly with one of the topics below and write a brief summary of them. Look for articles which explain how companies handle or should handle these employee problems. (Make sure you include a full bibliography.) Once your research is completed, develop a written "model" policy statement for a medium-sized manufacturing company for the topic you selected. Be sure that your statement specifies the rules and disciplinary procedures that apply.

Topics
1. Stealing/Theft/Dishonesty
2. Absenteeism
3. Insubordination
4. Tardiness
5. Alcohol/Drug Abuse
6. Safety Rule Violation
7. Sexual Harassment

LABOR RELATIONS, COLLECTIVE BARGAINING, AND CONTRACT ADMINISTRATION

75. CASE

Union Organizing at SGA Industries

Introduction

President White sat in his office at SGA Industries thinking about the union election taking place down at the plant auditorium. He felt that the company had waged a successful campaign to persuade workers that their best interests would be served only if the company remained union free. As he awaited the election results, his mind began to wander back to the events leading up to today's election.

Background

SGA Industries is best known as the world's largest producer of women's hosiery and employs approximately 6,500 people in ten plants in five communities in Georgia and South Carolina. The company's headquarters is located in Anderson, Georgia. The company's sales subsidiary, SGA Inc., has 12 offices in major market areas throughout the United States and sells its products directly to distributors around the world. The company's strategy of strong identification with the customer has made the SGA name one of the most recognized in the entire hosiery industry.

SGA was founded in 1907 by Sam Gerome Anderson. Anderson built the company and the community was named after him in 1910. Ever since, the fortunes of Anderson residents have been interwoven with those of SGA. Over the years the company supported the community, donating land and money for churches, schools, and hospitals and providing jobs for nearly a third of the town's residents. As the years passed, further expansion and product diversification occurred, and the company gained a reputation as an industry leader in the design, production, and marketing of women's and men's hose and undergarments.

Contributed by Gerald E. Calvasina, The University of North Carolina, Charlotte.

After the death of the last family member, Alexandra Anderson, SGA was managed by four chief executive officers in less than a dozen years before the company was purchased for $250 million by Jack Phillips. The new owner was a well-known Atlanta entrepreneur and business leader. Soon after the purchase, Phillips appointed Ted White as President of SGA.

Labor-Management Relations

Over the years SGA enjoyed a reputation as a steady job provider in an unstable industry. The company provided for its workers and treated them like family members. Many believe that the company's generosity to its employees and the town of Anderson helped to defeat an earlier union organizing drive by the Textile Workers of America by a vote of 3,937 to 1,782. At the time of the vote, the Chairman called it "an expression of confidence by employees." The SGA vote was viewed as a severe blow to union organizing efforts in the South.

When Phillips purchased SGA, he announced that his major goals would be to improve the community and to improve the quality of life for SGA employees and their families. Phillips invested over $100 million to reach these goals. The total included funds for pay increases, new job benefits, capital improvements, including the use of robots, community improvements, and other contributions. These improvements were also accompanied by a shift in management philosophy. The theme of the new management approach was self-sufficiency, and it signaled an end to the benevolent paternalism that had so long characterized employee relations at SGA. Greater emphasis was placed on employee performance and productivity.

During the mid-eighties, the entire hosiery industry experienced major problems. Growing foreign competition and imports had a negative impact on domestic hosiery manufacturers. Many manufacturers attempted to reverse the impact by intensive capital investments in new technology, reorganization and downsizing of plants, and by instituting programs to improve employee productivity and efficiency. SGA was not spared from this competition. Its international sales fell dramatically from $26 million to $10 million. Faced with increasing imports and weak consumer sales, the company was forced to lay off 1,500 employees, reduce pay scales, and to rescind many of the perks that the workers had enjoyed under the Anderson family. Many of these changes drew worker protests and created a good deal of tension between workers and management.

Wages in the industry had been rising steadily but were still lower than wages in the manufacturing sector in general. On a regional basis, the differential was still quite wide, with a study showing that wages ranged from $5.56 per hour in South Carolina to $8.90 in Michigan. In addition, as technology advanced, more skilled operatives were required, thus increasing the cost of turnover to companies. Employers in the industry also were becoming increasingly more dependent on women and minorities for employees.

At SGA 40 percent of the employees were women and 35 percent of the total work force were minorities. Minorities and women made up less than 2 percent of the management staff.

The Election Campaign

Despite its earlier defeat, the Amalgamated Clothing and Textile Workers Union (ACTWU) was back in Anderson, armed and ready for an organizing effort that would divert the attention of SGA management for several long and tense months.

While many employers learn of union organizing efforts by their employees only after the National Labor Relations Board informs them, the ACTWU's efforts to organize SGA employees were clearly out in the open a full nine months before the election. With a union office in downtown Anderson and a healthy budget, the ACTWU, led by Chris Balog, engaged in one of the most sophisticated union organizing efforts ever seen in the area. Using computerized direct mailing to stay in touch with workers and extensive radio and television advertising, the union effort at SGA attracted wide attention. Many observers felt that the outcome of ACTWU's drive would have significant implications for the ability of labor unions to make inroads into traditionally nonunion regions of the country.

Union's Campaign

The campaign issues developed and communicated to workers were for the most part predictable. Job security was brought to the front early and was easily introduced to the campaign in the wake of over 1,500 layoffs and selective plant closings by SGA management. In addition, in attempting to become more competitive in the face of increasing foreign competition, increased workloads and reduced wage rates were key issues raised by the union. The union repeatedly accused Phillips of engaging in unfair labor practices by threatening to sell or close the company if the union were to win bargaining rights for SGA workers. To a certain extent, the union did expand on the traditional wages, hours, and working conditions issues typically raised in organizing efforts. As the campaign progressed, Phillips became a focal point of union rhetoric, and the union attempted to portray Phillips as a greedy and ruthless city slicker from Atlanta who was not interested in the long-term survival of SGA and its employees.

Management's Campaign

While Phillips became a focal point of union criticism as the campaign wore on, his role in management's response to the organizing efforts was critical throughout the months preceding the election. With President White leading the anti-union campaign, backed by a sophisticated strategy developed by an Atlanta law firm specializing in anti-union campaigns, SGA was able to quickly respond to every issue raised by the union.

The SGA strategy to defeat the union organizing effort included extensive meetings with community, business, and religious leaders in an attempt to influence workers' views about the union. Extensive use of anti-union films was required viewing for workers on company time. Letters sent to workers' homes by President White and Phillips emphasized the need for team spirit, not only to keep the union out, but to overcome the threat created by hosiery imports. President White put it this way: "We intend to do everything that is proper and legal in this campaign to defeat the union. This is essential if we are to remain competitive in the hosiery business. Every day we are facing more and more foreign competition. Not only do our workers understand this, but I think the public does also. We have been able to communicate with our workers in the past, and we don't need a third party voice. We all must work together as a team. The only way SGA can beat the encroaching foreign competition is to streamline and consolidate our operations."

White and Phillips made repeated visits to plants to shake hands and listen to workers' concerns. The weekly employee newsletter was filled with anti-union letters written by workers and community members. Late in the campaign a letter was sent to SGA workers from Jack Phillips explaining why they should vote against the union (see Exhibit 5.4). In response to the union claim that Phillips was attempting to sell the company, Phillips also told the workers that "SGA is not for sale, but if I determine that the company cannot operate competitively, I can and I will cease to operate SGA. This is entirely up to me and nobody can stop me—including this union."

Employees' Views

The employees were divided over the union organizing campaign. Several employees formed an Anti-Union Committee which organized an SGA Loyalty Day. A statement by Terry Floyd, a shift leader, summed up the view expressed by some employees: "We, as employees of SGA, do not feel that it is in the best interest of our company and its employees to be represented by ACTWU. Many generations of the same families have worked at this plant; part of our strength is family heritage. I'm afraid a union will destroy that strength. We feel that a union is not needed and that we can work with management as a team." At one rally sponsored by the Anti-Union Committee, "No Union" badges, "Be Wise—Don't Unionize" t-shirts, and "Vote No" hats were worn by several hundred employees.

Others workers expressed support for the union. One worker stated, "We need a union for protection. At least it would give us a voice. Supervisors can be too arbitrary." Others pointed to pay increases and bonuses for top management in the wake of wage cuts and layoffs for plant workers. Many older employees, who remembered the generosity of the Anderson family, also expressed bitterness toward SGA and worried about their pensions.

Questions

1. What was the impetus for the union organizing effort at SGA Industries?
2. Discuss SGA's strategy in managing the representation campaign.
3. Discuss any potential unfair labor practice charges SGA management might face as a result of their campaign strategy.

EXHIBIT 5.4   *Letter to SGA Employees*

TO ALL SGA EMPLOYEES:

It is only fair for you to know SGA's policy on unions. Our policy is quite simple. We are absolutely opposed to a union at any of our plants. We intend to use every legal and proper means to stay non-union.

As you know, the hosiery industry has been under great pressure and competition from foreign firms. Sales in the industry have dwindled over the past few years, and we are in a poor profit position. Our government has done little to protect your jobs and stop the imports from eroding our sales. Only you and I can save this company and your jobs.

Our whole industry has been forced to modernize our production process to make it more efficient. In fact you know that many firms have merged together to strengthen their market position. Our company, too, will have to explore the possible advantages of pooling resources and products. In the long run such strategy can only benefit employees and management alike. I know bringing in the ACTWU at this time will only drive up our operating expenses and jeopardize our chances of making such arrangements. Only management has the right to decide how to operate this company. If we find we cannot operate this company profitably, we may be forced to consider other options.

We are convinced that unions have the tendency to create an adversarial relationship between employees and management. Cooperation and teamwork cannot exist in such a hostile environment. It is only through cooperation and teamwork that we will get through the crisis.

No SGA employee is ever going to need a union to keep her job. We know that ACTWU cannot help this company or you and will probably cause us to lose even more of our market and threaten your job security. I urge you—do not vote for the union. Let's all pull together and remember the goodwill of the Anderson family and how it has stood behind you all of these years.

Sincerely,

Jack Phillips

Jack Phillips
Chief Executive Officer

76. CASE

The Frustrated Quality Circle Team

Background

During the 1980s, one of the many U.S. Postmaster Generals initiated an innovation in labor management relations labeled "Employee Involvement—Quality of Work Life" (EI/QWL). The purpose of the innovation was not to supplant collective bargaining but to supplement it with a program of employee participation. Consequently, the mission of the program was to improve working conditions in any areas which did not contradict the collective bargaining agreement negotiated between the U.S. Postal System and the National Association of Letter Carriers.

The structure of the program included a local team, the manager of each facility, and the local Joint Steering Committee for the metropolitan area. The local team always included a member of management, a union representative, and two to five union members (depending on the size of the facility). The team met once a week for one hour during the workday to discuss ways of improving working conditions in their own facility. Only areas where there was total consensus could be written up and submitted for approval to higher levels.

Once a consensus on a proposal was achieved, the team wrote up a document detailing the need or problem, reasons for the problem, the proposed solution, and the benefits to the postal facility. This proposal was then sent to the facility manager (the second level in the structure). The manager had to approve or disapprove the proposal within seven days. If the proposal was rejected, reasons had to be given and the team could appeal to the third level in the structure.

The third level was the Joint Steering Committee, which consisted of higher-level union officials (i.e., the President of the union) and top management officials in the larger geographical area. The role of the Joint Steering Committee included training local team members, facilitating the process, resolving problems, and making final decisions regarding rejected proposals appealed from the local level.

The EI/QWL Program

A particular postal carrier facility in the Southwest began an EI/QWL program two years ago. The team consisted of a supervisor, a union shop steward, and three union members who had volunteered for the program. Among the proposals on which the team achieved consensus and recommended to the facility manager were ceiling fans to improve air circulation, fatigue mats for carriers to stand on while sorting mail, and a photocopy machine for the building to avoid driving to the downtown post office.

All of these proposals were accepted in writing by the facility manager within the required seven-day period. The team leader was told that the work orders for these three items had been issued. Other proposals such as eliminating time clocks were also considered but consensus was not achieved on them.

After ten weeks, the team was becoming frustrated because none of the items which were "on order" had arrived. Team members, who had shared their approved recommendations with other carriers, began to hear complaints that the process was a "farce," "nothing is going to change," and "you guys are wasting your time." Again, the team leader checked with the facility manager and was told everything was "on order."

After four more weeks without results the team decided to check with the Joint Steering Committee since copies of all paperwork connected with the EI/QWL system were automatically sent to them. The team was told that, as far as the steering committee knew, none of the items had been ordered. Other than the initial approval by the facility manager, there was no other paperwork. The team then decided to ask the facility manager for copies of the work orders. They were told that none of the work orders had been kept (even though postal system rules require retention of work orders until the item is received).

The Decisions

By then, the team was extremely frustrated. Two team members suggested simply not meeting again until the approved items were received. Several other teams in the metropolitan area had done just that as a result of similar frustrations. However, the team eventually decided to use the system rather than abandon it. This meant they would bring the problem to the attention of the Joint Steering Committee and hope that the committee would put pressure on the facility manager to implement the recommendations.

The team spent two weeks discussing how to go about implementing this approach. All members of the team agreed on a course of action except for the supervisor. The problem was that the supervisor reported directly to the facility manager. The supervisor was concerned about his own promotion prospects and salary increases if he signed the problem statement indicating the facility manager was the problem. Since all proposals had to be a consensus, he reluctantly agreed to sign the document which accused the facility manager of approving all proposals but not implementing any. It took a lot of pressure from other team members before his signature was obtained, since the facility manager evaluated him for merit salary increases and promotions. The team leader then gave the facility manager a copy of this document and sent the original to the Joint Steering Committee.

Questions

1. Describe the nature and causes of the problem in this case.
2. How would you explain the facility manager's behavior? What is his management style? What were his goals and objectives? Why?
3. Given the total situation, how would you evaluate the actions of the local team? Did they handle the situation properly? Did the supervisor make the right decision? Why or why not?
4. If you were a member of the Joint Steering Committee, what would you do now? How would you insure that this type of problem did not recur in this or any other postal facility?
5. Are innovations in labor-management relations, such as EI/QWL, a passing fad or a permanent part of the labor-management structure?

7 7 .   C A S E

The Give Back: A Case of Union Busting

Three years ago, Local 974 of the United Tireworkers of America made significant contract concessions to the North American Tire plant in Bailey, Georgia. The union concessions were made for the company's economic survival and for the plant to remain open. Now, riding the tide of one of the longest economic booms in U.S. history, North American Tire and its union were back at the bargaining table. This time, though, the union was not looking to give back but to receive. The union wanted not only to get back what was given up in previous negotiations, but also to get their share of the economic prosperity pie that past contract concessions had made possible. However, the company had other goals for negotiations.

The company's proposals did not satisfy the union's negotiating team, a strike resulted, and both sides indicated their resolve was strong. While picket lines and demonstrations at the plant were rather uneventful, a war of words was fought in the media. On the one hand, full page ads appeared in the local papers condemning the company for going back on their word to make up for the give backs of the past. On the other hand, the company claimed it needed to maintain its competitive position in an industry undergoing a shakeout of under-performing competitors. North American's parent company, Swiss Financial, of Alpsland, Switzerland, reported that operating profit rose 20 percent to $68 million on sales of $1.1 billion in the most recent quarter. North American's other non-union plants were operating at capacity, and the company recently announced the purchase of Mexico's largest tire-maker.

Negotiations broke down when the union rejected what management called its best offer. The company stated that the contract proposal was well above average for the Bailey, Georgia, area. However, the union countered that it was well below industry standards. In addition, the union filed unfair labor practice charges with the National Labor Relations Board. The union alleged that the strike was caused by unfair labor practices including the company's refusal to bargain over medical insurance or to bring its decision makers to the bargaining table.

Supervisors and clerical employees kept the Bailey tire plant operating at less than 30 percent of capacity, and plans were made by management to hire strike replacements. Striking employees were invited to return to work, but only a small insignificant percentage returned. The company began to advertise, interview, and hire strike replacements. Although the labor market was tight and Bailey's unemployment rate was less than three percent,

Contributed by Gerald E. Calvasina and Joyce M. Beggs, University of North Carolina, Charlotte.

there was no shortage of applicants. The company increased production at the Bailey plant, and production was also stepped up at its non-union plants. While the union cried foul, the company continued to increase production. A federal mediator was appointed to get both sides back to the bargaining table to resume negotiations.

Questions

1. What are the pros and cons of the firm's strategy of hiring replacement workers?
2. Assume that the firm's goal is to break the union, what are the advantages and disadvantages of this strategy?
3. What standard should the firm use in setting wage rates? (industry or geographic)

78. EXERCISE

Collective Bargaining Role Play— Bush Corporation

I. *Objectives:*
   A. To allow you to experience the collective bargaining process.
   B. To help you to understand the skills necessary to successfully negotiate a union contract.
II. *Out-of-Class Preparation Time:* 2 hours
III. *In-Class Time Suggested:* 45 minutes
IV. *Procedures:*
   A. The instructor will divide the class in half. Each half will be divided into a union team and a management team. There will be two simultaneous bargaining sessions (A and B).
   B. Read the description of the situation at Bush Corporation before class and familiarize yourself with the current contract and bargaining issues. Also read the role sheets for the union and management provided by the instructor.
   C. Before class each negotiation team should meet to develop a strategy for achieving a favorable agreement. Each team should consider three items: (1) degree of flexibility on each provision; (2) issues which are most critical; and (3) willingness to take a strike. Preparation of the bargaining strategy should take no more than 10 minutes. Alternatively, teams may meet prior to class to develop their strategy.

      D Your instructor will designate the amount of time for the actual bargaining session.

      E. Each team should appoint a chief negotiator and a secretary who will complete Form 1 indicating all the issues agreed upon in each of the areas under negotiation.

Negotiating Rules

1. At the beginning of the bargaining session, each team's chief negotiator should present an opening statement (one minute or less) stating its objectives.
2. Each team is allowed two three-minute caucuses during the bargaining session.
3. Each team is required to bargain in good faith and make every effort to reach an agreement. Failure to reach an agreement will lead to a strike.
4. Once a settlement is reached on a contract provision, that issue cannot be reopened.

Situation

Bush Corporation is a general aviation and business aircraft firm located in a large western city. The company manufactures aircraft, aircraft parts, avionics, and other aircraft accessories in addition to providing aircraft maintenance and overhaul services. The company's major aircraft models—fanjets and propjets—are generally used for business and recreational flying. The company's products have fared well in a highly competitive market. However, in the first half of the last decade there has been a slump in the market for new general aviation aircraft. Industry experts attribute this slump to high aircraft costs and overcapacity in corporate flight departments. Many large corporations are increasingly turning to on-demand charter flights to meet their business flying needs. A combination of weak market demand and high product liability insurance rates have plagued the industry and have forced many to cut back production and lay off workers. Economic forecasts indicate that demand may pick up in the latter half of the decade as international sales increase. Top management at Bush is very concerned about keeping down labor costs in order to remain competitive. Last year the company had to close down one production line and lay off 450 workers for six weeks. The aerospace industry is becoming increasingly automated, and Bush is planning to increase its use of robots in the production process.

A majority of Bush's 2,500 production employees are members of the International Association of Machinists. A relatively good labor-management relationship has become somewhat strained because of the large scale layoffs last year. While the union is aware of the company's economic situation, it is most concerned with employment security and a better position in terms of benefits. The present three-year contract (see Exhibit 5.5) is set to expire, and contract negotiations are set to begin. Union and company bargaining proposals are shown in Exhibit 5.6.

EXHIBIT 5.5   *Major Provisions of Present Three-Year Contract Between Bush Corporation and the International Association of Machinists*

1. Wages	Average union hourly wage	= $16.48
2. COLA adjustment	Prepaid increase of 2% and 1 cent for each 0.3 point rise in CPI; adjustments made annually	
3. Shift differential	15 cents/hour for third shift	
4. Overtime	All overtime paid at time and one-half	
5. Layoff notice	Minimum of two weeks notice	
6. Paid sick leave	2 but less than 4 years of service	= 1 day
	4 but less than 6 years of service	= 2 days
	6 but less than 8 years of service	= 3 days
	8 but less than 10 years of service	= 4 days
	10 but less than 25 years of service	= 5 days
7. Vacations	1 but less than 3 years of service	= 1 week
	3 but less than 10 years of service	= 2 weeks
	10 but less than 17 years of service	= 3 weeks
	17 but less than 25 years of service	= 4 weeks
	25 or more	= 5 weeks
8. Holidays	7 (Christmas Day, New Year's Day, Good Friday, Fourth of July, Memorial Day, Thanksgiving Day, and Labor Day)	
9. Life insurance	$10,000 group life plan; accidental death and dismemberment (AD&D) $7,500	
10. Health insurance	Major medical: $250,000 lifetime; company pays 75 percent of individual medical insurance	
11. Pensions	$20 per month per year of credited service	
12. Union security	All employed by the company who fall under the jurisdiction of the union shall, as a condition of employment, become members of the union at the expiration of the sixty (60) day probationary period.	

EXHIBIT 5.6   *Bargaining Program: Union and Company Proposals*

Issue	Union Proposal	Company Proposal	Industry Average
1. Wages	$1.25 general wage increase per hour	75 cents	Average hourly rate $18.94 in aerospace industry (local labor market $15.75 for skilled workers)
2. COLA adjustment	1 cent increase for 0.175% CPI rise; adjustments made quarterly	Keep current provisions	1 cent increase for 0.3% increase in CPI; adjustments made quarterly
3. Shift differential	20 cents/hour second shift; 30 cents/hour third shift	Keep current provisions	40 cents/hour for third shift only
4. Overtime	Double time for all hours worked outside of normal assigned shift; time and one-half for Sunday and holiday work	Keep current provision	All overtime paid at time and one-half
5. Layoff notice	Minimum of four weeks	Keep current provision	Three weeks
6. Paid sick leave	7 days per year after 10 years of service	Keep current provision	5 days per year after 10 years of service
7. Vacations	1 but less than 3 yr = 2 weeks 3 but less than 10 yr = 3 weeks 10 but less than 17 yr = 4 weeks Over 17 years = 5 weeks	1 but less than 3 yr = 1 week 3 but less than 10 yr = 2 weeks 10 but less than 17 yr = 3 weeks Over 17 years = 4 weeks	1 but less than 5 yr = 2 weeks 5 but less than 10 yr = 3 weeks Over 10 yr = 4 weeks
8. Holidays	Additional 3: Christmas Eve New Year's Eve Friday after Thanksgiving	Keep current provision	11 holidays
9. Life insurance	$15,000 group life insurance policy; $10,000 AD&D	Increase AD&D to $8,500	$15,000 Life Insurance; $8,000 AD&D

(continued)

EXHIBIT 5.6   *continued*

Issue	Union Proposal	Company Proposal	Industry Average
10. Health insurance	$750,000 lifetime major medical; company pays 85% of individual medical insurance	$500,000 lifetime major medical; company pays 75% of individual medical insurance	$500,000 lifetime major medical; company pays 90% of individual medical insurance
11. Pensions	$24 per month per year of credited service; increase retirees' monthly benefits by $.50 for each service year	$20 per year for past service; $22 for future service	$22 per month per year of credited service
12. Union security	Union membership required after 30 days	Keep current provision	60 day requirement

Other Bargaining Issues Not Covered by Present 3 Year Contract

Management would like to:

A. Include a contract clause to establish a lower-wage structure for new employees beginning in the new contract year. These new employees would have an average hourly rate of $11.50 versus the present entry rate of $13.50.

B. Establish a joint committee to work toward containment of health care costs.

Union members would like to:

A. Include a contract provision to protect workers affected by new technology. This provision would require Bush to:

1. Notify the union six months in advance of the purchase or projected introduction of any technological change that would affect employees' jobs or job content.
2. Provide the union with full information about this new technology.
3. Handle any reduction in work force through normal attrition and turnover.
4. Not reduce the pay of any employee who is transferred or displaced because of the new technology.
5. Provide workers with cross-training and retraining for jobs created by the new technology.
6. Provide employees who cannot be retained with training for jobs outside of the company and outplacement assistance.

B. Include a contract provision providing for an employee savings plan with a Section 401K feature.

FORM 1 *Issues Agreed Upon in Each Area*

1. Wages

2. COLA adjustment

3. Shift differential

4. Overtime

5. Layoff notice

6. Paid sick leave

7. Vacations

8. Holidays

9. Life insurance

10. Health insurance

11. Pensions

12. Union security

13. Other issues

79. EXERCISE

Applying the NLRA

How Do You Respond?

  I. *Objectives:*
   A. To help you understand the application of the National Labor Relations Act (NLRA).
   B. To help you understand the court's interpretation of the NLRA.
   C. To help you understand the meaning of the terms "decertification election," "union salting," "strike replacements," "Excelsior List,"and the rights of supervisors under the NLRA.
 II. *Out-of-Class Preparation Time:* 60 minutes
III. *In-Class Time Suggested:*   45 minutes
IV. *Procedures:*
   A. Read the exercise, review the National Labor Relations Act, and any additional reading assigned by the instructor.
   B. The class should be divided into groups of four.
   C. Each group should read each of the case incidents that follow and develop responses to each situation.

1. You are finishing up some paper work at the end of a hard day. As the Human Resources Manager, you have been involved in the company's negotiations with the union regarding the truck drivers' new contract with your firm. The negotiations have not been going well and all indications are that a strike will be called in a matter of days. As you are preparing to leave your office, three long-time truck drivers ask to have a word with you in private. They inform you that they are not happy with their union and that a number of the other drivers feel the same way. They ask you to help them "get rid of the union."

2. You have been interviewing an applicant for a production line opening. The applicant seems to have all of the necessary KSAs to do the job. You feel certain that he will be one of the three candidates you recall for a second interview with the production manager. As you are about to close the interview, the applicant informs you that if he is hired, he intends to encourage his co-workers to form a union.

3. The negotiations between your company and the union representing the 110 production workers in your firm has reached a dead end. Union members have already voted to go on strike. At a meeting of the key managers involved in running the company, the production manager suggests utilizing the remaining clerical, accounting, and managerial staff

Contributed by Gerald E. Calvasina, The University of North Carolina, Charlotte.

as replacements to keep the plant running. She also suggests contacting a temporary employment agency to help fill any remaining critical positions while the union members are on strike. As the Human Resources Manager, how would you respond to this suggestion?

4. You are the Human Resources Manager of a 150-employee retail establishment. The mix of employees in the store is: 50 full-time sales associates; 50 part-time sales associates; 20 full-time shipping and receiving employees; and 30 supervisory/managerial employees. You receive a call from the regional office of the National Labor Relations Board (NLRB) informing you that a petition for a representation election has been filed by your sales associates. Three weeks later, the NLRB informs you that an election has been ordered. The NLRB representative calls again and asks you to send him a copy of your current payroll complete with names and addresses of the employees in the potential bargaining unit. This list, you are told, will be turned over to the local union seeking to organize your employees.

5. You are the store manager for a regional supermarket chain. Your store is nonunion. When a local union attempts to organize your employees, you receive orders to terminate those employees of your store who have signed union authorization cards. Your regional manager also orders you to prepare termination slips for each of the fired employees detailing false reasons for their termination.

80. EXERCISE

Labor Arbitration

I. *Objectives:*
  A. To familiarize you with the arbitration process.
  B. To give you practice in presenting a case before others.
  C. To examine issues relating to contract administration.
II. *Out-of-Class Preparation Time:* 40–50 minutes
III. *Procedures:* Either at the beginning of or before class each student should read the exercise. To start the exercise, the instructor will divide the class into the following three groups:
  A. Union representatives (approximately five individuals)
  B. Company representatives (approximately five individuals)
  C. Arbitrators (all remaining participants, divided into groups of three to five members)

Contributed by Gerald E. Calvasina, The University of North Carolina, Charlotte.

The union representatives should meet together and carefully examine "The Union Position" and prepare to argue and defend this position. The company representatives should do the same with reference to "The Company Position." Meanwhile the arbitrators should read both the union position and the company position and discuss among themselves the arguments for and against each position.

After both the union and company representatives have prepared their position statements, each should present their case to the arbitrators. Each group will be allowed five minutes for their presentation, then an additional five minutes to counter the other group's position.

After all presentations are complete, each group of arbitrators will be given ten minutes to discuss the case and reach a decision. These decisions should be presented, along with the reasoning behind them, to all participants.

Finally, the instructor may (optionally) present the arbitrator's actual decision in this case.

The Issue

Was the grievant discharged for just cause? The company claimed the employee's negligence of duty resulted in the discharge and the union claimed poor performance was the issue. If the union is right, what should be the remedy?

Pertinent Provisions of the Union Agreement

Article I. Purpose of the Agreement. 1.3 The management of the company and the direction of the working force, including the right to plan, direct, and control operations, the right to hire, suspend, transfer, or discharge for just and sufficient cause, to relieve employees from duties because of lack of work or for other legitimate business reasons and the right to introduce new or improved methods or facilities of production is vested exclusively in the company; provided, however, that such rights shall not be exercised for the purpose of discriminating against any employee, and such rights shall not conflict with the provisions of this agreement.

Article 33. Discipline and Discharge. 33.1. In cases of poor job performance, the following procedure dealing with discipline will be accomplished with written notification to the Union:

a. Formal written warning in the first instance with copy to the employee.
b. In subsequent instances, formal written warning and/or suspension without pay for a period not to exceed five working days.
c. In the event three or more instances occur, one of which results in a suspension, within any two-year period, discharge for just cause will be accomplished.

33.1.1. For purposes of this article, job performance shall include consideration of the following factors:

a. Attendance record, including absenteeism, tardiness, and proven abuse of sick leave.
b. Adherence to industrial safety rules.
c. Adherence to Company house rules.
d. Ability to perform assigned tasks satisfactorily.

33.2 In cases of personal misconduct, the disciplinary action taken, including discharge, will be consistent with the gravity of the offense.

Background

The grievant was employed as a service technician for the ABC Petroleum/Gas Company from August 1984 to April of 1993. On January 26, 1993, grievant was dispatched to a customer who reported a strong odor. Grievant's service report showed that he spent 26 minutes on the call, that no leaks were found, and that no repairs were made. The grievant did not take a pressure/manometer test.

Later that same day, in response to a second call, another technician was sent to the customer's home. The second technician checked the gas tank and gauge readings, added some gas, used the track, and did the pressure/manometer test. He tested the lines and isolated the source of the gas odor at a leak in the heater connector after the shutoff valve on the heater. The leak was located less than two feet from the pilot light on the water heater, which was lit. The technician replaced the heater connector and put the old one in the back of his truck. Subsequently, the grievant's immediate supervisor talked with the second technician and examined the damaged heater connector. On January 28, 1993, the supervisor met with the grievant and informed him that he was being suspended, pending an investigation. The reason for the suspension was "Negligent in responding to report of gas odor on January 26, failure to perform leak investigation according to company procedures/leaving party with hazardous condition." By letter on April 16, 1993, grievant was notified that he was being terminated based on the company's findings indicating that "the incident was of such serious nature that we would be remiss in continuing your employment as a technician."

The Company's Position

The company contends that the grievant failed to follow normal procedures necessary to determine whether there was a gas leak, and that leaving the customer in a hazardous condition constituted just cause for discharge. The grievant's failure to find or repair the gas leak was not poor performance but negligence of duty. The company defined poor performance as involving a lack of skills or intelligence and that the grievant's behavior was not caused by a lack of skills or innate inability. The company specifically refers to Article 1.3 which permits the company to discharge an employee for "just cause" and that under Article 1.3, no prior warnings are required. The company also noted in its presentation that the employee was previously suspended for 5 days in 1990, and that he has been reprimanded on numerous occasions for various infractions.

The Union's Position

The union contends that the grievant should have been disciplined under Section 33.1 for poor job performance. The union contends that grievant performed three of the four tests usually performed and that at worst used poor judgment in not pressure testing the system. Further, the union contends that the company failed to give grievant adequate notice of the rule or the consequences of his action. The grievant did not have knowledge that he could be discharged for negligence in performance of his duties. Further, the union claimed that the company did not conduct a proper investigation and relied solely on the report of the second technician sent to the customer's home. The company made no attempt to visit the job site to determine first-hand if grievant had followed company rules.

81. SKILL BUILDER

Employee Communications During Union Campaigns

I. *Objectives:*
   A. To give you practice in preparing an effective company communication during a union campaign.
   B. To help you understand the practical application of the National Labor Relations Act.
II. *Time Required to Complete:* 1 hour
III. *Instructions:* Your company, Fruit Canners, Inc., has recently become aware that the United Food and Commercial Workers Union is attempting to convince employees in your plant to sign authorization cards. Management is somewhat surprised by the campaign because employee relations have generally been good. Prepare a one-page letter to be sent to all plant employees stating the company's position on the union drive and the company's desire to remain nonunion. Be certain that the content of your letter does not violate the provisions of the National Labor Relations Act.

PART 6

EXPANDING HUMAN RESOURCES GLOBALLY

82. CASE

Selecting a Manager for a Nigerian Facility

Victoria Oilfield Equipment is a supplier of drilling equipment for oil and gas exploration. Its headquarters is located near Houston, Texas. The company has seven offices and warehousing facilities near potential markets for its equipment. Only 30 percent of Victoria's profits come from selling equipment; the rest comes from leasing. Within its leasing operations, half the profit comes from supplying operators for the equipment. Victoria has over 25 years of experience in Texas and Louisiana and 10 years of experience in several Latin American countries. Most of its customers are large multinational oil companies. However, approximately 20 percent of its contracts are with small, independent exploration companies.

Victoria has just completed construction of a new facility near Port Harcout, Nigeria—its first venture into Africa. The machinery, trucks, and equipment to operate this facility are to arrive within the next three months. You are the Assistant Personnel Officer for Victoria, and you have been instructed to review the records of the three leading candidates for manager of this new facility. You must recommend one of the three to your boss, the Human Resource Director.

Before you examine the records, you make a list of factors that you believe should be taken into consideration:

1. General criteria: education, experience, job knowledge, desire, and stability.
2. The Nigerian facility will be in the start-up phase.
3. Victoria wants to develop some of its current managers in international operations.
4. Few Nigerians have experience in the technical aspects of drilling for oil, yet Victoria has built its reputation on the expertise of its managers and customer acceptance of its managers as knowledgeable professionals.
5. Although some of Victoria's managers have had experience in Latin America, none have had experience in Africa.
6. Political power within the Nigerian government shifts periodically, and many of those with whom Victoria negotiated its move into Nigeria are no longer in the government.
7. The supply of trained oil-drilling equipment operators in Nigeria is much less than the demand.

Contributed by Sam C. Holliday, formerly with the University of Southern California.

The three candidates are:

Henry Smith:

Age 34, United States citizen, graduate of Texas A & M, served three years in the Army and then joined Victoria. In his ten years with Victoria, his record has been outstanding, and it is often said that he will be president of Victoria someday. He has never been outside of the United States.

Juan Lopez:

Age 46, Venezuelan citizen, has been with Victoria for 21 years and worked his way up in several offices in Latin America. He spent two years in company headquarters planning operations in Latin America and is well respected throughout the company. He currently manages Victoria's facility in Ecuador.

Matthew Ohwueme:

Age 52, Nigerian citizen, educated in England, member of the Ibo ethnic group. He is the owner/manager of the largest Honda dealership in Lagos but has had no experience with oilfield equipment.

Questions

1. Would it be best for Victoria to select a manager who is a local (citizen of Nigeria), a home country national (citizen of the United States), or a third-country national (citizen of some country other than Nigeria or the United States)?
2. Which of the factors to be considered would favor the selection of Henry Smith? Juan Lopez? Matthew Ohwueme?
3. Which candidate would you recommend? Why?

83. CASE

Fred Bailey: An Innocent Abroad

Fred gazed out the window of his 24th floor office at the tranquil beauty of the Imperial Palace amidst the hustle and bustle of downtown Tokyo. Only six months ago, Fred had arrived with his wife and two children for this three-year assignment as the director of Kline & Associates' Tokyo office. Kline & Associates is a large, multinational consulting firm with offices in 19 countries worldwide. Fred was now trying to decide if he should simply pack up and tell the home office that he was coming home or whether he should try and somehow convince his wife and himself that they should stay and try to finish the assignment. Given how excited Fred thought they all were about the assignment to begin with, it was a mystery to Fred as to how things had gotten to this point. As he watched the swans glide across the water in the moat that surrounds the Imperial Palace, Fred reflected on the past seven months.

Seven months ago, the managing partner, Dave Steiner, of the main office in Boston asked Fred to lunch to discuss "business." To Fred's surprise the "business" was not the major project that he and his team had just finished but was instead a very big promotion and career move. Fred was offered the position of managing director of the firm's relatively new Tokyo office which had a staff of 40, including seven Americans. Most of the Americans in the Tokyo office were either associate consultants or research analysts. Fred would be in charge of the whole office and would report to a senior partner who was in charge of the Asian region. It was implied to Fred that if this assignment went as well as his past ones, it would be the last step before becoming a partner in the firm.

When Fred told his wife about the unbelievable opportunity, he was shocked at her less than enthusiastic response. His wife Jennifer (or Jenny as Fred called her) thought that it would be rather difficult to have the children live and go to school in a foreign country for three years, especially when Christine, the oldest, would be starting middle school next year. Besides, now that the kids were in school, Jenny was thinking about going back to work—at least part-time. Jenny had a degree in fashion merchandising from a well-known private university and had worked as an assistant buyer for a large women's clothing store before having the two girls.

Fred explained that the career opportunity was just too good to pass up and that the company's overseas package would make living overseas terrific. The company would pay all the expenses to move whatever the Baileys wanted to take with them. The company had a very nice house in

Contributed by J. Stewart Black, Amos Tuck School of Business Administration, Dartmouth College.

an expensive district of Tokyo that would be provided rent free. Additionally, the company would rent their house in Boston during their absence. Also, the firm would provide a car and driver, education expenses for the children to attend private schools, and a cost-of-living adjustment and overseas compensation that would nearly triple Fred's gross annual salary. After two days of consideration and discussion, Fred told Mr. Steiner he would accept the assignment.

The current Tokyo office managing director was a partner in the firm but had only been in the new Tokyo office for less than a year when he was transferred to head-up a long-established office in England. Because the transfer to England was taking place "right away," Fred and his family had about three weeks to prepare for the move. Between getting things at the office transferred to Bob Newcome, who was being promoted to Fred's position, and the logistical hassles of getting furniture and the like ready to be moved, neither Fred nor his family had much time to really find out much about Japan, other than what was in the encyclopedia.

When the Baileys arrived, they were greeted at the airport by one of the young Japanese associate consultants and the senior American expatriate. Fred and his family were quite tired from the long trip and the two-hour ride back to Tokyo was a rather quiet one. After a few days of just settling in, Fred spent his first day at the office.

Fred's first order of business was to have a general meeting with all the employees of associate consultant rank and higher. Although Fred didn't really notice it at the time, all the Japanese staff sat together and all the Americans sat together. After Fred introduced himself and his general idea about the potential and future directions of the Tokyo office, he called on a few individuals to get their ideas about how the things for which they were responsible would likely fit into his overall plan. From the Americans, Fred got a mixture of opinions with specific reasons about why certain things might or might not fit well. From the Japanese, he got very vague answers. When Fred pushed to get more specific information, he was surprised to find that a couple of the Japanese simply made a sucking sound as they breathed and said that it was "difficult to say." Fred sensed the meeting was not fulfilling his objectives, so he thanked everyone for coming and said he looked forward to their all working together to make the Tokyo office the fastest growing office in the company.

After they had been in Japan about a month, Fred's wife complained to him about the difficulty she had getting certain everyday products like maple syrup, peanut butter, and quality beef. She said that when she could get it at one of the specialty stores it cost three and four times what it would cost in the United States. She also complained that the washer and dryer were much too small and so she had to spend extra money by sending things out to be dry cleaned. On top of all that, unless she went to the American Club in downtown Tokyo, she never had anyone to talk to. After all, Fred was gone 10 to 16 hours a day. Unfortunately, at the time Fred was preoccupied, thinking about a big upcoming meeting between his firm and a significant prospective client—a top 100 Japanese multinational company.

The next day Fred, along with the lead American consultant for the potential contract, Ralph Webster, and one of the Japanese associate consultants, Kenichi Kurokawa, who spoke perfect English, met with a team from the Japanese firm. The Japanese team consisted of four members—the VP of administration, the director of international personnel, and two staff specialists. After shaking hands and a few awkward bows, Fred said that he knew the Japanese gentlemen were busy and he didn't want to waste their time so he would get right to the point. Fred then had the other American lay out their firm's proposal for the project and what the project would cost. After the presentation, Fred asked the Japanese what their reaction to the proposal was. The Japanese did not respond immediately and so Fred launched into his summary version of the proposal thinking that the translation might have been insufficient. But again the Japanese had only the vaguest of responses to his direct questions.

The recollection of the frustration of that meeting was enough to shake Fred back to reality. The reality was that in the five months since the first meeting little progress had been made and the contract between the firms was yet to be signed. "I can never seem to get a direct response from a Japanese," he thought to himself. This feeling of frustration led him to remember a related incident that happened about a month after this first meeting with this client.

Fred had decided that the reason not much progress was being made with the client was that Fred and his group just didn't know enough about the client to package the proposal in a way that was appealing to the client. Consequently, he called in the senior American associated with the proposal, Ralph Webster, and asked him to develop a report on the client so the proposal could be reevaluated and changed where necessary. Jointly, they decided that one of the more promising Japanese research associates, Tashiro Watanabe, would be the best person to take the lead on this report. To impress upon Tashiro the importance of this task and the great potential they saw in him, they decided to have the young Japanese associate meet with both Fred and Ralph. In the meeting, Fred and Ralph laid out the nature and importance of the task. At that point Fred leaned forward in his chair and said, "You can see that this is an important assignment and that we are placing a lot of confidence in you by giving you this assignment. We need the report this time next week so that we can revise and re-present our proposal. Can you do it?" After a somewhat pregnant pause, the Japanese responded hesitantly, "I'm not sure what to say." At that point Fred smiled, got up from his chair and walked over to the young Japanese associate, extended his hand, and said, "Hey, there's nothing to say. We're just giving you the opportunity you deserve."

The day before the report was due, Fred asked Ralph how the report was coming. Ralph said that since he had heard nothing from Tashiro, he assumed that everything was under control, but that he would double check. Ralph later ran into one of the American research associates, John Maynard. Ralph knew that John was hired for Japan because of his language ability in Japanese and that, unlike any of the other Americans, John often went out after work with some of the Japanese research associates including Tashiro. So, Ralph asked John if he knew how Tashiro was coming on the report. John then recounted that last night at the office Tashiro had asked if Americans sometimes fired employees for being late with reports. John had sensed that this was more than a hypothetical question and asked Tashiro why he wanted to know. Tashiro did not respond immediately and since it was 8:30 in the evening, John suggested they go out for a drink. At first Tashiro resisted, but then John assured him that they would grab a drink at a nearby bar and come right back. At the bar John got Tashiro to open up.

Tashiro explained the nature of the report that he had been requested to produce. Tashiro continued to explain that even though he had worked long into the night every night to complete the report it was just impossible and that he had doubted from the beginning whether he could complete the report in a week.

At this point Ralph asked John, "Why the hell didn't he say something in the first place?" Ralph didn't wait to hear whether John had an answer to his question or not. He headed straight to Tashiro's desk.

The incident just got worse from that point. Ralph chewed Tashiro out and then went to Fred explaining that the report would not be ready and that Tashiro didn't think it could have been from the start. "Then why didn't he say something?" Fred asked. No one had any answers and the whole thing just left everyone more suspect and uncomfortable with the other.

There were other incidents, big and small, that had made especially the last two months frustrating, but Fred was too tired to remember them all. To Fred it seemed that working with Japanese both inside and outside the firm was like working with people from another planet. Fred felt he just couldn't communicate with them, and he could never figure out what they were thinking. It drove him crazy.

Then on top of all this, Jennifer laid a bombshell on him yesterday. She wanted to go home, and yesterday was not soon enough. Even though the kids seemed to be doing okay, Jennifer was tired of Japan—tired of being stared at, of not understanding anybody or being understood, of not being able to find what she wanted at the store, of not being able to drive and read the road signs, of not having anything to watch on TV, of not being involved in anything. She wanted to go home and could not think of any reason why they shouldn't. After all, she reasoned they owed nothing to the company because the company had led them to believe this was just another assignment, like the two years they spent in San Francisco, and it was anything but that!

Fred looked out the window once more, wishing that somehow everything could be fixed, or turned back, or something. Down below the traffic was backed up. Though the traffic lights changed, the cars and trucks didn't seem to be moving. Fortunately, in the ground below, one of the world's most advanced, efficient, and clean subway systems moved hundreds of thousands of people about the city and to their homes.

Questions

1. What factors (individual, work, and organizational) contributed to Fred and Jenny's lack of adjustment to Japan?
2. What mistakes did Fred make because of his lack of understanding of Japan?
3. What criteria would be important in selecting employees for overseas assignments?
4. What special training and development programs might have been beneficial to Fred and his family prior to his assignment in Japan?
5. Assume you are Dave Steiner and you receive a call from Fred about his difficulties in Japan. How would you respond? What should be done now?

84. SKILL BUILDER

Going International

I. *Objective:* To give you an understanding of the human resource issues that emerge when a company establishes foreign operations.
II. *Time Required to Complete Assignment:* 5–6 hours
III. *Instructions:* Your instructor will divide the class into teams and assign each team one of the countries listed in the scenario described below. Your team is to conduct research on another country and prepare a report addressing the two questions listed in the scenario. Each team should be prepared to make an oral presentation of its research findings and recommendations.

There are a number of excellent sources of information on foreign countries. In addition to the sources your team may locate, you might try the following:
A. Consulate offices in the U. S. for each country
B. The World Factbook
C. Asia Pacific Management Forum
   (http://www.mcb.co.uk/apmforum/nethome.htm)
D. Institute for International Human Resources
   (http://www.shrm.org/docs/IIHR.html)
E. U.S. Department of Commerce International Trade Administration
   (http://www.ita.doc.gov/)

Scenario

Piedmont Electronics produces paging devices. The demand for the company's products has grown rapidly in the last few years. The company's new strategy includes a direct investment initiative to establish assembly and manufacturing plants in countries. The long-term objective is to establish operations in key markets throughout the world. Piedmont is considering the following host countries:

Malaysia
China
India
Brazil
Mexico
Malawi
Philippines
United Kingdom

The company's president has asked a human resource team to prepare a research report on each country. The report should:

1. Describe:
   a. labor and employment laws;
   b. wage rates and worker benefits;
   c. education and literacy of labor force;
   d. labor availability;
   e. living standards;
   f. cultural norms and values of the country.
2. Discuss the implications of the research findings in terms of how Piedmont should set up human resource management practices in the host country.

PART 7

HUMAN RESOURCE AUDITS/
TERM ASSIGNMENTS

85. TERM PROJECT

Human Resource System Evaluation

I. *Objective:* To help you critically analyze a human resource management system, identify problems, and recommend constructive improvements.

II. *Out-of-Class Preparation Time:* 30–40 hours per group (10–15 hours per individual student)

III. *In-Class Time Suggested:* None, unless an oral report is required by the instructor

IV. *Procedures:* You should identify a real organization, form groups of two to three people, and receive permission from either the CEO or the Personnel Director to study the organization. Once permission is received, your group should arrange to interview as many of the following as possible: the Human Resources Director, other human resource department employees, employees performing different functions at different levels in the organization, and labor union officials (if any).

V. *General Purpose:* The study will focus upon the selected organization's human resources and employee relations objectives, structures, policies, practices, and selected administrative problems. It will give you the opportunity to learn firsthand about the management of human resource systems in actual organizations. It will also provide you with the opportunity to develop field research methodologies and evaluation skills that should prove beneficial in future academic and professional assignments. Finally, for the organization cooperating with each of the student projects, the results of these studies should be helpful in future efforts to improve the efficiency and effectiveness of their human resource systems.

The final product of this study will be a comprehensive written report to be submitted no later than one week before the end of the term. Each of you should assume the stance of an outside consultant who has been called in to evaluate the human resource system of the particular organization. At a *minimum*, the paper should reflect the items contained in the Evaluation Guide that follows. Alternatively, your instructor may permit each group to focus on one or a few selected parts of the organization's human resource system.

Evaluation Guide

I. *The Organization and Its Mission*
  A. When and why was this organization established?
     1. Under what statutory or legal authority was it created?
     2. What are the principal needs and objectives that the organization is designed to fulfill?

    B. What are the structural components of the organization?
- **1.** How is the organization organized to carry out its objectives?
- **2.** Where is the focus of decision-making authority for carrying out these objectives?
  - **a.** How centralized or decentralized is the decision-making process with respect to
    - **i.** organizational planning?
    - **ii.** operational management?
  - **b.** What is the relationship between the leadership of this organization and
    - **i.** elected public officials?
    - **ii.** other public officials?
    - **iii.** leaders in the private sector?
    - **iv.** representatives of employee organizations or associations, if any?
    - **v.** professional and technical staffs?
- **3.** What budgetary constraints confront the organization?
  - **a.** What are the sources of revenue for this company?
    - **i.** for capital expenditures?
    - **ii.** for operating expenditures?
  - **b.** What changes have occurred in the organization's budget in recent years?
    - **i.** Have there been any noticeable increases or decreases in revenues?
    - **ii.** Have there been any new sources of funding?
    - **iii.** Have any old sources of funding been reduced or eliminated?
    - **iv.** How have these trends affected management of the organization?
- **4.** What is the total employment complement of the organization?
  - **a.** How are these employees distributed throughout the organization?
    - **i.** by department or operational function?
    - **ii.** by skill, e.g., managerial, professional, technical, clerical, skilled craftsperson, semi-skilled operatives, unskilled laborers, etc.?
  - **b.** What have been some of the noticeable employment trends in recent years?
- **5.** Does the organization operate overseas?

    C. What are the major problems and opportunities confronting this organization? Up to this point, how well has the organization responded to these challenges? What are your recommendations? Why?

    D. Does the organization have a strategic management plan including goals, objectives, and timetables?

II. *The Role of the Human Resource Function*
   A. Does this organization have a formal and identifiable human resource function (department)?
      1. When was this department or function formally established and why?
      2. How is the human resource function or department organized to carry out the objectives of the organization?
      3. How many individuals are directly associated with the human resource function or department?
      4. What are the academic and employment backgrounds of those involved in the function or department?
   B. What is the focus of decision-making authority on personnel matters within the company?
      1. Who establishes the objectives and policies related to human resource matters?
      2. What is the relationship between the human resource functions and other operations of the organization in the administration of personnel policies and practices?
   C. To what degree has the human resource function used information technology to manage information?
   D. To what degree is the Internet used in the human resource function? How?
   E. What is the perceived importance of the human resource function or department relative to other functional operations of the organization?
   F. Does the human resource function provide support in foreign countries? What problems or challenges does this present?
   G. What recommendations do you have (if any) for reorganizing the human resource function? Why?
III. *Employment Decisions*
   A. To what degree is human resources management integrated into the strategic management of the organization? How?
   B. Who is responsible for human resource planning and forecasting for the organization?
      1. What methods are used to determine staffing needs?
      2. Does the organization focus primarily upon short-run or long-run human resource needs, or both?
      3. Are job analyses and job descriptions made for each position in the organization? To what degree are they updated periodically?
      4. What specific problems have been encountered in the human resource planning process?
         a. To what can they be attributed?
         b. What are the major alternatives for resolving these problems?
         c. Which solutions are most feasible, and why?

5.   If no human resource planning is done:
   a.   Why not?
   b.   Has the lack of human resource planning had any negative impact? Why?
6.   Does the organization provide career planning and career counseling for employees? Why or why not?

C.   Once staffing needs are established, what procedures are utilized for filling job vacancies?
   1.   Who is responsible for staffing the organization—the human resource department or the respective functional departments?
   2.   What methods are used to recruit new employees?
   3.   What methods and criteria are used for evaluating and selecting job applicants? Have these methods been validated? How?
   4.   To what extent are new employee recruitment, evaluation, and selection procedures aided or restricted by:
      a.   established policies or practices of the organization?
      b.   provisions contained in employment laws?
      c.   factors associated with local labor markets?
   5.   To what degree does the organization seek to fill existing job vacancies from among present employees or by recruiting new employees, and why?
   6.   To what degree does the staffing reflect the skills, knowledge, and abilities necessary to successfully implement the strategic goals of the organization?
   7.   To what degree and how does the organization support a goal of diversity in the workplace?
   8.   What does the organization do to enhance the work and family interface?

D.   What specific problems have been encountered in the employment staffing process?
   1.   To what can these be attributed?
   2.   What are the major alternatives for resolving these problems?
   3.   Which solutions are most feasible, and why?

IV. *Determination of Working Conditions and Rewards*
   A.   Is an occupational classification system utilized by the organization?
      1.   Who is responsible for determining the classification system?
      2.   What are the basic features of this system?
         a.   Does the classification system appropriately reflect variations in job skills?
         b.   Is it used effectively as a mechanism for identifying career paths? Explain.
         c.   Have there been any recent reviews and evaluations of the performance of the classification system in relation to organizational and personnel goals?

B. How are wage and salary levels and annual improvements determined?
1. Does the organization conduct periodic internal and external wage surveys?
2. Are salary levels adequate to enable the organization to attract and maintain an effective work force? Why or why not?
3. Do differentials in salary grades appropriately reflect differentials in skills and responsibilities?
4. Are large proportions of employees grouped into particular salary grade levels?
5. How do salary levels compare with those of other comparable organizations for the same or similar occupational and experience groupings?
6. Does the current reward system adequately reward employees with the requisite knowledge, skills, and abilities necessary to implement the strategic plan?
7. What trends have taken place in salary levels over the past few years?
8. To what degree is incentive compensation used and in what areas?

C. What methods are used for evaluating employees for the purpose of determining their effectiveness and any merited salary increases?
1. Do employee performance appraisal systems actually reflect job performance? Why or why not?
2. How adequate or inadequate are the performance appraisal methods currently being used? Why?
3. Do they reflect the knowledge, skills, and abilities needed to successfully implement the particular department's strategic goals?

D. How adequate are non-wage fringe benefits?
1. How are they determined?
2. How do they compare with those of other organizations?
3. How have they changed in recent years and how will they change in the future?

E. Has the organization introduced any special programs or activities to improve safety and health conditions on the job?

F. What efforts, if any, are utilized to maintain employee morale and job satisfaction?

G. Does the organization provide for flexible work options such as telecommuting or job sharing? Please provide details.

H. To what degree is outsourcing used and in what specific areas?

I. What retirement options are currently offered and how are they expected to change in the future?

J. What improvements in compensation and employee motivation should be made? Why?

V. *Employee Training and Development*
  A. Has the organization supported programs for employee training and development? Why or why not?
    1. What kinds of programs have been established? Have they been oriented toward:
      a. job skills?
      b. supervisory and leadership skills?
      c. basic educational skills?
      d. knowledge, skills, and abilities necessary for strategic goal attainment?
    2. How do these programs relate to the organization's strategic and operational objectives?
    3. Does the organization maintain its own training staff or are outside organizations used for training purposes?
    4. What proportion of employees have participated in training and development programs supported by the organization?
  B. To what extent has the organization's programs of employee training and development been used in making decisions related to promotions and transfers within the organization?
    1. Are promotion decisions based primarily upon the measured and observed abilities of employees or upon their seniority in the job?
  C. What problems, if any, have been encountered in the administration of employee training and development programs within the organization? What suggestions for improvement can you make? Why?

VI. *Employee Frictions*
  A. What methods and procedures are available for resolving employee complaints and grievances?
    1. Have there been large numbers of such grievances? Why?
    2. Has the volume of grievances been growing or declining? Why?
    3. What are the major problems eliciting the majority of employee grievances?
  B. Have there been many employee discipline problems?
    1. Are there clearly spelled out formal procedures within the organization for handling discipline cases? What are they?
    2. How often are employees disciplined or discharged?
      a. What are the major causes of such problems?
      b. How have these been dealt with by the organization?
  C. To what extent have employee tardiness, absenteeism, and turnover been problems?
    1. Have these problems been studied to determine their most likely causes? What are they?
    2. What steps have been taken to resolve these problems, if they exist? What steps should have been taken? Why?

    D. Have any of the employees sought to join labor organizations for the purpose of engaging in collective bargaining over wages, hours, and working conditions? Explain.

        1. Why have, or have not, such organizing activities taken place?

        2. What is the official position of the organization toward acceptance or rejection of unionism for its employees?

        3. If a labor union exists in this organization, what effect has the union had upon:

            a. overall decision making within the organization?

            b. the efficiency and productivity of the organization?

            c. the administration of the personnel function?

            d. the relations between the managers of the organization and its non-managerial personnel?

            e. the interpersonal relationships among non-supervisory employees?

    E. What has been the relationship between management and union leaders? (e.g., cooperative; neutral; cold; hostile)

        1. Have there been any noticeable changes in the nature of this relationship in the recent past? Why or why not?

        2. Have there been any work stoppages among employees of the agency in order to pressure management into agreeing to union demands?

            a. What were the issue(s)?

            b. Why did the dispute occur?

            c. How was it resolved?

            d. What has been its subsequent impact upon:

                i. the operation of the company?

                ii. employee performance?

                iii. the work environment?

                iv. the decision-making process involved in personnel matters?

    F. What suggestions would you make for minimizing employee grievances and improving the labor relations climate (if applicable)? Why?

VII. *Summary and Evaluation*

    A. How effectively is the human resource function of this organization contributing to the fulfillment of its mission, objectives, and strategic plan?

    B. What are some of the problems of human resources management that have been adequately solved or are now in the process of being solved by the organization?

    C. What are some of the major human resource problems that remain to be confronted and solved?

    D. What would appear to be among the most desirable solutions to these problems? Provide specific detail and justification for your recommendations.

86. TERM PROJECT

Human Resource Manager Interview

   I. *Objectives:*
   A. To analyze the role of human resource managers in organizations.
   B. To allow you to gain a better understanding of the nature of a human resource manager's job.
   C. To help you understand the interface between human resource and line managers.
   II. *Out-of-Class Preparation Time:* 8–10 hours
   III. *In-Class Time Suggested:*   None unless instructor wants an oral report
   IV. *Procedures:*
   A. This assignment is to be done individually by each student.
   B. Locate a human resource manager to interview. You may select a human resource generalist or a human resource specialist. After the manager understands the research project and agrees to cooperate, conduct the interview. The interview should take about 45 minutes to one hour.
   C. Also interview a line manager in the same organization to gain his or her views of human resource management.
   D. A suggested interview outline is given (in Exhibit 7.1) for the questions to be asked. You are expected to prepare additional questions. The final interview questions and the name of the organization and manager you will interview should be turned in to your instructor for approval prior to conducting the actual interview. Additionally, you should gather research information on the company before the interview if possible.
   E. Prepare a report (8–10 pages) of the results of the interviews which covers: (1) a description of the overall operations and role of the human resource department; (2) a description of the human resource function you explored in-depth; (3) the type of interaction between human resource and line managers; and (4) the extent to which the organization's human resource management practices conform to theoretical prescriptions. If differences are found, discuss why they exist.

EXHIBIT 7.1   *Interview Outline*

Part I: Organization Information

a. Type of business/industry/organization
b. General description of company's products/service/operations
c. Brief company history
d. Number of employees: managerial, clerical, operative, etc.
e. Organization structure
f. Size and structure of the human resource department

Part II: Background of the Human Resource Manager

a. Title
b. Academic preparation (highest degree earned and field of study)
c. Years with organization
d. Years of personnel experience
e. Other work experience
f. Professional associations/organizations

Part III: Human Resource Management Functions

Ask the human resource manager to check off and rate the human resource activities listed in Form 1.

Part IV: Role of Human Resource Department

Ask the human resource manager the following general questions:
a. What is the role of the human resource department in your organization?
b. To what extent is the human resource staff/department involved in strategic business planning? Explain.
c. In your opinion, what are some of the most pressing human resource issues faced by organizations today? Why?
d. What was the most difficult organizational problem faced by the human resource department in the last five years? How was it resolved? Why?

Part V: In-depth Review of HRM Function

Explore in depth one of the HRM functions with the human resource manager (for example: recruiting, selection/staffing, compensation, training and development, performance evaluation, etc.). You should first review the material in the text on the human resource function you choose and then prepare a set of questions for the manager relating to how that function is carried out in the organization. During the interview be sure to get enough information so you can describe their function in detail. Ask the executive to comment on the effectiveness of the function and his or her interaction with line managers in carrying out the activity. Try to obtain examples of forms and/or materials used.

Part VI: Interface with Line Managers

Once you have interviewed the HRM manager, also interview one of the line managers in the organization. The purpose of this interview is to understand the way in

(continued)

EXHIBIT 7.1   *continued*

which the human resource function "interfaces" with other managers in the organization.

Ask the manager:
a. To rate the activities listed in Form 2.
b. What kinds of things are done by the human resource department that support you in your position?
c. What do you "ideally" expect from the human resource department in performing your job?

FORM 1   *Form for Ranking of Human Resource Activities by Human Resource Manager*

Instructions: Place a check next to the human resource activities under your responsibility and indicate the importance of these responsibilities using a scale of 1 (very important) to 5 (not very important).

	Human Resource Activities	**Importance**
_____	**1.** Ensure fair and consistent implementation of human resource policies and procedures.	_____
_____	**2.** Advise and counsel management on employee problems.	_____
_____	**3.** Design appropriate staffing and recruiting policies and programs.	_____
_____	**4.** Assist department managers in interviewing, selecting, and hiring of employees.	_____
_____	**5.** Design and implement performance evaluation system(s).	_____
_____	**6.** Administer direct and indirect compensation programs.	_____
_____	**7.** Ensure compliance with federal and state fair employment laws and other legal restrictions in all employment practices.	_____
_____	**8.** Counsel employees on job-related and/or personal problems.	_____
_____	**9.** Develop and maintain employee human resource records.	_____
_____	**10.** Develop EEO policy and communicate EEO policy to all managers.	_____
_____	**11.** Ensure compliance with safety and health standards.	_____
_____	**12.** Oversee fair application of employee grievance procedures.	_____
_____	**13.** Provide state-of-the-art solutions to employee relations problems.	_____
_____	**14.** Plan for future human resource needs.	_____
_____	**15.** Work with top management on human resource implications of business plans and strategies.	_____
_____	**16.** Design and implement employee training and career development programs.	_____

(continued)

FORM 1   *continued*

_____**17.** Negotiate the collective bargaining agreement.   _____

_____**18.** Administer and enforce provisions of the collective bar-   _____
gaining agreement.

_____**19.** Other(s) write in.   _____

_____

_____

_____

_____

_____

FORM 2   *Form for Ranking of Human Resource Activities by Line Manager*

Instructions: Here is a list of typical activities performed by human resource departments in organizations. Please indicate the importance of the activities performed by the human resource department in your organization using a scale of 1 (very important) to 5 (not very important).

Human Resource Activities   **Importance**

1. Ensure fair and consistent implementation of human resource   _____
policies and procedures.

2. Advise and counsel management on employee problems.   _____

3. Design appropriate staffing and recruiting policies and programs.   _____

4. Assist department managers in interviewing, selecting, and hiring   _____
of employees.

5. Design and implement performance evaluation system(s).   _____

6. Administer direct and indirect compensation programs.   _____

7. Ensure compliance with federal and state fair employment laws   _____
and other legal restrictions in all employment practices.

8. Counsel employees on job-related and/or personal problems.   _____

9. Develop and maintain employee records.   _____

10. Develop EEO policy and communicate EEO policy to all managers.   _____

11. Ensure compliance with safety and health standards.   _____

12. Oversee fair application of employee grievance procedures.   _____

13. Provide state-of-the-art solutions to employee relations problems.   _____

14. Plan for future human resource needs.   _____

15. Work with top management on human resource implications of   _____
business plans and strategies.

16. Design and implement employee training and career development   _____
programs.

(continued)

FORM 2   *continued*

17. Negotiate the collective bargaining agreement.   _____

18. Administer and enforce provisions of the collective bargaining   _____
agreement.

19. Other(s) write in.   _____

_____

_____

_____

_____

_____

87. GROUP DEBATE PROJECT

Controversial HRM Issues

I. *Objectives:*
   A. To help you understand both sides of controversial human resource
      management issues.
   B. To allow you to apply human resource management concepts in
      understanding the policy implications of the issues.
II. *Out-of-Class Preparation Time:*   Equivalent to time required for students
    to complete a major term paper assignment
III. *In-Class Time Suggested:*   45 minutes
IV. *Procedures:*
   A. Each debate will consist of two teams: an affirmative team which
      upholds the proposition and a negative team which opposes it.
      Debates can be scheduled throughout the semester to coincide with
      course content. For example, the comparable worth debate should
      be held after compensation is covered in the course. Alternatively, all
      debates could be held at the end of the term.
   B. Students should be divided into groups of three or four depending
      on the number of debate topics to be covered during the semester.
      The number of debaters on each side should be equal and the time
      allowed for each side is the same.
   C. Each group should be assigned to either the affirmative or negative
      side of a topic.

D. Each team conducts research on its topic. Because of the current nature of the debate topics, you are encouraged to consult current periodicals (e.g., use the *Business Index, Business Periodicals Index,* etc.) in addition to academic journals and books. You may want to review the list of journals in the Skill Builders in Part 1.

E. Each team prepares a written paper (8–10 pages) analyzing both sides of the topic in addition to presenting its arguments. The paper should be divided into three major parts: Introduction, Discussion, and Conclusion. (See additional instructions that follow.)

F. The debate is held in class and the two sides present their argument with the affirmative side opening and closing the debate.

G. A chairperson presides over the debate and keeps time.

H. The debating teams' presentations are evaluated by the rest of the class and the instructor (see Form 1).

Additional Instructions for Debate Teams

Structure of Classroom Debates

First Affirmative	6 minutes
First Negative	6 minutes
Second Affirmative	6 minutes
Second Negative	6 minutes
Rebuttals: Negative	5 minutes
Affirmative	5 minutes
Audience Cross-Examination	10 minutes

Tips on Oral Presentation

1. All of the speeches in the debate, *except* the first affirmative speech, should be given extemporaneously by the debaters. They should not be read. Essentially, the debaters' comments must reflect what was presented in the previous speech.

2. The first affirmative speech should be used to build the affirmative case. It is a good idea to give an overview of the major arguments you will use to uphold the proposition.

3. The first negative speech must be presented with the content of the first affirmative speech in mind. The aim of the negative speech is to cast doubt on the affirmative's arguments. The second speeches on both sides attempt to elaborate and build arguments as needed.

4. The rebuttal should directly address the arguments made by the other side.

5. Two excellent sources on debating are: Arthur N. Kruger, *Modern Debate: Its Logic and Strategy* (New York: McGraw-Hill, 1960) and Thomas K. Hanley, *An Introduction to Debate* (Boston: Ginn & Company, 1965).

Suggested Debate Propositions

1. Resolved: That Affirmative Action is a fair method of achieving equal opportunity in the workplace.
2. Resolved: That employment-at-will or termination-at-will should remain the basic doctrine governing employee dismissal and should not be subject to legislative control.
3. Resolved: That federal legislation should be passed to prohibit discrimination against homosexuals in the workplace.
4. Resolved: That employee diversity enhances organizational performance.
5. Resolved: That telecommuting enhances employee productivity and morale while reducing turnover.
6. Resolved: That employers should develop and enforce policies prohibiting dating between co-workers.
7. Resolved: That family-friendly policies which benefit only employees with dependent children are unfair to other employees.
8. Resolved: That U.S. immigration laws should be changed to allow more immigration by technical specialists from emerging/developing countries.
9. Resolved: That the use of contingent workers is an effective and efficient means of staffing.

Suggested Paper Format

Your written paper will follow a form known as a "full brief"—a comprehensive analysis of both sides of a given proposition, outlined logically from which the debater can develop his or her case. Each team should have a minimum of ten references (in most cases you will have many more). The paper will consist of three parts: Introduction, Discussion, and Conclusion:

Introduction:
a.   Statement of the proposition and your group's position.
b.   Why is the issue important?
c.   Origin and history of the issue—keep brief.
d.   Outline the conflicting arguments—why is there a controversy?
Discussion: (This is the major section of your analysis.)
a.   Present your arguments to support your position.
b.   Back up your arguments with sound reasoning and evidence.
Conclusion:
a.   Summarize the main points of the discussion—recapitulate your major points.
b.   End with an affirmation or denial of the proposition (depending on whether you have the affirmative or negative position).

FORM 1   *Debate Evaluation Form*

DEBATE:

Use the following Scale to write in a rating on each item below for each team.

	1 POOR	2 FAIR	3 GOOD	4 SUPERIOR

	Affirmative Team	Negative Team
I. Analysis (Was the analysis reasonable, complete, and clear?)		
II. Reasoning and evidence (Were the arguments structured soundly based on research facts and examples? Were arguments logical?)		
III. Organization (Was each speech clearly and cogently organized so that you could follow the structure of the debate?)		
IV. Rebuttal (Were unsupported points and assertions challenged by the opposing team?)		
V. Delivery (Was each speech effectively presented? Consider voice inflection, eye contact, and tone.)		
VI. Questions (Did the team adequately answer audience questions?)		
VII. Overall team rating		

(Continued)

FORM 1   *continued*

In my opinion, the better debating was done by
the _____
    (Affirmative or Negative)

Comments for Affirmative Team:

Comments for Negative Team: